THE EMPOWERMENT TRADITION IN AMERICAN SOCIAL WORK

Empowering the Powerless: A Social Work Series
Alex Gitterman, General Editor

D1042966

Organizing for Power and Empowerment
Jacqueline B. Mondros and Scott M. Wilson

―

EMPOWERING THE POWERLESS: A SOCIAL WORK SERIES
Alex Gitterman, General Editor

THE
EMPOWERMENT
TRADITION
IN
AMERICAN
SOCIAL WORK

A HISTORY

Barbara Levy Simon

Columbia University Press
New York

Columbia University Press
New York Chichester, West Sussex

Copyright © 1994 Columbia University Press
All rights reserved

Library of Congress Cataloging-in-Publication Data

Simon, Barbara Levy
The Empowerment Tradition in American Social Work:
A History/Barbara Levy Simon
p. cm. – (Empowering the Powerless)
Includes bibliographical references and index.
ISBN 0-231-07444-1
ISBN 0-231-07445-X (pbk.)
1. Social service–United States–History.
2. United States–Social policy.   I. Title.   II. Series.
HV91.S55   1994   93-39813
361.973–dc20
CIP

Casebound editions of Columbia University Press books
are printed on permanent and durable acid-free paper.

Printed in the United States of America
c 10 9 8 7 6 5 4 3 2 1
p 10 9 8 7 6 5 4 3

To Paula

Contents

Editor's Note

Barbara Levy Simon's *The Empowerment Tradition in American Social Work: A History* inaugurates a new Columbia University Press social work series entitled Empowering the Powerless. The miseries and human suffering encountered by social workers in the 1980s and 1990s are different in degree and kind from those encountered in the fifties, sixties, and seventies. An obvious significant change is the increasing degradation and distress faced by large sectors of the client population. Growing number of persons are discriminated against, experience severe stress, and feel powerless to influence the forces that affect their lives. They face without hope such devastating issues as family and community violence and neglect, chronic unemployment, social and physical disability, including AIDS, homelessness, and substance abuse.

Social workers in practice today deal with profoundly vulnerable populations, overwhelmed by oppressive lives and the circumstances and events they are powerless to control (Gitterman 1991). Many social work clients' problems persist, in large part, because powerful groups in society, such as corporate and political systems, withhold access to resources and opportunity structures (Germain 1990). For example, our public schools are funded in a way such that the affluent receive a richer education, and, therefore, access to essential opportunities, while minority and poor children receive significantly less education, less hope, less of our concern (Kozol 1991). The recent Republican convention bashing of single mothers, welfare recipients, and gay/lesbian persons made explicit how these groups institutionalize poverty and vulnerability. Withholding and the abuse of power create chronic unemployment and underemployment of those whom the schools fail to educate, insufficient low-cost housing, and inadequate health care for poor children and adults. When community and family supports are weak or unavailable, and when internal resources are impaired, these populations become very vulnerable to physical, emotional, and social deterioration. These harsh realities lead to increased feelings of impotence and futility and conspire to institutionalize vulnerability and powerlessness.

The task of helping these populations has become significantly more difficult to fulfill. For the stubborn truth is that problems have been increasing while resources to mitigate them have been decreasing. Those with less get less! While public and private social agency budgets are being slashed and caseloads are increased to unmanageable levels, these agencies are concomitantly blamed for programmatic failures and financial mismanagement (Orfield 1991). Thus, social workers also feel overwhelmed, suffer burnout, and, like their clients, feel powerless and hopeless.

Within this social context a series on the subject of Empowering the Powerless is timely. In the series' first book, *The Empowerment Tradition in American Social Work: A History*, Professor Simon rigorously traces the concept of empowerment: its historical roots, intellectual and political traditions, salient themes, recurring issues, contributions by the social work profession, current directions, and future implications. Social work students, in their search for professional identity, need to be familiar with the important historical contributions made by our profession. Professor Simon, a creative scholar and gifted writer, makes our history come alive. We hope social work students will be given the opportunity to read this book and to develop an appreciation of their professional roots.

The second book in the Empowering the Powerless series will present community organizing concepts and case materials. Future books will conceptualize and illustrate empowerment practice with specialized populations (e.g., depression, substance abuse) and with oppressed populations (e.g., people of color). The series will also present creative empowering professional roles (e.g., social worker as educator) and examine the linkage between clinical practice (i.e., "private troubles") and social and organizational reform (i.e., "public issues"). In the series empowerment practice is viewed as the process and outcome of helping clients and staff to increase their personal, interpersonal, and political power so that they can exert greater control and influence in their personal and professional lives. While various political ideologies and theoretical perspectives have evolved that limit the concept of empowerment to helping people develop increased feelings of personal power without attempting changes in structural resources and opportunities, or, in contrast, to organizing people for collective action and increasing their political power, the Empowering the Powerless series will emphasize the integration of personal, interpersonal, and political power.

I present the series' first book, *The Empowerment Tradition in American Social Work: A History*, with excitement and pride in Professor Simon's contribution to the profession's literature.

Alex Gitterman
General Editor

Preface

The concept of *empowerment* has become one of the murkier terms in the American political and cultural lexicon. *Empowerment* has achieved the dubious distinction of being among the tiny handful of concepts, along with *freedom, equality,* and *welfare reform*, that signify opposite meanings to political antagonists. To contemporary champions of laissez-faire economics and minimal government, empowerment means handing off to people in local areas the responsibility for making their everyday lives better. To present-day advocates of an activist democracy—a polity that embraces the vigorous pursuit of a socially secure condition for all citizens by all of those citizens and their government and their corporate leaders—empowerment invokes the principle of subsidiarity, by which "larger and more powerful political and economic institutions sustain smaller communities instead of dominating them . . . and encourage 'a new experiment in participatory democracy' in the American workplace and polity" (Bellah et al. 1991:282).

It is the premise of this book that the second meaning of empowerment has been a central philosophy of one stream of social work for approximately a century. Though the coinage of the word *empowerment* is relatively recent, the perspective connoted by that term is not. The inspirations for empowerment-based social work and its changing manifestations over time are the subjects of this inquiry.

Social work's commitment to helping marginalized and impoverished people empower themselves is as old as the occupation itself. Since the last decade of the nineteenth century, social work's empowerment tradition in the United States has comprised one vital segment of the larger profession. It is a tradition shaped by practitioners and theorists from diverse epistemological orientations and varied modes of practice who work in highly diverse settings. A century of empowerment social work has unfolded in public institutions, voluntary organizations, proprietary sites, sectarian institutions, secular agencies, unions, corporations, and private practices.

The American empowerment tradition within social work has required of its participants five elemental processes: 1. constructing collaborative partnerships with clients, client groups, and community leaders, 2. emphasizing the capacities of clients and client groups rather than their incapacities, 3. sustaining a dual working focus on individuals and their social and physical environments, 4. recognizing clients and client groups as active subjects with interrelated rights, responsibilities, needs, and claims, and 5. directing professional energies in a consciously selective manner toward historically disempowered groups and their members.

This book will attempt three projects. First, it will define, describe, and illustrate the fundamental properties of U.S. social work practice since the 1890s that have been devoted to client empowerment, "a process through which clients obtain resources—personal, organizational, and community—that enable them to gain greater control over their environment and to attain their aspirations" (Hasenfeld 1987:478–479). In illustrating and analyzing practice that has supported client empowerment, it will be important to examine obstacles to empowering practice. It will also be necessary to investigate the nature and contours of paternalistic practice, the orientation most antithetical to the empowering impulse.

Second, this book will trace the century-long evolution of social work practice that has been devoted to client empowerment and will explore the social movements, ideas, and beliefs that have been most influential in the thinking of those who have forged the empowerment tradition. Finally, the book will examine implications for future practice that have been extracted from the first one hundred years of empowerment-oriented social work.

It is important to note that this book is not a history of the social work profession. Instead, it is a selective, diachronic exploration of a particular, long-lived strain of practice within the United States. That strain has been known by many terms between the 1890s and the 1970s and only came to be called "empowerment" practice when Barbara Solomon formally introduced the term into the profession's discourse with her pathbreaking book, *Black Empowerment* (Solomon 1976).

The text has been written in gender-neutral language. However, some of the quotations that are included were spoken or written in an earlier time—long before anyone was aware of the destructive effects of reinforcing the invisibility of women and girls through the generic use of male forms of pronouns and nouns. Out of respect for the integrity of the original quotations, I have left them intact.

The text uses the terms *black* and *African American*. Since the two terms are used in contemporary writings and speech by black and African American activists and scholars in the United States, and since each term has its advocates, I have employed both.

Acknowledgments

The suggestion to write this book came from Alex Gitterman, editor of the Columbia University Press social work series Empowering the Powerless, in which *The Empowerment Tradition in American Social Work: A History* appears. His posing of the project, encouragement of my work at each phase, and editorial vision and suggestions proved invaluable to me in the creation, shaping, and completion of the book. Furthermore, Alex Gitterman offered these several forms of assistance with steady goodwill during a period of knotty internal politics at the institution in which we both serve as faculty members. Regardless of difficult workplace tensions and strains, he succeeded completely in providing safe harbor for our collaboration as editor and author. For that high level of professionalism, I am deeply appreciative. Indeed, his principled way of fostering and editing my work in the midst of complex organizational stressors is a model that I would try to emulate in the future, should that opportunity ever arise.

The enthusiasm of Jonathan Stanton and Tracy Stanton helped motivate me while I pursued this project. Doren Slade was a wise, reliable, and savvy guiding force throughout the entire process. Her arduous efforts to write, revise, and secure publication for her own admirable book, *Making the World Safe for Existence: Celebration of the Saints Among the Sierra Nahuat of Chignautla, Mexico,* while she worked at a highly demanding full-time job, continually refueled my reserves of hope and commitment.

Paula Hooper Mayhew sustained and advised me through every step of the project. The depth of her generosity, curiosity, and intelligence continues to astound me, despite more than eleven years of being the direct beneficiary of her unstinting largess. Her faith in me is, happily, infectious. I thank her for her steadfastness and love.

Finally, I want to express appreciation to the countless practitioners and theorists of the empowerment tradition in American social work since 1893. Some of them have directly educated subsequent generations of social workers through their publications, speeches, or practice; many more have passed on their legacy indirectly and anonymously. Whether they have been acknowledged explicitly or not, their example and perspective continue to inform, challenge, and inspire their successors.

THE EMPOWERMENT
TRADITION IN AMERICAN
SOCIAL WORK

CHAPTER ONE

Empowerment and Social Work Practice

And hardest of all is it to understand that a person to "make good" psychologically must be allowed not only to make good by his own efforts, but to make good in his own way.

If we must resist impulses to threaten or punish, or grant or withhold favors, how much harder to see that each individual must make his own solution, not in the sense that he is master of his fate and captain of his soul in a reckless defiance of external reality, but that his goals and life objectives are *unique for him*. Hopefully, society itself will achieve a wider and deeper liberty based on more security, more co-operation, and less competition—so that the client's choices will be less determined by anxieties and frustrations, but the choices will remain his, not ours.

—Gordon Hamilton

Introduction

Empowerment practitioners of social work since the 1890s, in each era using different language to characterize their work, have viewed clients as persons, families, groups, and communities with multiple capacities and possibilities, no matter how disadvantaged, incapacitated, denigrated, or self-destructive they may be or may have been. The job of the social worker committed to client self-empowerment has been to devise a working relationship with clients that is premised upon the clients' particular abilities, resources, and needs and that supports the client or client group in making daily life more rewarding and in exercising "shared power in partnership with others" (Cook 1992:16).

The purpose of this partnership is to foster clients' use of their own strengths in the process of searching for and consolidating enhanced self-esteem, health, community, security, and personal and social power (Weick 1982, 1990). For example, in working with a teenage girl who has been referred to a social worker in a public school because of an excessive number of school days that she has missed since the start of the school year, the school social worker who is guided by an empowerment orientation would quickly ascertain the girl's special interests, aspirations, and areas of confidence. Then he or she would pursue with the girl ways to express and act on her interests more directly at school and in after-school programs, while discussing with school officials institutional accommodations that might be helpful to the teenager. Meanwhile, of course, the worker would also be assessing any and all obstacles to the girl's full participation in school and contributing factors to her truancy as a prelude to devising with the client and her family a conjoint plan of action (Meyer 1993:29). The teenager's particular interests and problem-solving energy would be sought out and mobilized from the outset, in empowerment-based social work, regardless of how many other layers of exploration and action were required over time.

Empowerment-based social work has sought to exploit the pockets of robustness in clients' personalities and the resourcefulness and resilience that may be found in their families, friendships, neighborhoods, and subcultures (Hartmann 1958, 1964). It has fostered client self-empowerment by taking clients and client groups seriously as experts on their own lives and as citizens and claimants, both within the specific domain of human services and within the larger polity. To illustrate, a social worker of the empowerment perspective, upon seeing for the first time in a public mental health clinic a client who is experiencing emotional depression because of the noticeable deterioration of his vision due to multiple sclerosis, would attempt several things. He or she would try to link the man with a self-help group of people who are living with multiple sclerosis, would learn from him the most telling ways in which his vision loss affects his daily activities, and would discuss with the new client the kinds of adaptations and resilience that he has already exhibited on his own in the course of coping with his illness and its effects.

Social work of the empowerment tradition has assumed that the central "story" to tell, both historically and contemporarily, is that of clients' own varied endeavors to gain resources that will enhance their "mastery over their affairs" (Rappaport 1987:122, Solomon 1976:315). Furthermore, it is a form of social work practice that has aided clients in finding meaning in and making sense of their situations, relationships, and problems (Saari 1991). In addition, empowerment-based social work has remained wedded to the conviction that only members of devalued and stigmatized groups are proper principals (Oberschall 1973, Solomon 1976).

Such practice has been fundamentally hopeful. Only practitioners who have believed deeply that people can change and that environments can be transformed have been able to work from an empowerment perspective in a sustained fashion. Without such a belief, recurrences and intensifications of the problems of clients leave social workers cynical or, at the very least, doubtful about the possibility of identifying and enhancing the authentic strengths of clients and communities. Since empowerment-based practice depends upon social workers to reach out aggressively to engage any and all capacities and initiative that a client, family, or community possesses, it is an approach that is incompatible with cynicism.

An example of the necessary hopefulness that underlies empowerment practice can be found embodied in social work at the Bedford Hill's Correctional Facility in New York State. There, the social workers on the staff of the Family Violence Program work with women prisoners who have endured and internalized years of abuse, both physical and emotional, within their families of origin and, later, in their relationships as adults. These are women who, in many cases, became perpetrators as well as objects of violence. Practice with the women inmates of Bedford Hills is long-term work, work interrupted by frequent setbacks, and work unsupported by a larger society that has little interest in giving any form of a break to female convicts. Consequently, the professionals who take on this challenge at Bedford Hills are, of necessity, believers in human beings' capacity to grow and change.

Indeed, the empowerment approach presumes that oppressed people and communities yearn for freedom, justice, and fulfillment. Like Paulo Freire, the Brazilian educator and leader of international literacy campaigns, empowerment-oriented social workers presuppose that historically disempowered people "struggle for their lost humanity"— often against difficult odds—because of human beings' "ontological vocation" (Freire 1970:28).

Social workers of an empowerment perspective have attempted assiduously to avoid twin dangers that loom large in the path of any would-be agent of change. Such practitioners have sought, on the one hand, to eschew fatalistic externalism—a tendency to see the world as a stage directed by powerful economic and political forces, an arena in which human consciousness and initiative have only "bit parts." At the same time, such social workers have forsworn hubristic grandiosity, an inclination to perceive human ambition and subjectivity as all-important, ignoring thereby the potency of social structures, historical forces, genetics, and human beings' immediate contexts (Freire 1970:35, Rose and Black 1985:44).

Practice from an empowerment perspective emerges from an understanding of a particular dialectical relationship that has been best characterized by Freire. He writes of the interplay between, on the one hand, the force of people and, on the other hand, the force of tradition, economics, social structure, and politics that contour key features of the settings and times into which people are born and raised (Freire 1970, 1990). This complex appreciation of human initiative, social forces, and the intersections between the two has crystallized when social workers have been able to adopt an attitude of "critical curiosity" about the possibilities and limits of the daily practices and environments of themselves and of their clients (Freire 1990:7–9).

Critically curious practitioners have been, concomitantly, both faithful listeners and bold interpreters who "uncover and make explicit a certain dream about social relations, which is a political dream" (Freire 1990:5). For both clients and social workers of the empowerment tradition, personal transformation and social change are necessarily interdependent and mutually reinforcing processes, each insufficient without the other (Gutierrez 1990).

Social work clients' pursuit of self-empowerment, that is, their pursuit of the intertwined goals of personal and social transformation, has taken place over the past century in the U.S. in many varied settings. Public welfare offices, voluntary social work agencies, both centralized and community-based, both traditional and nontraditional, both sectarian and secular, proprietary social work agencies, alternative social work and social movement organizations, employee assistance programs in corporate and union settings, and social work private practices have served as primary sites of empowerment practice.

Competing Social Work Traditions

Social work history in the United States has proved to be, of course, much more than a tale of activities in support of empowerment. It also has been a narrative of relationships, policies, and programs that have reduced, either unintentionally or purposefully, the actual and perceived power and choices of clients, client groups, and communities.

Indeed, paternalistic social work's imposition of priorities upon clients' worlds has constituted as integral an element in our professional past and present as has the empowerment tradition's deference to initiatives jointly arrived at between clients and workers that are anchored in clients' own experiences and aspirations (Reynolds 1934, Rose 1990b, Simon 1990).

Social work, after all, has never been one harmonious chorus of unified practitioners and theorists. To the contrary, the evolving profession has been an arena of ceaseless internal debate, tension, and conflict since the 1880s. Contention has ruled the day at least as often as internal accord (Austin 1985:16).

Professions in general, among them the social work profession, are clusters of heterogeneous segments whose members are seeking diverse objectives through diverse means (Bucher and Strauss 1961:326). Predictably, deep divisions emerge in professions concerning epistemology, methodology, and technique, both between specialities and within them (Bucher and Strauss 1961:328). Professions even splinter internally concerning the question of what activities and values constitute their core (Bucher and Strauss 1961:328).

Nonetheless, some professions are able to cohere, despite near-chronic inner discord, provided that they have met two conditions. Professions prevail if their multiple internal fragments have a shared history of taking on common tasks linked to unclaimed problems, "jurisidictional vacancies," that no other profession has been able to appropriate yet as its own (Abbott 1988:60–91). Second, a profession survives its own internal fragmentation and external competition if it convinces the public that its cluster of techniques and body of abstract knowledge are essential for solving or ameliorating a recognized problem (Abbott 1988:3–62).

The social work profession is an amalgamation of diverse actors and groups who have agreed at only the most general levels of abstraction about common tasks, problems to be solved, techniques to employ, and knowledge bases upon which to rely. Far from being a community of like minds, social work's occasions of internal agreement have been the outcomes of hard-fought, in-house battles about the profession's aims and means. It is not surprising, therefore, to find that empowerment-based social work constitutes only one historic tradition of several within the social work profession (Beck 1983, Gray, Hartman, and Saalberg 1985, Gutierrez 1990, Hegar and Hunzeker 1988, Hirayama and Hirayama 1985, Pernell 1985, Pinderhughes 1983, Sherman and Wenocur 1983, Solomon 1976, 1982).

Empowerment-based social work has competed historically with two important rival traditions in the paternalistic mode. One weighty paternalistic rival has been that of the *benefactor*. The benefactor tradition is one in which workers treat clients as victims who are part of a group of unfortunate people that, apparently, have managed their lives less well than have the social workers who are offering care (Pinderhughes 1983). The work of benefactors is informed by two unconscious elements: their unacknowledged sense of being superior to their clients in managing life, and their unacknowledged sense of powerlessness in the face of the complexities and seeming intractability of clients' troubles. Benefactors project the latter feeling onto their clients and, as a result, perceive them to be inadequate and incompetent (Pinderhughes 1983).

Social workers of this strain usually borrow a view of clients from the medical profession—one that attends primarily to clients' deficits. Needs, to the benefactor social worker, are symptoms and outgrowths of pathology in clients' past and present. Clients' needs are also understood to be indications of the mismatch between the vigor of environmental demands and the frailty of clients' responses.

Another rival tradition to that of empowerment practice is that of the *liberator*. The liberator is a social work organizer and advocate who, like the benefactor, views clients as victims of their life circumstances. However, unlike the benefactor, the social work liberator does not perceive clients to be personally scarred by oppression. Instead, he or she views members of oppressed groups as intact; it is the surroundings of the oppressed that require restoration and transformation. Environmental and organizational metamorphosis, not clients' personal change, is called for to restore the dignity and freedom of disenfranchised groups and their members. Social workers of the liberator tradition attempt to contribute to social change both through exercising forceful and foresighted leadership and through developing leadership among those who are disenfranchised.

The liberator tradition is an admixture of elements that have been illustrated in, first, the stewardship of Moses, which entailed heroic forms of moral and strategic leadership on the part of the anointed head, and, second, Lenin's "vanguard," a corps of revolutionaries who tried to lead an oppressed group out of feudalism by virtue of the vanguard's advanced consciousness, discipline, and sacrifice (Lenin 1935). Both Moses and Lenin's vanguard were thought to be possesors of a vision of a better world and of a path to that world. Their respective followers relied on them for exactly that.

Paternalism has undergirded both these forms of practice. Practice is paternalistic if conducted on behalf of people without their consent (Spicker 1988:54). Paternalism has two elements, the intent to do good for another and the effect of violating another's known wishes (Abramson 1985:389–390). Empowerment-based social work practice conceives of paternalism as alien to its essential values and purpose. Averse to assuming either the posture of the benefactor or the liberator, the social worker functioning within the empowerment tradition seeks neither to lift a client "up" to the professional's level nor to lead clients out to a promised land mapped out previously or independently by the professional.

Instead, the social worker who is intent upon client empowerment attempts to initiate and sustain interactions with clients and client groups that will inspire them to define a promised land for themselves, to believe themselves worthy of it, and to envision intermediate approximations of that destination that they can reach, in a step-by-step fashion, while remaining in reciprocal connection with each other and with a professional guide who offers technical and emotional help. Adherents of the liberator approach have encouraged clients to seek complete autonomy from professions and professionals; practitioners of the empowerment tradition have interpreted clients' pursuit of personal and interpersonal power as a process of taking initiative and establishing their integrity, dignity, agency, and claims within relations of interdependence. Drawn in recent years more toward paradigms that stress intersubjectivity—like those of the Stone Center's "power-in-relation" school and self-psychology—than toward an Eriksonian emphasis on autonomy and maturity, empowerment social workers have tended to view strength as that which one exercises in concert with others rather than alone or in contradistinction to another (Chodorow 1991, Erikson 1950, 1956, Gilligan 1990, Miller 1986, Noddings 1984). Professional assistance, in this view, is not by definition an obstacle to client empowerment. It can, however, easily devolve into a barrier if the social worker interferes with supportive networks that clients have created for themselves or if she or he harbors a private definition of the helping relationship's purposes, means, and criteria for determining achievement of the end.

Building Collaborative Relationships

One essential property of social work practice that is dedicated to empowerment is the collaborative nature of the relationship that forms between the practitioner and the client. Collaboration is not equivalent to a cooperative relationship between an expert helper and a client in which the flow of inspiration and aid is essentially unidirectional. Nor is it a partnership of actors who are equal in interpersonal and organizational power (Hasenfeld 1987).

Instead, in empowerment-based social work, collaboration resembles closely the "alliance" between social worker and client conceptualized in 1951 by Bertha Reynolds. For her, an alliance is a relationship that hinges upon three elements: 1. a shared sense of urgency concerning the problems confronting the client, 2. a conjoint commitment to problem solving in as democratic a manner as possible, and 3. a shared emphasis, initiated by the worker, on the common humanity of both members of the relationship, despite what may be marked distinctions in social class, race, life chances, and education (Reynolds 1951:162, Freedberg 1989:35). Such collaboration entails ongoing availability, reciprocity, engrossment, and acute receptivity to the client's perceptions and experiential truths on the part of the professional who has been charged, professionally and organizationally, with the responsibility to be "carer" (Noddings 1984). The sine qua non of authentic collaboration is an ongoing reciprocity of effort, ideas, resources, and, most important, respect. Both parties are "fellow strugglers" in a partnership in which "the specialized know-how for negotiating and surviving the morass is sometimes possessed by social worker, sometimes by client, sometimes by neither" (Wood and Middleman 1989:11). In circumstances in which neither holds the requisite expertise, it is the social worker's obligation to engage the client, client group, or community in a conjoint pursuit of the necessary knowledge and skills.

Multiple roles may be played by both the professional social worker and the client within a collaborative relationship, as long as the client remains the primary "engine" of change. A professional need not and, indeed, ought not be passive as a collaborator, provided that she or he consults and works out agreement regularly and carefully with the client about the nature, direction, and pace of activity that each will undertake. The professional social worker as collaborator will, together with the client, select interventive roles—"conferee," broker, mediator, advocate, counselor, caseworker, case manager, group leader, organizer, assessor, administrator, or policy formulator—that are dictated by the problem at hand rather than in an a priori fashion reflective of the methodological proclivities or ideological preferences of the practitioner (Practice, Programming, and Supervision Faculty 1990, Goldberg and Middleman 1974, Meyer 1987:413 1970:115–121, Wood and Middleman 1989:98). Within the empowerment tradition, each province of practice—work with individuals, groups, families, organizations, and communities—has been an important locus of collaborative relations with clients. The focus and emphasis of that collaborative work, predictably, differ in each of the five modalities.

In practice with individuals, one chief challenge to the social worker as collaborator has been that of earning sufficient trust from the client initially and then progressively over time so that the latter chooses to participate as fully as he or she is able. A client's participation is crucial in identifying issues, aims, and tasks to address and in remaining committed to working on agreed upon projects in times of extreme self-doubt, despair, interpersonal conflict, or setback. Another major challenge has been that of avoiding the practitioner's common error of turning one's own helplessness in the face of clients' sustained hostility, passivity, self-destructiveness, or intransigence into punitive reactions, overtly controlling behavior, or the passive-aggressive surrender to a benefactor's stance of focusing primarily on clients' pathology.

In work with groups, collaboration has taken at least three concomitant forms. A professional's encouragement of members of the group to help each other in a collaborative way is clearly as crucial as establishing a cooperative and reciprocal bond with the group as a whole and with each person in it. Empowerment practice with groups has an advantage that dyadic work does not. Clients can derive almost immediately a sense of personal and interpersonal power from the collectivity that is able, to some degree, to reduce the structural power imbalance between the social worker and his or her clients. For that reason, among others, many empowerment practitioners who work within the one-on-one format urge and help their clients also to join support groups or treatment groups made up of people with common needs and issues.

Similarly, in empowerment work with nuclear, extended, and alternative families, heavy emphasis has been placed on strengthening existing relations of mutual assistance among adults. Empowerment practitioners have attempted to interrupt unidirectional patterns of helping in which one family member characteristically comes to the rescue of other adults, who usually have not in the past reciprocated and have not been expected to reciprocate when the "rescuer" needs help. Reciprocity among adult family members is encouraged along with self-reliance, instead of a continuance of a family system in which one member carries the psychosocial burdens of several others. Another common form of collaborative practice with families involves efforts to assist abused women and children in recognizing their right to a life without violence, in putting a stop to their abuse, or in getting help to find safety and to end abusive relationships (Rodriguez-Trias 1992:663). Additionally, empowerment practitioners call upon collaboration when working with socially or physically isolated families. Here, a frequent tack of empowerment social work has involved helping family members to interconnect with other families, friends, neighbors, and community resources (Hartman and Laird 1983).

In practice with organizations, social work administrators and consultants who concern themselves with empowerment priorities have placed heavy stress on the involvement of direct practitioners as full collaborators with managers in the planning, evaluation, and reconfiguration of service delivery. Empowerment practice with organizations has rejected "scientific management," or "Taylorism." Frederick Taylor and his followers in the 1880s and 1890s worked to separate completely planning functions from implementation in the interests of maximizing efficiency and management's control of the work process. By contrast, empowerment approaches to administration and organizational development have presumed that sustained organizational effectiveness hinges upon bringing the insights of direct practitioners to bear directly on the processes of conceptualizing the design and redesign of programs and services (NYC Chapter of NASW 1992, Rothschild and Whitt 1986, Martin 1990). Client empowerment and organizational empowerment, simple logic suggests, depends upon worker empowerment. Worker empowerment, in turn, springs from participatory program planning processes that involve administrators and line workers as partners in thought, action, and the evaluation of action.

Community social work has also been a major bailiwick in which empowerment practitioners have employed their collaborative talents over the past century. Whether seeking to strengthen the natural helping networks of neighborhoods, to include community residents and service recipients directly in councils, committees, and boards of every description, or to confront head-on issues of institutional discrimination, community workers have located collaboration between themselves and community members at the heart of their project (B. B. Solomon 1985:253–255).

Despite the centrality of collaboration to social work dedicated to client empowerment, collaborative practice has faced multiple obstacles in all practice modalities. An understanding of the concept and practice of collaboration hinges on a careful inspection of the social, institutional, and psychological barriers to the development of partnerships between social workers and clients.

Some Obstacles to Collaboration

The imbalance of power within a working relationship between professional social workers and their clients is one obstacle to sustained collaboration. Partners in empowerment-directed collaboration are not equal in power when one member of the relationship is a professional social worker and the other is a client in an agency setting or in an institution. On this subject, Reynolds early on expressed her doubts that equality between worker and client could ever be achieved in a hierarchical society in which the professional social worker is an intermediary between the enfranchised and the disenfranchised (Reynolds 1934, Freedberg 1989:34). More recently, social workers of an empowerment orientation who hold a similar point of view to that of earlier empowerment theorists like Reynolds have extended our understanding of the nature of power imbalances and their effects on clients and the client-worker partnership. The most earnest of collaborators, for example, can be ensnared by "power traps" (Weick 1982:177–179). Power traps are disruptions in mutuality that intrude when the "learned helplessness" of historically devalued clients converges with a profession's intent upon retaining legitimacy through keeping control over technical and abstract expertise (Weick 1982:177, Abbott 1988:3–64, Seligman 1992, Seligman and Groves 1970). One example of a common power trap is the temptation to mystify one's professional base of skill and knowledge, thereby making it less likely for the client to understand his or her own contribution to the healing or problem-solving process. Mystification temporarily gains the practitioner unearned authority in the client's eyes. Another power trap is the tendency to distance from clients by issuing diagnoses that are devaluing and by adhering in an undifferentiated manner to the "abstinence rule," the orthodox psychoanalytic taboo against responding directly to a client's expressed need and against answering a client's questions about the professional's life (Jacoby 1990:194–195, Weick 1982:177–179).

The power asymmetry between worker and client is unavoidable in any situation in which one person reaches out for help from a professional who is endowed with expertise, interpersonal skills, and authorized membership in an organization that controls critical resources needed by clients, such as access to their children or income supports (Hasenfeld 1987:470–471). In an asymmetrical working bond in which all key actors remain devoted to client empowerment, the client and worker would be utopian fools to seek equality of power. Instead, they would be wise to pursue "equal moral agency," a condition in which both endorse the equality of dignity and existential human worth of each while simultaneously acknowledging the imbalance of power and authority between them in their agency-based relationship (Handler 1992:286).

Compounding the structural inequality in power in client-worker relationships is a dangerous psychological variable that accompanies most, if not all, relationships that social workers have with their clients or constituents—the desire to feel superior (Reynolds 1942:30). Reynolds's warning about the appeal of feelings of superiority has been encapsulated by Ann Hartman:

> Championing an egalitarian relationship in practice, she [Bertha Reynolds] deplored the hierarchical relationship between helper and helped, feeling that such a situation provided "a safe harbor in ourselves for all the unconscious desires to be superior." Like the rounded back of the farm laborer, the tendency to superiority was for social workers, she felt, an occupational hazard. (Hartman 1986:86)

Dovetailing all too conveniently with the unconscious magnetism for professional helpers of feelings of superiority is the collusive tendency, on the part of many individuals from historically devalued and oppressed groups, to feel inferior to members of historically valued groups (Weick 1982:174, Memmi 1967:87). As an outgrowth of profound self-hatred and sustained self-doubt, members of disempowered groups often assume that wisdom lies outside themselves and that it resides in others who are as little like themselves as possible (Miller 1986). A Manichean world is thereby imposed by racism, sexism, and imperialism on the psyches of marginalized people, who, then, like those in privileged cultural groups, mistakenly equate power with goodness and powerlessness with badness (Fanon 1968:41, 1967, Miller 1986). This tragic confusion is a predictable one in societies that privilege one gender over another, one race over another, one sexual orientation over all others, and moneyed people over poor ones.

As a consequence, empowerment-based social work has the salient task of assisting clients to examine, in groups with others who share a similar situation, the mythical and degraded self-portraits that they have internalized unconsciously as members of a stigmatized group (Memmi 1967:87). Additionally, the social worker, in a dyadic partnership with the client, can investigate the nature of the bonds that that client forms with more powerful individuals and the nature of the trade-offs attached to those bonds. Then, slowly, that person can commence on a journey toward "self-recovery," a lifelong process that entails the conscious rejection of the oppressor's matrices of merit and the construction of fresh categories with which to order the world and to view and value oneself in that world (Memmi 1967:151–152).

Social workers who treasure empowerment, meanwhile, have as much psychological work to do as do their clients. Professionals must recognize and explode the categories of thought that separate their internal world into dualistic polarities between superior and inferior, the helper and the helped, the well and the sick. Like the search for "self-recovery" of disenfranchised clients, social workers of the empowerment tradition recognize the necessity to struggle to identify, surface, comprehend, and deconstruct unconscious proclivities toward psychic imperialism through a daily and ongoing process of self-reflection. This ongoing excavation of the self is "a progressive obsession," the aim of which is to bring closer together one's intentions and one's actions as a professional helper (Freire 1990:6–7).

Emphasizing Client Strengths

Empowerment-based social work has rejected throughout the past century a "Pollyanna" perspective, one based on the denial of the deficits and limitations of a client, family, group, or community with whom one is collaborating. Social work that has begun from and built upon client strengths and resources in the course of bringing about personal and environmental change has done so with full and detailed attention to the depth of damage—psychological, physical, cultural, economic, social, and political—incurred by individuals, their families, and their communities in the face of decades of poverty, discrimination, and multiform deprivation. Empowerment-based social work has attended carefully to the underside of clients' lives, to the developmental lags and lacunae in people's abilities, resources, relationships, and communities that may well emerge when hardship, hostility, and violence permeate schools, neighborhoods, workplaces, and families. Social workers devoted to client empowerment have borne witness to the derailments of human growth and development that are embodied in clients' drug addiction, alcoholism, chronic emotional depression, masochism, abuse of children, battering of women, abandonment of the dependent elderly, and criminal activity. Social work that has failed to take full stock of clients' present limitations as well as strengths has been a form of wishful thinking that offers false promises and eventually leaves clients with deepened despair.

Empowerment-based social work, by contrast, has highlighted the importance of reinforcing and expanding clients' extant capabilities and resources while attempting to help people heal their traumatized bodies, minds, spirits, and neighborhoods. Far from being practice that sees with "rose-colored glasses," it is an approach that has acknowledged the many sides of clients' realities and that has chosen, for strategic and existential reasons, to emphasize the patches of health and power that clients present (Weick 1990).

To build on client strengths is, first, in dialogue with clients, to identify their nature, location, and uses, both realized and potential. Second, empowerment social workers over and over again bring to clients' or client groups' attention numerous and specific illustrations of the ways in which their existing strengths contribute to their survival, development, and sustenance in the face of protracted difficulties. A third step in the effort to build on client strengths is to engage clients in dyadic and peer group discussions in which they identify and enumerate their own internal and external resources and then link them operationally to the everyday challenges they encounter at home, at work, in interpersonal relationships, in their neighborhoods, and in the larger community. Fourth, empowerment social workers assist clients and client groups in mapping out, in the light of their articulated aspirations, the additional skills, talents, and resources they want to develop as extensions of their existing capacities. Throughout the process of building on client strengths, practitioners of each modality explore with clients or client groups the juxtaposition of the latter's strengths and deficits, the relationship between client strengths and the salient problems that challenge them, and the possibilities of linking clients' strengths with those of other people and groups who have needs in common.

Some Obstacles to Emphasizing Client Strengths

As with the development of bona fide collaboration between clients and workers, the project of building upon clients' capacities has its predictable impediments and deterrents, whether one is working with individuals, groups, families, organizations, or communities. One such stumbling block is the pervasiveness of the human service practice of viewing reductively a client or client group as a "part object," that is, as a presenting problem, as a cluster of deficits, as a set of demands, as a bundle of needs, or as damaged "Other" (Klein 1975, de Beauvoir 1953:33). If, as a practitioner, one falls into such reductionism, one risks reinforcing unwittingly the longstanding disempowerment of the very individual or group who has come for help in transcending stigma, poverty, or the internalized blocks to self-realization that mirror so faithfully external barriers (Solomon 1976). Often, unconscious defensive processes such as splitting, projection, or displacement lead the social worker to view a client as a "problem." One antidote is to think consciously of both one's clients and oneself as "whole objects." Whole objects are human subjects who have complex and changing motivations, needs, capacities, histories, and contextualized possibilities. To remain conscious of the wholeness, agency, and complexity of clients or client groups is demanding and indispensable labor for the social worker who wants to assist people with obtaining greater power over and opportunities within their everyday lives.

Another obstacle to enacting practice that emphasizes client strengths is the readiness of many clients and client groups from historically disadvantaged populations to believe the worst about themselves (Miller 1986). Oppression, once internalized, takes a number of self-denigrating forms, including the toxic self-hatred and self-doubt that cripple individuals and groups who have been subject over many decades to the contempt of members from more powerful groups. Practice that emphasizes client strengths must first erode long-held habits of client self-loathing experienced at both conscious and unconscious levels of being.

A Dual Focus on Person and Environment

The century-long struggle to make one unified track out of a two-railed interest in attacking social ills and in aiding individuals and families in need has characterized both the overall social work profession and the empowerment stream within the profession. The pursuit of unity amidst bifurcation began within empowerment ranks in the settlement houses and charity organization societies of the 1890s and continues in the present. Creating a psychosocial equation that is not lopsided, that neither tilts toward the *psycho* or the *social*, is a project that has strained the hearts and minds of the most creative of empowerment theorists and practitioners in every generation since Jane Addams and Mary Richmond.

In recent decades, ecological theorists of social work practice have brought forward frameworks that construct an understanding of human beings as subjects who are part of particular generations, environments, and times and whose accrued interactions with their social contexts constitute a pivotal focus of exploration, collaboration, and intervention. Creators of "situational," "transactional," "person-in-situation," and "person-and-situation" theories have made clear that the environment is linked integrally and intimately with the daily lives of individuals, families, groups, organizations, and communities who people that environment. To change successfully the opportunity structure of an individual or family, one must apprehend and change the opportunity structures of the physical, economic, social, cultural, and political context in which that individual or family dwells and works. To improve the equity and quality of a society, polity, institution, or community, one must assess and add to the life chances of identified persons and groups within those settings. Practice that focuses only on changing society and community or only on changing persons and families has, in short, been ruled out by ecological social workers who have viewed the interconnections between persons and their contexts as the solar plexus of a client or client group's systemic universe (Germain and Gitterman 1980, Hartman and Laird 1983, Meyer 1970, 1983, 1987, 1993).

For these scholars, each in her or his distinctive way, client-centered practice has proscribed the privileging of psyche over context and vice versa. Instead, they have maintained that empathic understanding of clients and constituents, accurate psychosocial and community assessments, and effective interventions—intrapersonal, interpersonal, and social—flow from simultaneous appreciation of the idiographic and the universal in each problem posed. In this existential and operational paradigm, the welfare of individuals and their families is linked inextricably with the well-being of their social contexts. Equally interwoven is the vigor of social movements with the overall strength of the individuals and families involved in those movements (Germain and Gitterman 1980, Goldstein 1973, Hartman and Laird 1983, Meyer 1970, 1983, Goldberg and Middleman 1974, Pincus and Minahan 1973, Siporin 1975).

Similarly, feminist theorists of social work practice have pointed to the necessarily intertwined nature of the private and public spheres of daily life. Feminist social workers from all branches of practice have decried the false dichotomy of treating the personal and the political as mutually exclusive realms. Feminist social workers have invoked Rosalind Petchesky's call to discern the "reverberations" and inter-connections among spheres of life, such as those between intimate relationships and market relations, even as they continue to be set in opposition to each other by the culture as a whole (Petchesky 1979:376, Bricker-Jenkins and Hooyman 1986, 1991, Sancier 1986–1992, Weick 1982, Dinerman 1986, Wetzel 1986, Hanmer and Statham 1989, Van Den Bergh and Cooper 1986, Morell 1987).

An Obstacle to Practice with a Dual Focus

Like all other Americans, social workers are subject to the centuries-old tendency in Western thought of conceiving of mind apart from body, autonomy as antithetical to communion, the sacred as separate from and superior to the profane, and the elect as wholly and irre-versibly distinct from the damned (Bakan 1966). Social work in the United States has been shaped within this dualistic tradition and, not surprisingly, has developed its own ingrained habit of dichotomous thinking about "micro" and "macro" concerns. Social work's history is one of metronomic movement between emphasizing aid to individuals in one era and a drive toward environmental change in the next (Morell 1987:145). The psyche often has been diagnosed apart from subjects' social lives and environs and discussed as if it were a pure essence shaped during a child's first five years of life by a mother or family in splendid isolation from society. Similarly, socioeconomic and political reform has been considered by some social work theorists as the "one true faith" that merits professional devotion and has been deemed more important than "band-aid" work with the psychosocial concerns of individual clients and their families. Dualism and hubris within U.S. social work ranks have thereby cursed both the house of intrapsychic excavation and the house of social change.

The Client and Client Group as Claimant

The client—whether an individual, family, group, organization, or community—is, in the tradition of empowerment-based social work, viewed as one who attempts to meet a set of particular needs by exercising the rights and responsibilities that flow from membership in a community and by asserting claims for resources, power, and relationships. The client is, at one and the same time, a subject who needs material goods and services, human interaction, and respect, a citizen or prospective citizen who exercises rights and responsibilities that are stipulated by specific polities, and a claimant who makes demands on a social order that reflect her or his emergent or full comprehension of both needs and rights. The client or client group as claimant begins (or continues) the self-empowerment process by articulating to a social worker a need, perhaps for a job, for aid in getting free from drug addiction, for subsidized child care, for help in securing a General Education Diploma (G.E.D.), or for assistance in making primary health care available in the neighborhood. The client comes forward initially (or is mandated to come forward or is an object of outreach) as one who needs, one who is in some sort of difficulty. This is a risky posture, one that places the client in danger of becoming lodged in the disadvantaged position of being perceived as childlike unless that client recognizes concomitantly, in the midst of the condition of needing, the constellation of rights that he or she is entitled to as an adult member of society (Rappaport 1981:1–2).

What rights are those? The answer is far from simple. Complicated both by historical contingency and the willingness of the group of which that client is a member to make claims, no fixed definition of rights is possible. For example, the client who is a convicted felon who seeks counseling while serving time in prison has many fewer rights as an adult member of contemporary U.S. society than does a client in an outpatient mental health program who has no criminal record. Or, for another example, the client who is an immigrant without formal citizenship in the United States does not have the same rights vis-à-vis voting, employment, or freedom of international movement as does the citizen. A third illustration is found in poor communities of historically disadvantaged people who have fewer rights that are honored, de facto, day-to-day by the police than do wealthy suburban neighbors twenty miles away, despite the identical nature of their rights, de jure.

Rights, in short, are not inalienable essences, but specific prerogatives granted by the commonwealth to groups and individuals who, at some point in history, have fought to define and obtain them. Rights, in other words, are powers and privileges to which members of a political entity are entitled, by designation and assignation of the state, which is the official representative of the public at large (Marshall 1950).

Citizenship is constructed and maintained through three forms of participation—civil, political, and social (Marshall 1950, Barbalet 1989, Turner 1986). Civil participation is the ongoing activity each person and group exercises to ensure the protection of constitutionally granted freedoms. Political citizenship is the collective pursuit through electoral politics of parliamentary, judicial, and administrative authority and power (Marshall 1950, Barbalet 1988:6–7, Turner 1986:108–110). Social citizenship involves the ongoing effort to establish economic and social security through accessible and equitable public schooling, a fair tax system, social services, income supports, and a refereed international marketplace of capital, commodities, services, and jobs (Marshall 1981).

Employing this three-tiered conception of citizenship, one can answer the question of what rights a client in need can rely upon in the process of making claims for resources and power. A client in the United States near the end of the twentieth century who is neither incarcerated nor an alien enjoys a cluster of civil rights, including but not limited to freedom of speech, religion, assembly, press, and self-defense, as well as the freedom from cruel and unusual punishment. In addition, that client, as an adult member of society, holds, among other legal powers, the right to vote, to petition the courts and administrative bodies for fair hearings and appeals, to remove, in conjunction with other citizens, officeholders from office, and to hold local, state, regional, and national office. Finally, a client has certain social and economic entitlements, contingent upon his or her age, social class, gender, employment history, and familial status. These entitlements may include a free public school education through the end of high school, social security retirement benefits, unemployment insurance, public protection of private pension plans, workers' compensation, income supports, health insurance in old age, and disability insurance.

One of the most pressing tasks of the empowerment-based social worker is to make sure that her or his clients have as comprehensive and up-to-date an understanding as possible of the civil, political, and social forms of participation to which they are entitled and the correlative procedures, prerogatives, and resources available to them. It would be a grave error to assume, without inquiring, that one's client has good knowledge of his or her rights as a citizen and as a consumer of services. After all, few of us who are professional social workers have a thorough understanding of our own rights and entitlements, some of which change significantly and rapidly over time.

It is also the duty of the empowerment-based social worker to assist a client with the complex process of defining his or her needs, whether emotional, material, or spiritual. Just as it would be a strategic mistake to assume that clients come to us with full knowledge of their rights and entitlements, so it would be foolish to assume that clients enter into relationships with social workers with clear and unconflicted comprehension of their short- and long-term needs. Again, the simple act of self-reflection on the part of the professional social worker will constitute a reminder that none of us knows, at any one moment in time, the exact nature and interrelationships of our key needs. The existence of the unconscious within the psyche keeps some needs temporarily secret from the self. Other needs remain unknown because one does not yet have the language with which to conceive and describe them. Still other needs go unrecognized because they conflict directly with already recognized and desired requirements of the self or with the expectations that valued others hold.

On occasion, clients may arrive at the doorstep of a social worker with a clear understanding of what his or her primary need and goal is. A husband may want a divorce, a couple may want to adopt a baby, a terminally ill person may want to find a means of committing suicide, a neighborhood may want to make its streets and playgrounds safer. In situations like these, one responsibility of the empowerment-oriented social worker is to devise with the client(s) a relationship that will enable that client to double check that his, her, or their stated desire is in close congruence with the overall interests, long-held values, and central commitments of that person, couple, or group. The social worker's responsibility is also, at this juncture, to use his or her engagement and assessment skills in assisting clients to evaluate, before acting, the implications of the fulfillment of this expressed primary need for other cherished elements of their daily lives.

The social worker who is guided by the empowerment perspective has, in short, a highly active part to play in the formation of a working partnership that taps the experience, expertise, and resources of both worker and client. The obligation of the social worker to initiate, engage, gather data, assess, contract, implement, intervene, and evaluate remains strong. However, unlike in the approaches of the benefactor and liberator, that obligation is a consistently joint one reliant upon ongoing, vigorous, and reciprocal problem solving, give-and-take, and challenge between client and worker.

Some Obstacles to Claimants

Regrettably, clients' full exercise of civil, political, and social rights and responsibilities is frequently obstructed. Illiteracy is one major obstruction. Adults and adolescents with minimal reading skills will have a severely limited opportunity to enact any one of the three forms of citizenship and to derive benefit from social services, health care, income supports, and job programs for which they may be eligible.

Lack of fluency in English constitutes a second major barrier to clients, particularly in those many states of the U.S. that do not publish public information or post signs in the first languages of immigrants. Consequently, it remains a standing challenge to empowerment-based social workers to help mobilize popular pressure to make available free or low-cost courses in adult literacy and English as a Second Language, as the settlement house movement provided in the first three decades of its existence. At the same time, empowerment practitioners join with community groups in lobbying for the development of bilingual and multilingual social services and health clinics for people who are in immediate need and far from fluent in English.

A related obligation of empowerment social workers and their clients is to continue to advocate and organize for quality public schooling that teaches children and teens to be fully literate and fully enfranchised. In an era of deficit reduction, intensifying intergenerational conflict, and Republican leaders' abandonment of the commitment to comprehensive public funding for public education under the transparent guise of offering "educational choice" for parents through vouchers, it behooves clients and social workers to redouble their efforts to join other citizens in reaffirming a social contract that ensures free and effective public education for all children and adolescents.

Another serious barrier to clients' full participation in civil, political, and social affairs is the shortage of social supports available to working parents in an age in which extended families are much less likely to live in the same neighborhood than a quarter century ago and in which child care is expensive and hard to secure. Especially for the millions of heads of families who are single, working mothers, participation in civic life is unlikely. Women's low wages and continuing occupational segregation in the poorest paid segments of the work force leave working mothers with little money to pay for the child care that is needed if they are to involve themselves in sustained community service. A shortage of time as well as of money hinders the involvement of working parents in political and social citizenship. Housework, including child care, remains disproportionately in women's hands in all but a tiny percentage of American households (Coverman 1983, Googins 1987, Hochschild 1989, Shelton and Firestone 1989). Therefore, working mothers' "second shift" at home further interferes with their capacity to take part in the vital civic work of protecting their own basic constitutional freedoms and ensuring that their interests are well represented in legislative and administrative governance (Hochschild 1989).

Still another major obstacle confronts clients as claimants. Many clients have been socialized into clienthood within a traditionally paternalistic social service and welfare system. Their roles, functions, repertoire of behaviors, and expectations as clients have been shaped, in many cases, in relations in which they have been treated as beneficiaries and recipients, not claimants. Thus, they must undertake a gestalt shift to move to an alternative self-conception.

Similarly, many practitioners have learned their trade under the supervision of benefactors or liberators, the former being more likely. Consequently, they know much about overruling client preferences, labeling client pathologies, inculcating values, and correcting "false consciousness." Most social workers, like their clients, have major revisions to make in their self-conceptions and in their way of building relationships with clients if they are to be able to honor empowerment traditions.

Particularly at those moments when a client's and worker's judgments collide, the opportunity arises for paternalism to seep into the working relationship through the backsliding of either partner. Learned postures of helplessness, victimization, or emotional dependency threaten to repossess the client. Meanwhile, the worker may find himself or herself overruling adult client preferences to further the client's "best interests." Or skills training may gradually devolve into values induction. Often, it is the client's claiming the claimant's role that triggers the resurgence of paternalism within the social worker.

How, then, does the empowerment practitioner sustain a collaborative approach when in conflict with a client or client group? How does she or he avoid falling back into condescending or defensive stances when faced with a client who is or has become a bona fide claimant? "The answer" can be found in self-reflection and in continuing dialogue with clients, a dialogue conducted with resolute commitment to maintaining a democratic approach to problem solving. The responsibility for sustaining a democratic connection in the midst of conflict falls more fully on the practitioner's shoulders than the client's because of the structural advantages of power and authority enjoyed by the professional in a worker-client relation.

Dialogue is, of course, not magic. It is, however, a convenient and useful medium that enables adults who are at odds with each other to take in the reasoning, feelings, and humanity of those with whom they disagree. Dialogue conducted in a mutually respectful manner, in which both or multiple parties listen carefully to each other and avoid ad hominem and ad feminam judgments, holds the promise of creating a new order of problem solving and relating. It also makes possible compromise, negotiation, the identification of shared ground, and the deferral of action until more data can be gathered or more reflection undertaken by one or more participants.

Selective Focus on Historically Disempowered Persons, Groups, and Communities

The fifth necessary ingredient of empowerment practice is selectivity of focus. In the United States, sadly, there has been no shortage of "customers" for social services since the 1890s. Public and voluntary sector agencies have had to create waiting lists to order the historic mismatch between basic human needs and available social resources. As a consequence, empowerment practitioners, like all social workers, have been confronted in every era with painful choices about whom to serve.

The original twin missions of social work, those of relieving the misery of the most desperate among us and of building a more just and humane social order, continue to command the allegiance of members of the empowerment tradition. These intertwined missions have proved to be durable and worthy criteria with which to choose lifework and to discard less compelling possibilities.

Client empowerment presupposes an existing condition of client disempowerment and marginality. Fitting subjects, therefore, of empowerment social work are socially despised persons, families, and groups. They may be poor in a country that values economic success, black in a culture that privileges white skin, chronically ill in a nation that equates health with productivity and productivity with merit, or old in a land that cherishes the vigor of youth and shuns symbolic and material reminders of human mortality. Or they may bear some other discernible attribute that evokes fear and dread on the part of Americans who identify more with the "center" than the "periphery" (Shils 1975). A stigmatized status, in sum, is the sine qua non of clients and client groups served by social workers of the empowerment perspective (Goffman 1963, Solomon 1976).

FIGURE 1.1

NECESSARY ELEMENTS OF AMERICAN SOCIAL WORK PRACTICE
IN THE EMPOWERMENT TRADITION

1. Collaborative partnerships with clients, client groups, and constituents
2. A central practice emphasis on the expansion of clients, capacities, strengths, and resources
3. A dual working focus on individuals and their social and physical environments
4. The operating assumption that clients are active subjects and claimants
5. The selective channeling of one's professional energies toward historically disempowered groups and individuals

---

Guidelines for Practice in an Empowerment Mode

Day-to-day practice that incorporates the five core elements of the empowerment perspective noted above takes what shapes? The shapes are as diverse as the communities, cultures, and organizations in which social workers function. Nonetheless, despite multifarious forms, contexts, and modalities, social work interventions that are infused with an empowerment perspective all honor nine essential guidelines.

The first guideline of empowerment-based practice has been, *Shape programs in response to the expressed preferences and demonstrated needs of clients and community members*. Practitioners' importation of issues and priorities to an agency or neighborhood is nothing more than intellectual and political colonialism—that most erosive and, in the long run, counterproductive of activities. The empowerment approach, by contrast, has decried such importation. Instead, the empowerment tradition has inspired its social workers to listen to clients and neighborhood members at great length before shaping programs and services. Empowerment work has long been premised on the study of clients' or constituents' articulated concerns and demonstrated needs, study involving attentive, systematic, and skilled inquiry into the meanings, consequences, causes, correlates, forms, and scope of problems. Empowerment-based social work depends upon the best of the concepts and methodological skills of the assessment tradition in social work, incorporating community assessment, psychosocial assessment, and behavioral assessment into its repertoire of diagnostic tools (Kellogg 1909, Mattaini and Kirk 1991, Meyer 1983, 1993).

The second guideline that has guided the development of empowerment-based practice is, *Make certain that programs and services are maximally convenient for and accessible to one's clients and their communities*. Geographic, financial, temporal, and transportational attainability, together with linguistic and cultural receptivity, are necessary components of accessible programs and staffs. Throughout most of twentieth-century social work, concerns for short-term cost containment have contended vigorously with the priority of ensuring the accessibility of services to clients. Creaming is one common adverse consequence of paying more attention to short-run efficiency than to longer-term effectiveness of service delivery. To prevent creaming and the disregarding of the most vulnerable of clients, empowerment social work has shouldered two particular obligations: championing the priority of the multidimensional accessibility of services and demonstrating technically the long-term wisdom, cost-efficiency, and efficacy of policies of inclusion.

A third guideline of empowerment-based social work practice has been, *Ask as much dedication to problem solving from one's client as from oneself*. To work collaboratively with clients who are accustomed to making extensive claims on themselves and on the people and systems around them is relatively easy. To work collaboratively with clients unaccustomed to recognizing their own needs, rights, and responsibilities, let alone making demands on themselves and others in recognition of those needs, rights, and obligations, is much harder to accomplish. Collaboration rests on a balance between participants of commitment to the joint project, of effort put into problem solving, and of respect for the dignity and ideas of the other. Paternalism slips almost unnoticeably into the relational mix when practitioners work harder than their clients to remedy a client's or client group's situation or to build a client's stock of interpersonal skills. To ask and keep asking clients for an investment and renewal of their hard work and commitment is to communicate respect and hope, provided, of course, that "a transactional definition of the problem"—an initial and frequently renegotiated compact about working goals and priorities—has been struck (Gitterman 1989:169). Careful exploration, confrontation, and comprehension of both transferential and countertransferential feelings and behaviors are called for on the part of the practitioner dedicated to client empowerment.

A fourth guideline of empowerment-based social work is, *Call and build upon the strengths of clients and communities.* In agency-based practice and outreach, it is not enough to conduct careful assessments and to factor into the design of programs the expressed needs and preferences of clients and community members. It also behooves empowerment-directed social workers to configure services that directly call upon the wisdom and experience of clients and of the client's family and community.

For example, the Center for Family Life in the Sunset Park section of Brooklyn, New York, has created a Foster Grandparent Program that relies on the parenting and teaching skills of older residents in the neighborhood who provide "in-home aid" to families of children who are at risk of abuse or neglect. Similarly, the Neighborhood Foster Care Program of the Center for Family Life calls upon the parenting expertise and generosity of Sunset Park residents who volunteer both to serve as foster parents for neighbors' children and to assist these foster children's biological parents with the process of learning or relearning how to parent (Lerner 1990:35). Empowerment involves recognizing and tapping the particular talents and capacities of clients or neighborhoods so that people or communities can come to their own aid in the most full and imaginative manner possible.

Yet, one hastens to add, empowerment does not imply abandoning a client group or neighborhood to its own devices. Few, if any, groups or neighborhoods in the U.S. have sufficient capital, raw materials, technology, jobs, commerce, schooling, housing stock, markets, leadership, public and social services, and domestic peace to make their own way successfully. In the global economy of the late-twentieth century, all communities in the U.S., including the most privileged, are entities that are heavily reliant upon governmental subsidies and infrastructures, other neighborhoods, and diverse societal institutions for goods, services, knowledge, and skills. It should, consequently, surprise nobody that historically marginal groups and communities, like their wealthier and less stigmatized neighbors, require contributions from a larger whole, in addition to their own strength and will, to survive and cohere.

A fifth guideline that has helped shape empowerment-based practice has been, *Devise and redevise interventions in response to the unique configuration of requests, issues, and needs that a client or client group presents. Resist becoming wedded to a favored interventive method.* By being a combination of both "client-driven" and "issue-driven," instead of "method-driven," empowerment practitioners and agencies have attempted to avoid reinforcing the historic dualisms of social work—"wholesale vs. retail," "cause vs. function," and "movement vs. service."

Instead, empowerment practitioners have sought to crosscut these distinctions with attention to the unique in each person or client group as well as to the universal in his, her, or their situation (Abramson 1985:390–392, Campbell 1978, Lee 1929, Meyer 1970:110–121, 1993, Morell 1987, Richmond 1930, Schwartz 1974). Consequently, social workers of the empowerment perspective have required skill in a significantly broader range of methodologies than other practitioners. As generalists "specializing" in empowerment, they have needed working competence in each of the traditional methods of social work to be able to answer fluidly the diverse calls that clients and client groups from historically disempowered communities have made. Responsiveness to individuals, families, groups, organizations, communities, and social causes all lie well within the purview of empowerment social work and each empowerment practitioner. A single case or group of people presenting a common concern could require a practitioner to enact, at various points, technologies from casework, group work, social work with families, community organization, program development, advocacy, administration, and policy analysis. In a world and culture of increasing specialization and compartmentalization of function, empowerment social work, paradoxically, calls upon its members to embrace an increasingly generalist outlook and approach. The integrity of individuals and their social groupings and the complexity of their contexts so demand.

The sixth guideline of empowerment-based social work has been, *Make leadership development a constant priority of practice and policy development.* To develop leadership is to assist individual clients, families, organizations, and community groups in acquiring and consolidating elements of daily living indispensable to the accrual and exercise of power at home, at work, and in political life.

And what are the constitutive elements of leadership? The short list includes: 1. a vision, derived from experience and dialogue, of the overall social goals, programs, and policies that would nourish oneself, one's family, and community; 2. the ability to articulate and transmit that vision in a clear and persuasive way to diverse constituencies; 3. first-hand knowledge of the problems at hand; 4. education in the accumulated wisdom of people and communities who have addressed similar problems; 5. supportive relationships; 6. interpersonal skills; 7. self-knowledge and confidence; 8. a firm ethical and cultural identity; and 9. alliances with strategically located authorities.

Leaders emerge, according to empowerment thinking, from ongoing processes of peer-to-peer inspiration and from programs in the voluntary, governmental, and corporate sector that are designed specifically to recognize and build on the strengths and knowledge of individuals, families, workplaces, and neighborhoods. The development of leadership also relies upon practitioners' alertness concerning the double-barreled ease with which professional practice can devolve into controlling and manipulative paternalism and clients from devalued groups can fall back into familiar patterns of deference, helplessness, and blaming.

Allegiance to a seventh guideline of practice, *Be patient, since empowerment takes substantial amounts of time and continuity of effort,* also characterizes empowerment-based contexts of practice. Undoing the emotional trauma of child abuse, generating employment opportunities for adults who have never before worked and who are functionally illiterate in both English and Spanish, or mobilizing a city and neighborhood to eradicate the danger of lead poisoning in a poor community with old and scarce housing stock are not jobs for those who are in a rush to transform society, wear the hero's mantle, or be a healing force. Empowerment flows from the trust that people develop in themselves, in their neighbors, and in the institutions in their communities, such as schools, hospitals, police precincts, and churches, upon which they must rely from childhood through old age. Trust grows slowly and warily among people who have been entrusted with little. Degradation and violation cause individuals and groups to lose faith in the possibility of creating a life that is neither degraded nor violated by such endemic forces as racism, poverty, and the battering of women and children. Helping people to reverse this despair and supplant it with hope in and labor toward the fulfillment of their own aspirations is the work of those practitioners who are constant and whose watch is long.

An eighth guideline of empowerment-based practice concerns social workers' relationships to power and oppression in their own lives (Weick 1990). *Take ongoing stock of social workers' own powerlessness and power at work.* If a social worker is to be able to have authentic empathy for a client or community struggling to understand and overcome internalized and external forms of oppression, that worker must be deeply knowledgeable about his or her own inhibiting and liberating "field of forces" in the present and in the past (Lewin 1951). Moreover, a social worker must have an especially clear-sighted sense of his or her authority and power on the job and the limits of the same, if he or she is to avoid attempting to dominate or punish clients out of the frustration that often attends work in underfunded and stigmatized social service bureaucracies with troubled and marginalized individuals and families (Lipsky 1980).

To assist with client self-empowerment, one requires a richly layered and textured comprehension of one's own strengths, limitations, and history of empowerment and disempowerment, a detailed understanding of one's power and limits of power on the job, and an excellent and broad set of assessment, engagement, and interventive skills.

Furthermore, one needs careful, ongoing supervision and training so as to ensure that one has a continually updated and contextualized comprehension of clients' calculi of daily experiences, of one's own countertransferential responses, and of the possibilities and constraints of the social worker's agency-based role.

A ninth and final guideline for practice in an empowerment mode has been, *Use "local knowledge" to contribute to the general good (Geertz 1983).* Practitioners of the empowerment branch of social work in the U.S. have, for a century, borne two concomitant responsibilities: to respond to historically dispossessed people who have signaled some form of immediate need and to help construct a more equitable and less cruel social order. Relying on detailed knowledge they have derived from extensive exposure to clients' problems, perspectives, and interpretations in direct practice, administration, and community social work, empowerment social workers have attempted to contribute their understandings to public discourse and social reform. Empowerment-oriented social workers have done so not only through their paid work on the specific concerns articulated by their clients and client groups but also through their direct involvement as citizen volunteers in social and political campaigns.

The chapters to follow will illustrate some of the many ways in which practitioners since the 1890s have borne witness through public testimony to the harsh conditions of living and working encountered by their clients. Attention will be paid to the efforts of empowerment-based social workers to document the consequences for their clients of destructive and dysfunctional social policies and to their participation with their clients in sustained lobbying and advocacy initiatives. Their attempts to shape and secure model legislation on numer-

---

FIGURE 1.2

GUIDELINES FOR SOCIAL WORK PRACTICE
IN AN EMPOWERMENT MODE

1. Shape programs in response to the expressed preferences and demonstrated needs of clients and community members
2. Make certain that programs and services are maximally convenient for and accessible to one's clients and their communities
3. Ask as much from one's clients as from oneself
4. Call and build upon the strengths of clients and communities
5. Devise and redevise interventions in response to the unique configuration of requests, issues, and needs that a client or client group presents. Resist becoming wedded to a favored interventive method
6. Make leadership development a constant priority of practice and policy development
7. Be patient since empowerment takes substantial amounts of time and continuity of effort
8. Take ongoing stock of social workers' own powerlessness and power at work
9. Use "local knowledge" to contribute to the general good

ous health and welfare subjects and their service as volunteer consultants to community-based organizations, self-help groups, and grassroots campaigns for social justice will also be highlighted. In sum, selective involvement in social and political causes and in public office has been an organic and logical part of the overall professional function for practitioners of the empowerment perspective.

Conclusion

Contemporary social work that is practiced from an empowerment perspective has acquired a complex heritage of ideas and examples from predecessors who have occupied every imaginable methodological and epistemological corner of the social work profession. These ancestors within the profession practiced and published long before the language of empowerment took hold. In their relationships with clients from historically devalued groups and in the interventive approaches they devised and implemented, earlier practitioners and educators established the five essential elements and nine guidelines of empowerment-based practice that this chapter catalogues retrospectively.

Social workers of the present also benefit from the knowledge of obstacles to the enactment of empowerment-based practice recorded by prior practitioners. We are reminded by our predecessors that the social worker who collaborates with clients in defining problems, establishing priorities, and selecting the means to employ in pursuit of agreed upon directions needs to remain acutely aware of the power discrepancies extant between professionals who are formal representatives of organizations that distribute scarce resources and their clients who need those resources. Further, we have been warned that empowerment-based social work is endangered on a daily basis by the collusive and destructive interplay at an unconscious level between professionals' internalized sense of superiority over those asking for help and clients' actual or potential self-hatred, particularly if clients are members of socially despised groups. Finally, present-day practitioners of social work who are guided by an empowerment perspective are taught by their forerunners that they function in a culture pervaded by dualistic structures of thought and feeling that favor not cooperation but competition "between ways of giving meaning to the world" and that privilege superordinate-subordinate relations between and among people rather than egalitarian collaboration (Weedon 1987:35, Bakan 1966). Dualistic thinking and the institutions in which dualisms are embedded mitigate against the construction and longevity of authentically collaborative relationships by making it difficult for both worker and client even to conceive of a mutually inclusive intersubjectivity in which both subjects retain full-fledged agency and dignity (Giddens 1982, Stolorow and Atwood 1992).

Nonetheless, despite serious obstacles, such genuine partnerships between clients and social workers have proved possible to build and sustain. This book will provide illustrations of the chain of such collaboration in social work history and explore the intellectual and political traditions that have inspired it.

To comprehend the continuity over time of the empowerment tradition within social work, a succession that will be documented in this book, one must first comprehend the religious, political, and intellectual sources of this tradition. These heterogeneous inspirations will constitute the focus of the next chapter.

CHAPTER TWO

———

The Roots of
Empowerment

I know of no safe depository of the ultimate power of the society but
the people themselves, and if we think them not enlightened enough to
exercise their control with wholesome discretion, the remedy is not to
take it from them, but to inform their discretion. —Thomas Jefferson

The concept of empowerment springs from many sources, some quite
remote and others more proximate. Social workers' conceptions since
the 1890s about human nature, the state, the community, and the
interrelationships among these three entities have been drawn from a
common cumulative reservoir of historical precedent and thought. In
addition, social workers have been subject to the power of particular
ideas and movements of their respective eras. Empowerment cosmol-
ogy and methodology are social constructions handed down from cultural ancestors that each generation of activists then has tailored to
resonate with the demands and visions of its own time and place.

   This chapter will focus upon social workers' shared inheritance of
ideas and themes that have formed the bedrock of empowerment
thinking in the United States. After examining this common legacy,
the discussion in subsequent chapters will shift to a chronological
examination of the particular zeitgeists that were conducive to the
spawning of empowerment approaches during three different periods
of social work history. The purpose of this investigation is to trace the
development of concepts of empowerment that continue to inspire the
thought and action of contemporary social workers. Hopefully, the
discussion will help present-day practitioners in the U.S. comprehend
the cultural anchors of their own commitment to assisting historically marginal people in gaining greater control over the terms of their
everyday lives.

To engage in the process of empowerment requires that one assume that human beings bear significant responsibility, in league with other human beings, for the enhancement of their condition on earth. Empowerment thinking is deeply antifatalistic. It insists that human agency is the central resource to call upon to improve the human condition. People engaged in self-empowerment may well call upon heavenly forces for help and strength in walking the path they have chosen. Nonetheless, the people who desire greater power and efficacy in their everyday affairs and a more responsive polity must themselves be the principal actors who initiate and sustain the pursuit of empowerment.

It is not a search that people can conduct alone. The ethos of empowerment bears no resemblance to the Horatio Alger theme of people "picking themselves up by their own bootstraps." To the contrary, the pursuit of self-empowerment is a campaign in which persons, families, and groups call upon the democratic state, the surrounding neighborhood, and a variety of professions to assist them in marshaling the skills, the knowledge, and the resources that they need if they are to enjoy the full fruits of citizenship and of community and family membership while carrying out the many obligations associated with those complex statuses.

The Intellectual and Political Foundations of the Concept of Empowerment

The Protestant Revolution

It is the Protestant Revolution of the sixteenth and seventeenth centuries that gave rise in the West to the popular belief that people are bound by duty to help shape their own earthly state. In R. H. Tawney's words: "To the Calvinist . . . the calling is not a condition in which the individual is born, but a strenuous and exacting enterprise to be chosen by himself, and to be pursued with a sense of religious responsibility" (Weber 1958:2). Luther and Calvin, argues Weber in his famous book-length essay, *The Protestant Ethic and the Spirit of Capitalism*, revolutionized Western thought by shifting the attention of many Christians who sought salvation from the next world to this world and, correspondingly, by shifting the burden of responsibility for salvation from God to the shoulders of those individuals who desired to demonstrate their worth to God through faith and "the fulfillment of duty in worldly affairs" (Weber 1958:80). Since the sixteenth century, "there remains, more and more strongly emphasized, the statement that the fulfillment of worldly duties is under all circumstances the only way to live acceptably to God. It and it alone is the will of God, and hence every legitimate calling has exactly the same worth in the sight of God" (Weber 1958:81). Thus follows the "Puritan's serious attention to this world, his acceptance of his life in the world as a task" (Weber 1958:88). From Lutheranism and Calvinism, then, have sprung the hope that any mere human can improve his or her lot through hard work and, therefore, bears the corresponding burden of doing so.

Furthermore, a variety of sects within the Reformation introduced into Christian thought the democratic notion that "the priesthood of all believers" could discern God's revelations directly by reading and interpreting the Bible (Weber 1958:60–91). The faithful need no longer turn to religious "experts," to intermediaries, such as priests, in order to comprehend God's will in this new Protestant world. Instead, a believer could, through her or his own attentiveness to the Bible and prayer, find Truth. This notion, too, is an important antecedent to the democratic proclivities within empowerment-based practice and to its dethronement of the unchallenged reign of experts.

Quakerism during the seventeenth century added still another democratizing premise to the storehouse of ideas that gave rise to the tradition of empowerment. Its contribution of the belief of the "inner light" present in all human beings, of the immanence of God within each person, with the consequent sanctity of all human life, extended respect, value, and redemptive possibilities to even the most stigmatized peasant, despairing debtor, or degraded prisoner (Frothingham 1972:119). Within the United States, especially, the Quaker tradition's reverence for the bit of God found in every woman and every man, whether slave or free, reverberated far beyond Quaker settlements and helped root the idea of the power and worth of the ordinary person in regions of the country and in institutions with which Quakers had no direct contact. Quakers also contributed the practice of seeking community consensus through extended dialogue, a form of decision making found in many contemporary self-help groups and community organizations (Silverman 1987, Rothschild and Whitt 1986).

Merchant and Industrial Capitalism

The spread of merchant capitalism and, later, industrial capitalism constitutes another distinct part of the background from which the empowerment tradition eventually emerged because of capitalism's peculiarly dislocating consequences for peasants, slaves, tenants, small landowners, artisans, industrial workers, and shopkeepers. The urbanization, colonization, industrialization, and emigration engendered by capitalism expanded exponentially the numbers of people who found themselves without land, intact extended families, jobs, income, community, or a recognized niche in society (Thompson 1966, Hobsbawm 1962, Katz 1986). The experience of powerlessness, rootlessness, and marginality became pronounced and widespread under capitalism in much of Europe during the fourteenth through the eighteenth centuries and in the United States by the 1830s among white settlers. (For many Native Americans and black Americans, disempowerment came much earlier, coeval with the earliest European settlements in the New World.) The pervasiveness of territorial, cultural, and economic dislocation provided a brutal but compelling impetus for arousing people to identify the causes of their shared misery and to speed their own pursuit of redress, emancipation, and empowerment.

Additionally, capitalism placed a premium on the taking of risks, the demonstration of initiative, the envisionment and planning of a more prosperous future, and the identification of others with whom one shared economic and social interests. These valued aspects of capitalist life, which had not been nurtured among common people in precapitalist systems, became implicitly desirable dimensions of the behavior of members of empowerment movements of the nineteenth and twentieth centuries.

Sad to say, the confluence of Protestantism and capitalism begot another cultural force, in addition to emancipatory and empowerment movements. These revolutions together also gave rise to a moral category new to Christendom, that of the "undeserving" poor. Whereas medieval Europe, under the manorial system and Catholicism, had preached *caritas*, generosity and charity toward all, especially the most impoverished, Protestant capitalism legitimated the moral condemnation and economic dismissal of those populations, families, and individuals who had been stripped of ancestral homes and common rights to land usage by the enclosure movements of Western Europe (Boswell 1988). Many millions of newly landless people found themselves uncompetitive in the emergent marketplace of labor on account of one or, usually, several reasons—old age, early childhood, poor health, disability, pregnancy, responsibility for young and old dependents, geographic displacement, technological obsolescence, drought, floods, locusts, placement in the familial birth order, poor timing, or bad luck. Under the new rules of Calvinist doctrine, worldly wealth reflected godliness; poverty revealed the opposite. Failure to prosper in the marketplace of land, labor, and commodities now signaled failure as a human being and as a Christian in contrast with earlier, feudal times, when failure to prosper had been a God-given station endured by the vast majority of people in the "great chain of being" (Lovejoy 1936:59–60).

Much later, in Great Britain and the U.S. of the late nineteenth century, Social Darwinists crystallized this harsh underside of the Protestant and capitalist messages into a three-part homily, one that insisted, first, that poor and despised people had brought their misery upon themselves by their own lack of foresight, initiative, and diligence; second, and in consequence, that their poverty, hunger, and even premature deaths were deserved; and third, that human beings as a "race" would only improve, Herbert Spencer, William Graham Sumner, and others argued, if they discarded their dregs, that is, abandoned to their own fates people who failed the test of the market, which was also the test of God.

Jeffersonian Democracy

Another central block in the foundation on which empowerment thinking was built is Jeffersonian democracy. Thomas Jefferson's translation into North American terms of John Locke's insistence "that all human beings are equal, rational, governed by principles of reciprocity and fairness, and, as such, capable of self-rule" had far-reaching consequences for the forms of formal and informal democracy and citizenship established in the United States (Hawkesworth 1990:24, Barber 1984). Incorporating Rousseau's belief in the equality, independence, innocence, and perfectibility of human beings into his own philosophy, Jefferson argued strongly and persistently for the necessity of an active citizenry, one that did much more than simply vote (Hawkesworth 1990:25–26, Zimmerman 1986:1–5, Miller 1987).

Fearing "too little democracy" rather than too much, Jefferson advocated for the development of many voluntary organizations, for the creation of vital local communities characterized by face-to-face relationships, and for a decentralized and regionalized form of government that would engage as many citizens as possible in its workings (Barber 1984:xi, Bullert 1983:30). He helped plant firmly in the political ethos of the United States a strong preference for localism and an abiding faith in the doctrine of popular sovereignty, the notion that power over an entire society rests "not in particular bodies of electors but in the 'people-at-large'"(Schwartz 1988:2, Wood 1972:164). Above all, he contributed a profound optimism about ordinary people's capacity for wise self-governance in matters big and small once they had had the opportunity through education to learn about and reflect on issues salient to the general welfare. The Jeffersonian preference for "bottom-up" democracy has remained an essential plank in the floor of the empowerment tradition as has his insistence on the need for literacy and education for all who would be called upon to act as citizens (Peterson 1985:79–85).

Transcendentalism

Only a few years after Jefferson's death in 1826, another philosophical force important to the creation of an empowerment tradition in the U.S. captured the imagination of many. Transcendentalism, an outgrowth of New England's Unitarianism, emphasized the dignity and divine possibilities of human beings and the power of their reason and intuition to discern revelations from an immanent God (Rose 1981:39–42, Hopkins 1940:4–8). As Ralph Waldo Emerson, a leading Transcendentalist, wrote in 1836:

> Therefore that spirit, that is, the Supreme Being, does not build up nature around us, but puts forth through us, as the life of the tree puts forth new branches and leaves through the pores of the old. As the plant upon the earth, so a man rests upon the bosom of God; he is nourished by unfailing fountains, and draws at his need inexhaustible power. Who can set bounds to the possibilities of man? (Emerson 1971:1:63–64)

This veritable hymn to human potentiality evidences an exuberantly optimistic outlook that placed human beings at the very center of the redemptive process—an empowering role, indeed. Emerson and his fellow Transcendentalists, Bronson Alcott, George Ripley, Margaret Fuller, Theodore Parker, Henry David Thoreau, Elizabeth Peabody, and the young Walt Whitman "simply claimed for all men what Protestant Christianity claimed for its own elect" (Frothingham 1972:108).

They borrowed from their Enlightenment-era predecessors a belief in the perfectibility and essential goodness of human beings and, at the same time, "rejected the mechanistic universe of the Enlightenment for a vitalistic, organic view of nature in which" individual choice and activity held central sway (Albanese 1988:10). Like Jefferson, the Transcendentalists placed high hopes in human reason, finding it to be the main source of revelation and the element that ensured that people could "rule themselves" (Whitman 1964:380).

Furthermore, Transcendentalism called for the "immediate application of ideas to life" (Frothingham 1972:106). Most of the leading Transcendentalists immersed themselves in a network of collective social reform movements, such as abolitionism, women's and Negroes' suffrage campaigns, prison reform, the development of kindergartens, and an early progressive education movement. Some, like George Ripley, who founded Brook Farm in 1841, created communal experiments in Transcendental living, planned communities that attempted to devise structures, dynamics, and rituals that would honor institutionally the divinity, equality, and freedom of its members. Transcendentalism of the 1830s and 1840s foreshadowed the later empowerment tradition's optimistic insistence that stigmatized people can transform their own personal, communal, and social existence using internal resources as a mainspring. Through its generous faith in human nature, its egalitarian belief in the power of each person's reason to serve as a guide to a divinely inspired existence here on earth, and its devotion to the immediate enactment of its ideals through social reforms and experiments, Transcendentalism prefigured empowerment activities. Indeed, Emerson's charge of fifteen decades ago would still play well in the contemporary empowerment movement: "Build, therefore, your own world" (Emerson 1971:1:45).

Utopian Communities

Transcendentalists were not the only social pioneers "building their own world" in the period between 1830 and 1850 in the United States. A cascade of social experimentation characterized these twenty years. Planned religious communities of Shakers, Mormons, Amish, Oneidans, and Rappites burgeoned (Albanese 1988). So also did nascent socialist communities of Fourierists and Owenites, groups of people horrified by the consequences of the early Industrial Revolution and, as Gianna Pomata (1986:33) suggests, groups keenly aware that industrialization and urbanization might result in an "impending and possibly irretrievable loss" of community and popular culture. Both Fourierist and Owenite experiments rested on the radically egalitarian belief that a good society would need to be a classless society— one made up of many small-scale communities operating on the basis of the free association of cooperating neighbors, equal in status, resources, and rights (Taylor 1983, Cahm 1989). They demonstrated both a "theoretical and practical commitment to women's liberation" and strengthened a long-standing tradition in the United States of relying on cooperation among people who shared commitments and space (Taylor 1983:1–22). These pre-Marxist socialist communities tested out and circulated ideas that later became central to the empowerment tradition concerning the transformable nature of interpersonal and community relations and the salience of relations of mutual aid in daily life.

Anarchism

Belief in mutual aid as a basis for social life proved to be the defining theme of anarchism, another political movement of the nineteenth century that created and instilled into the ethos of the United States principles and preferences that made their way eventually into the core of empowerment-based social work practice. Appalled both by industrial capitalism's destruction of people and nature and by the spread of estranging bureaucracies, Pierre Proudhon of France, Mikhail Bakunin and Peter Kropotkin of Russia, and Emma Goldman of the United States made many attempts, together with their compatriots, to develop a social order and "morality out of the practice of mutual aid," while recognizing that "self-assertiveness of the individual was also an important factor for progressive evolution because it helped break the bonds that society imposed on the individual when institutions began to petrify" (Cahm 1989:6).

Anarchism sought to replace competition with cooperation and to supplant centralized authority with free associations of individuals and small groups that were to be "constantly modified to meet the multiple aspirations of all" (Cahm 1989:3). Reacting strongly against social Darwinism, anarchists believed in a "naturally . . . cooperative order," evolving through improvisation and experimentation, in which mutual aid was a far more central "natural" force than selfishness and the competitive struggle for survival and supremacy (Roth-schild and Whitt 1986:15, Kropotkin 1989).

Following Proudhon's conceptions of "mutualism" expressed initially in the 1840s, anarchists in the last third of the nineteenth century proposed that centralized states be abolished and replaced by two forms of social institutions: "communes" and "workers' councils." Communes were to be small and local territorial units collectively controlled by cooperating residents; workers' councils were parallel units in the workplace, also small and collectively controlled by workers. Anarchists proposed that communes federate territorially with other communes, while remaining autonomous. Concomitantly, workers' councils would federate industrially with other workers' councils, also retaining local autonomy. In addition, federations of communes and federations of workers' councils would provide each other mutual aid and exchange (Rothschild and Whitt 1986:16).

Undergirding these proposals was a deep mistrust of hierarchy and centralization that Bakunin articulated clearly in a speech of 1868, at a time when he was engaged in a titanic struggle with Marx concerning the preferred direction for international socialism to take:

> I am not a communist because communism concentrates and absorbs all the powers of society into the state, because it necessarily ends in the centralisation of property in the hands of the state when I for my part want the abolition of the state. . . . I want society and collective property to be organised from the bottom upwards by means of free association and not from the top downwards by means of some sort of authority. (quoted in Cahm 1989:36)

Bakunin and his followers challenged Marx's leadership of international socialism at the congress of the International at the Hague in 1872 over the issue of the use of state authority. They lost decisively. That loss split socialism into two opposing camps: Marxists, who supported a centralized approach to managing society collectively, and anarchists and socialists, who sought a decentralized and popularly controlled form of society. The former camp, as is well known, had immense influence on the twentieth-century history of Russia, eastern Europe, and parts of Asia and Africa, but relatively little significance in the United States.

Anarchism, according to Rothschild and Whitt (1986:16), was dismissed from a central political role on the world stage but, nonetheless, succeeded in popularizing in Western Europe and the United

States a commitment to five key ideas: 1. social organization and functioning through small, decentralized voluntary associations, 2. the importance of creating federations among autonomous voluntary associations, 3. "the goal of creating functional organization without hierarchical authority," 4. a two-track plan in which "communities control . . . community functions and workers control . . . workplace decisions," and 5. an emphasis upon "the unity of means and ends," an insistence that the way one attempts to achieve change is inseparable from the lasting outcomes and value of the effort (Rothschild and Whitt 1986:16–18). Furthermore, anarchism's particular conception of community took firm root in this country, a conception that emphasized relations among members that are many-sided, direct, unmediated by representatives or leaders, and characterized by reciprocity (Taylor 1983:26). Reciprocity for anarchists involved a combination of mutual aid and sharing that was understood to be at one and the same time short-term altruism and long-term self-interest (Taylor 1983:28–30).

The empowerment philosophy and activities of social workers since the 1890s, I suggest, have been enriched significantly by these anarchist principles, but only indirectly. In the U.S., popular knowledge about anarchism, until the New Left's "rediscovery" of its central principles, was extremely limited and skewed. American press coverage had focused on the violent minority of anarchists who, for example, assassinated President McKinley in 1901. The nonviolent anarchism of William Godwin, Proudhon, and Kropotkin received little direct attention or appreciation in the U.S. outside of scholarly circles until the 1960s. The severe repression of anarchists by the U.S. government and the contempt for anarchism of the Marxist left contributed to making it the most misunderstood and underestimated of the diverse cultural and political philosophies that have formed the basis of American empowerment thought. Nonetheless, anarchism's influence in the U.S. has far exceeded its reputation. Anarchist ideas have, for more than a century, been filtered into American workplaces, community groups, social movements, and families through the discourse and priorities of populism, the labor union movement, Progressive-era campaigns for "free love" and birth control, food, farming, and housing cooperatives, the Catholic Left, and the women's movement.

Expanding Notions of Citizenship

Another essential building block in the foundation of empowerment thought was the eighteenth-century conception of citizenship forged by a succession of philosophers of the French Enlightenment. It is a conception that has been expanded and modified during the past two centuries as a consequence of the elaboration of capitalism, the upsurge of nationalism, the spread of enfranchisement movements, and the creation of socialism (Marshall 1950, Barbalet 1988, Turner 1986).

Citizenship is a dynamic and socially constructed concept of participative membership in a community or society, membership that carries with it rights and status that reflect the time and place in which members live and the degree of success enjoyed by those members, in combination with their peers, in the delineation, protection, and exercise of their rights (Marshall 1950).

Citizenship entails three distinct elements: civil, political, and social participation (Marshall 1950, Barbalet 1988, Turner 1986). Civil participation is a notion that springs from eighteenth-century beliefs about the natural rights of "man" and the protection of those rights in relation to a state or sovereign. The United States' Bill of Rights is a classic statement of the set of civil protections that the Founding Fathers, deeply influenced by Diderot and Voltaire, thought essential to preserving the liberty of the individual. The institutions of the law and the courts were seen as those most directly linked to the preservation of an individual's civil freedoms. In this conception of citizenship, civil rights were essentially judicial and legislative defenses against intrusions on a person's life, liberty, or pursuit of happiness by a government, army, tyrant, or church.

Soon, however, during the nineteenth century, this notion of citizenship proved too circumscribed for leaders and members of groups historically excluded from membership in the citizenry by virtue of race, gender, or lack of property. A succession of enfranchisement movements made up of artisans, small farmers, African Americans, industrial laborers, and women sought inclusion into the ranks of those citizens who were entitled to full civil liberties. The growth of citizenship was "stimulated both by the struggle to win those rights and by their enjoyment when won" (Marshall 1950:92). To become enfranchised, many varied groups and individuals, such as Frederick Douglass and Susan B. Anthony, found it necessary to demand active roles in the formal exercise of political power, roles that involved voting and holding office in legislatures and local governing bodies. The exercise of citizenship came to mean not only the "eternal vigilance" needed to guard individual liberty but also the aggressive and organized pursuit and enactment of political power in parliamentary arenas. The concept of citizenship thereby was transformed by emancipation and suffrage movements to involve both civil protections and the right to multidimensional political involvement (Marshall 1950, Barbalet 1988:6–7, Turner 1986:108–110).

Still later, in the twentieth century, social democrats and socialists in Great Britain, Scandinavia, and the United States proposed adding a social dimension to the concept of citizenship. T. H. Marshall of Great Britain and others argued that people in a condition of prolonged economic disadvantage within capitalist societies do not in practice have the same access or ability to exercise the formal legal and political rights of citizenship as do economically privileged people (Barbalet 1988:2). Poor people can rarely, for example, find legal representation that equals in competence that secured by corporate leaders. Nor can they afford to lobby Congress in the sustained manner that wealthy special interests can. Running for national office is a formal right open to any citizen but, practically speaking, an impossibility for many who do not have the seed money necessary for initiating expensive campaigns. Disproportionate levels of illiteracy among impoverished people decrease the likelihood that that their civic participation will be as full as that of more economically secure neighbors (Marshall 1975, 1977).

Members of the movement for social citizenship in Western Europe and the U.S., like Paul Kellogg and Michael Harrington, sought to reduce the inequalities of resources that, they believed, lead to limitations on civic and political participation. The construct of social citizenship meant assuring economic security for all citizens by means of a welfare state, maintaining a progressive and solvent taxation system that could finance social services, income supports, and education, and ensuring the continuity of a free economic market for the production of wealth, the generation of jobs, and the distribution broadly of educational services (Marshall 1981). The key institutions needed to create and sustain social citizenship within capitalist societies were thought to be welfare bureaucracies devoted to reducing economic inequities, a vital international marketplace for commodities, services, and labor, and, of equal import, a diverse and accessible educational system that prepares all citizens and prospective citizens for critical thinking and social productivity.

Leaders of the movement for social citizenship elaborated carefully their conception of the institutional requirements of social citizenship because they believed that rights have no meaning outside of particular institutional contexts and "are thus only realizable under specified material conditions" (Barbalet 1988:6). Therefore, full participation by citizens in the social contract hinges, for architects of social citizenship and, I will argue, for empowerment-based social workers, upon the interrelated trinity of civil liberties, political rights, and socioeconomic entitlements.

FIGURE 2.1
INTELLECTUAL AND POLITICAL FOUNDATIONS
OF THE CONCEPT OF EMPOWERMENTS

Year	*Elements of the Foundation*
2000	Notions of Social Citizenship
1900	Anarchism
	Notions of Political Citizenship
	Utopian Communities
	Transcendentalism
1800	Jeffersonian Democracy
	Notions of Civil Citizenship
	Industrial Capitalism
1700	
1600	
	Merchant Capitalism
	Protestant Revolution
1500	

Conclusion

The central conceptual threads of civil, political, and social citizenship are interwoven with those of the Reformation, merchant and industrial capitalism, Jeffersonianism, Transcendentalism, utopian (pre-Marxist) socialism, and anarchism to make up a fabric of symbols, ideas, and beliefs that serves as a backdrop for empowerment thinkers and actors. It is a vibrant and complicated weave whose colors, at times, have complemented each other and have, at other times, clashed.

Empowerment is, at one and the same time, an end, a set of means to that end, and an unfolding historical process, one in which actors have made choices that are deeply affected by the orthodox and heterodox ideas and forces that converge in the time and place in which they have lived. Inspired by a long and complex skein of traditions, movements, and social experiments, empowerment-based social work practice since the 1890s in the United States has drawn its inspiration from a common cultural stock of themes and ideals about community, liberty, human agency, human possibilities, social institutions like the family and state, mutual aid, and citizenship.

Additionally, as the next seven chapters will discuss, social workers who are dedicated to empowerment have grafted onto that common stock of ideas notions specific to the historical moment in which they practiced. As a consequence, social workers who have evolved an empowerment approach to working with devalued and stigmatized people have done so with language, concepts, and passions that mirror their respective time periods. We turn now to a chronological exploration of empowerment thought and practice, beginning with the Progressive era.

CHAPTER THREE

The Early Period: Context and Influences, 1893–1917

> May I warn you against doing good to people, and trying to make others good by law? One does good, if at all, *with* people, not *to* people.
> —Jane Addams

The Context of Social Work's Earliest Phase

The expansion and acceleration of the interrelated processes of industrialization, immigration, migration, and urbanization, at rates unprecedented in the recorded history of the world, forged the context into which the social work profession was born during the three decades prior to World War I (Katz 1986:146–150, Ehrenreich 1985:19–30). Already by 1890, twenty-three thousand child laborers were working in thirteen states of the American South alone (Carruth 1979:351). During this period of the late nineteenth century, more than 90 percent of U.S. factory production took place in cities, displacing commerce as the economic foundation of urban areas and giving rise to the formation of suburbs by 1890 (Katz 1986:151, Leiby 1978:73).

Between 1890 and 1915, approximately seventeen million people poured into cities in the United States from rural communities in Europe in the hopes of finding economic security or increased political and religious freedom (Ehrenreich 1985:21). By 1890, New York City was home for twice as many Dubliners as lived in Dublin and for two and a half times as many Jews as lived in Warsaw (Carruth 1979:350). Millions more came to the city from farms and rural villages here at home, leaving behind, as had most of the European immigrants, the support systems of rural communal life (Mandler 1990:6, Ehrenreich 1985:21). By the end of the nineteenth century, New York

City's Lower East Side housed 250,000 persons per square mile, and, in certain precincts, 750,00 per square mile, rates of population density that rival those of contemporary Bombay (Carruth 1979:403, Mandler 1990:9).

Equally significant in shaping this period was the rapid concentration and consolidation of economic and political might. Rockefeller, his associates, and his lawyers had organized by 1883 the Standard Oil Trust, a cartel of many oil and gas companies (Carruth 1979:329). At the turn of the century, the New York Central Railroad controlled ten thousand miles of track in five of the country's largest cities: Chicago, Cincinnati, St. Louis, New York, and Boston (Carruth 1979:389). By 1890, 1 percent of the population of the U.S. owned more than the other 99 percent (Carruth 1979:355).

To increase the productivity of industry and, therefore, the consolidation of wealth, steelmakers replaced the artisan's way of working with "scientific management," an industrial approach that subdivided and routinized the work process into many separate functions performed by many different workers. Borrowing methods from engineers, chemists, and metallurgists that had proved useful in the transformation of physical objects in the laboratory, Frederick Taylor and others devised and disseminated a method of measuring, analyzing, and segmenting human labor that sped up production. Of equal importance, scientific management removed from workers on the production line all decision making about the work process, centering control for the first time in managers' hands alone (Hamilton 1989:71, Edwards 1980, Braverman 1976).

Faced with an ethnically, culturally, and linguistically diverse workforce made up of many men, women, and children recently arrived from rural communities in Europe and the United States, scientific managers labored to impose a standardized work ethic and discipline that would supplant diverse work schedules carved out within heterogeneous ethnic cultures (Hamilton 1989:84). "Industrial time" replaced preindustrial rhythms that had been honored for centuries in societies dominated by agriculture and crafts (Hareven 1982).

Whereas the sun, for millennia, had governed the start and end of the workday, the clock now became the proctor of the work cosmos. The workday grew ever longer, regardless of the season, absorbing even the night into the pursuit of production and profits. Shift work emerged, forever fragmenting the family as a collaborative work unit. Children as well as adults were pressed into twelve-, sixteen-, and eighteen-hour shifts, limited only by the outer boundaries of human endurance and concentration (Hareven 1982).

In the past, the long and hectic workdays of seed time and the harvest had been followed by the far less pressured seasons of late fall and winter. Industrial time obliterated altogether the moderating and compensating influences on work of the succession of seasons.

The pace of work also was accelerated dramatically by the industrial process and its timekeepers. Workers no longer determined the speed of their metaphorical plow. Factory owners, through their shift supervisors, now established the pace of the machinery and of the laborers attached to that machinery (Hareven 1982, Braverman 1976).

As the sweeping impact of the introduction of industrial time into workers' lives suggests, the United States, during the formative quarter century of the social work profession's emergence, was a society of explosive growth, sustained social dislocation, and deepening internal divisions. The distinctions between urban and rural experience became more stark as a burgeoning middle class began to enjoy a quality of life that urban commerce and newfangled amenities helped make possible. Department stores, indoor plumbing, central heating, electricity, elevators, and street cars made city life even farther removed from the ways of most people in the country. Contrasts also became more vivid within cities between the everyday lives led by the rich who had been well served by the boom periods of the Gilded Age and the lot of the numerous urban poor, for whom the economic depressions of the mid-1880s, 1893–1894, and 1907 constituted major threats to their very existence.

The interests of industrialists and managers, on the one hand, and of the managed, on the other, clashed repeatedly in incidents of bitter and bloody industrial warfare in which federal troops, state troopers, or Pinkerton forces were called in to put an end to labor unrest and strikes. Reports of the railroad strikes of 1877 in Pittsburgh and Martinsburg, West Virginia; the famous Homestead strike of 1892 at the Carnegie Mills; and the Pullman strike and attendant general railway strike called by Eugene Debs of the American Railway Union in 1894 alerted the American public to the profound disparities between the demands of laborers and those of their bosses.

Within the middle and upper classes, the contrast between the occupational and professional opportunities open to men and those open to women was heightened as female graduates of the new

women's colleges and of the few coeducational colleges and universities that admitted women found themselves excluded from all but a
handful of vocations. To have earned a B.A. from institutions like
Smith, Oberlin, or Cornell, yet be barred, nonetheless, from entering
the worlds of industrial and commercial management, diplomacy,
government service, medicine, law, the ministry, engineering, the
physical sciences, the emergent social sciences, and the professiorat
drove many an educated woman into either psychogenic illness, pro-
tosocial work, or both (Chambers 1986:6, Frankfort 1977, Muncy
1991, B. M. Solomon 1985).

Also glaring in this period was the chasm between the formal and
informal prerogatives, opportunities, and safety available to white
people and those available to black people, at every class level and in
every region of the country. Many blacks were only one generation
away from slavery by 1890 and still shouldered its legacy of poverty,
fear, violence, illiteracy, and exclusion from most arenas of education,
employment, and justice. Older free-born blacks, ironically, found
themselves facing more physical danger and fewer legal protections,
dollars, social roles, and choices than they or their free-born parents
had enjoyed prior to the passage of the Thirteenth and Fourteenth
Amendments (Foner 1989). With the end of Reconstruction in 1877,
the creation of Jim Crow segregation in the 1890s, and the upsurge in
recorded lynchings, 1,914 blacks between 1882 and 1901 alone, the
conditions facing black Americans near the turn of the century were
unenviable and unlike those of white citizens and legal aliens (Shapiro
1988:31–21).

Another distinction of major import during the last decade of the
nineteenth century and the first two decades of the twentieth was that
between the life chances of the native-born and those of foreign-born
Americans. Xenophobia, a political and cultural staple of nineteenth-
century American politics and social relations, flourished during the
1880s and 1890s as massive immigration flows from Southern and
Eastern Europe and Ireland fueled native-born citizens' preexisting
fears (Higham 1988). Overt and covert quotas kept Irish, Italian, Jewish, Polish, Russian, German, and other groups of foreign-born people and their children out of many residential communities and many
lines of work and study (Higham 1988). Some groups, like Chinese-
Americans, could no longer bring families members to the U.S. or
become naturalized because of the Chinese Exclusion Act of 1882,
which was regularly renewed and expanded to include people of other

Asian countries in addition to China during the first two decades of the next century (Takaki 1990).

Citizens, immigrants, migrants, paid workers, and unpaid family workers had multiple responses to these yawning social, cultural, and economic divisions. Middle-class women's recognition of the growing divisions and widening misery in the United States in the last decades of the nineteenth century gave rise to "maternalism," an ideology and movement that sought to glorify women's capacity to mother and to embed the maternal values of nurturance, kindness, and morality in the institutions and processes of the whole of society (Koven and Michel 1990:1079). Historians Koven and Michel document the two-front nature of maternalism, the exaltation of the private merits of women's domesticity—conceived of as quotidian caring for the vulnerable young, old, and sick at home—and, simultaneously, the sanctioning of women's public roles as "natural" caretakers of politics, government, the community, the school, the workplace, and the marketplace (Koven and Michel 1990:1079). It was a tiny step, indeed, from maternalist thinking to the actual involvement of women in early social work and Progressivism.

A variety of other social movements also congealed amidst the social transformations and deepening divisions of the late nineteenth century. Populism, the trade union movement, and the Niagara Movement for African American advancement, each of which is discussed in the next section of this chapter, articulated the desires, claims, and demands of constituents who were underrepresented or unrepresented in the domains of political and economic decision making of the last portion of the nineteenth century.

The extremes of wealth and poverty and of unbridled power and disenfranchisement in the Gilded Age spawned widespread revulsion. A spirit of public interest arose at the turn of the century in reaction to the excesses of the 1870s and 1880s. An outpouring of concern for public welfare and for the downtrodden was catalyzed by the muckraking of Lincoln Steffens, Ida M. Tarbell, Ray Stannard Baker, David Graham Phillips, and Upton Sinclair, among many others (Schlesinger 1986, Wiebe 1967). Early social workers joined with muckrakers in efforts to protect the public from adulterated foods, contaminated water supplies and milk, injuries and death at work, and the false claims of merchants and manufacturers.

Some Americans pursued remedies for accelerating social dislocation in the realm of knowledge. They sought to use reason and empirical inquiry to understand the nature of their increasingly plural society and to prevent social fragmentation. The birth of the social sciences as formal disciplines and of their applied counterparts in the United States sprang in part from this form of rationalist response to change and conflict.

In the U.S., in particular, architects of fledgling social sciences saw themselves as secular missionaries helping to discover ways of sustaining the health of a republic that they saw as an exception to the corruption and tyranny of older republics in the Old World. Early social scientists in the U.S. were believers in "American exceptionalism," a nationalist ideology that presupposed that the United States was a unique republic that was unrelated to the tortuous history of the Old World. For devotees of American exceptionalism, the U.S. constituted a millenial domain of unprecedented civic virtue, liberty, and opportunity that the founders had created de novo in accordance with natural laws (Ross 1991:22–50).

A cascade of organizations was founded to help with this noble project: the American Social Science Association in 1865, the National Prison Association in 1870, the American Public Health Association in 1872, the National Conference of Charities and Corrections in 1879, the American Historical Association in 1884, the American Economic Association in 1885, the National Statistical Association in 1888, the American Academy of Political and Social Science in 1889, and the American Psychological Association in 1892. The organizational forms, the research methods, and the data gathered by these nascent groups and their individual members soon became tools indispensable to the work of reversing the decay of the political and social millenium into which Progressive-era social scientists believed themselves fortunate enough to have been born (Ross 1991:144–149).

It was an era of unprecedented growth and, at the same time, of frightful rupture of the social fabric. Both optimism about expansion and fear of social conflict and decay preoccupied the intellectuals, professionals, and activists of the day.

Influential Movements, Ideas, and Beliefs

The men and women who set out to practice inchoate forms of social work in settlement houses, charity organization societies, hospitals, neighborhood health stations, child welfare agencies, courts, schools, and social reform movements of the 1890s and the Progressive era were affected not only by their first-hand observations of misery and poverty, but also by the discourse of the period that narrated, explained, and interpreted in diverse ways the nature, scope, causes, and consequences of the crises at hand. The meaning that these early social workers ascribed to the hardship and turmoil that they witnessed emerged from the interaction of the symbolic properties of the crammed tenements, tubercular children, and noxious sweatshops with the cognitive categories of those who documented them as caseworkers, settlers, or inspectors on civic commissions of inquiry (Van Maanen 1988:41). Social workers brought conceptual categories to their experiences that they had drawn from both their culture's background and its foreground. It is to the cultural foreground that this chapter will now turn in the process of probing the immediate influences on the categories of thought and perception of those Progressive-era social workers who were particularly attuned to the problem of the powerlessness and misery of those with whom they worked.

Populism

Far from the urban haunts of the earliest social workers, populists created the National Farmers Alliance and Industrial Union, a significant force of black and white farmers in the Southwest, South, and Great Plains region between 1884 and 1896. In fighting the monopolies that controlled railroad shipping, grain elevators, and the prices of seeds, fertilizer, and farm equipment, populist farmers elected state legislators, congressmen, and governors; created more than 1,000 newspapers; mobilized a multistate lecturing system; and secured 10 percent of the vote in 1892 for their presidential candidate (Goodwyn 1986:19–29, 1978, Ehrenreich 1985:26) In so doing, they reinvoked the Jeffersonian tradition of calling upon ordinary citizens to resist collectively and actively the concentration of power and resources in the hands of elites. In the stead of centralized and consolidated government, Populists envisioned decentralized local control of economic and political affairs, ceilings on the amount of property any citizen would be permitted to own, and the restoration of the intimacy that had characterized life in preindustrial towns (West 1986:208).

Economic reprisal, fraudulent elections, and the racism and xenophobia of some subgroups within populism brought about its rapid disintegration in 1896, but not before the movement reinvigorated and popularized an ethos of grassroots participation and cooperation (Riessman 1986:54–55). Populist sentiments lingered long after the demise of the Populist Party because of its success in fueling a sense of outrage with the damage done by elites to the common good and to common people (Boyte and Riessman 1986:8).

In the 1880s and 1890s, Populists demonstrated to both rural participants and urban onlookers the possibility of the joint reclaiming of dignity and power for common people and, in the process, modeled a democratic method for involving people (Goodwyn 1986:29). Empowerment-oriented social workers near the turn of the century were among those who took careful note.

The Social Gospel

"Now that God has smitten slavery unto death, he has opened the way for redemption and sanctification of our whole social system," declared the Reverend Edward Beecher in 1868 (Hopkins 1940:9). An early spokesperson for the Social Gospel movement, which was another prominent element in the cultural foreground of early social workers, Beecher revealed in his statement the encouragement and momentum that the success of abolitionism provided socially conscious Christians following the Civil War.

This ardent enthusiasm for social reform within some Protestant circles in the period between 1870 and 1920 was both accelerated and sobered by the shock of the railway strike of 1877, the Haymarket riot of 1886, and the labor strife and economic depression of the 1890s (Handy 1966:9). Stimulated by the Christian socialism of British clergy such as Thomas Chalmers and Charles Kingsley, the Social Gospel movement in the United States, was led by Washington Gladden, Richard Ely, and Walter Rauschenbusch. They and their followers called for the fulfillment of Christ's promise of heaven on earth through expansion of human cooperation and the creation of a collectivist society that would abolish poverty and capitalism (Handy 1966:3–10, Cort 1988:227–232). This philosophy drew a strong following from among Congregationalists, Episcopalians, northern Baptists, Methodists, and Presbyterians and eventuated in the creation of the Federal Council of Churches in 1908 (Handy 1966:12). Informed by a deep belief in progress, the goodness of human beings, and the nearness of a benevolent God, Social Gospel leaders in parishes and such seminaries as Union Theological Seminary in New York City called for immediate and sustained enactment of the social principles of the historical Jesus (Handy 1966:10). Enactment meant abolishing poverty, infant deaths, homelessness, and the monopolization of power and property by the rich. Founders and staff members of the settlement houses, workers in the charity organization societies, and social reformers in Progressive-era campaigns took to heart these lessons of the Social Gospel.

Unionism

Unionism, the movement of working people to organize themselves collectively at the workplace to retain control over the production process and to improve their wages and working conditions, was also a formative influence on empowerment-oriented social workers during the earliest years of the profession's evolution (Ehrenreich 1985). Organized labor, in its protracted wars with the owners and management of the steel, textile, mining, meatpacking, shipping, and railroad industries of the late nineteenth century, provided a philosophy, language, cluster of symbols, and example that reverberated in many subsequent movements and ideologies.

Respect for the "ordinary" working person, an ethic of self-help, and a rejection of oligarchy were unionist ideas that translated easily into terms directly applicable to social work with disadvantaged people (Foner 1947). So also were labor unions' belief in the power and necessity of collective strategies and tactics for bettering workers' lives and their egalitarian commitment to the welfare of all who became members of "the brotherhood" ("an injury to one is an injury to all").

Of particular interest to empowerment-oriented social workers of the profession's early period were the Industrial Workers of the World (I.W.W.). Known as the "Wobblies," the I.W.W. was a revolutionary union movement of roughly a million members between 1905 and 1919 that concentrated on forming unions of workers in ill-paid occupations that had never before been organized in the United States, like mining, forestry, and janitorial work. Unlike the American Federation of Labor (A.F.L.), which organized only skilled workers, the "Wobblies" consciously sought to build a movement of workers from all skill levels. Intent upon maximal inclusivity and the abolition of workplace and societal discrimination on the basis of race, gender, religion, and country of origin, the I.W.W. counted many recent immigrants, African Americans, women, and rural laborers among its members (Foner 1947).

Some of the key themes of empowerment of the past and present— of "struggle with oppressors," of "solidarity among sisters and brothers," of "rank-and-file control"—flow directly from the labor movement tradition established by unions within the A.F.L. and the I.W.W.

Though few social workers were themselves members of unions during the first three decades of social work's history, many were alerted by the labor movement to the plight of the unemployed and the underpaid and to the strength that lies in numbers of those who gather together to make common claims.

Feminism

Feminism, also, made its distinctive mark on the thinking and vision of early social workers who took notice of the powerlessness and desperation of their clients. Since many early social workers were college-educated young women from the middle and upper-middle classes for whom the labor market had few niches, it is not surprising that the message of "first-wave" feminism held great appeal for them (Chambers 1986, Donovan 1990, Muncy 1991).

The feminist demands of suffragists such as Elizabeth Cady Stanton, Sojourner Truth, and Susan B. Anthony and of cultural radicals like Amelia Bloomer and Charlotte Perkins Gilman required little explication for early female social workers. They knew firsthand about the conditions and constraints of womanhood in the late nineteenth century (Barry 1988, Gordon 1992). Life within male-dominated families, institutions, and society had served as a primer in their own need for empowerment and had escalated the rise of their social feminist sensibilities, those that perceived women's rights to be an integral and indispensable part of a wider agenda of social reforms. The highest priority of the social feminist agenda was the prevention of pauperization among urban adults and children (Cohen and Hanagan 1991:470, O'Neill 1969, Gordon 1992:44). The expansion of women's civil and political rights were one means to that all-important end.

Pragmatism

Another salient set of ideas circulating in the cultural universe of early social workers was that of Pragmatism. A uniquely American philosophic tradition shaped in the last two decades of the nineteenth century and the first decade of the twentieth by Charles Peirce, William James, and John Dewey, Pragmatism advocated that truths about the world and guidelines with which to govern human behavior are to be found not, as Kant had believed, in the search for a priori rules and first principles, but by examining the consequences of human activity.

The Pragmatists understood human experience to be the key and only source of wisdom to which human beings have access, provided that that experience is subjected to a systematic process of inquiry by a community of investigators, not just by one individual (Cruz 1987, Barber 1984, Bullert 1983, Moore 1961:267). Peirce, James, and Dewey's emphasis on the centrality of action and its effects, their respect for experience as a guide, their futuristic outlook, and their view of truth as that which is communally derived established an epistemological, ethical, and metaphysical bias in the United States toward experimentalism and activism, a bias that both directly and indirectly influenced Progressive-era social workers and social reformers. It is no coincidence, for example, that John Dewey was a devoted friend of and frequent correspondent with Jane Addams for more than thirty years. Dewey had come to know Addams while he was in residence at Hull House in 1900 (Barber 1984). He was also a founding member of the National Association for the Advancement of Colored People (NAACP) and of the Men's League for Women's Suffrage, two groups of deep interest in the early decades of the century to empowerment-oriented social workers (Bullert 1983:35).

The Pragmatists also stressed the interdependent nature of human existence, a condition that, they felt, has at least four dimensions. First, they advanced the notion of the interconnectedness of subject and object, rejecting the notion that they are two sides of a dualistic polarity. Instead, they were early proponents of the idea that subjects and objects create joint and interactive realities that are continually being constructed socially. The Pragmatists also argued that ends and means cannot be divorced, that the merit of one deeply affects the value of the other. Third, Pragmatism promoted the idea that actors and actions only have meaning with their context (Moore 1961, Smith 1978, Barber 1984, Westbrook 1991). Indeed, it is this school of thinkers who introduced the concept of "transactive" relationships between human beings and their environments, an idea that later formed an essential element of Lewinian field theory, systems theory, and ecological approaches to social work practice. Fourth, Peirce, James, and Dewey believed human beings to be interdependent with each other, to be social beings whose survival, happiness, and success in sustaining a meaningful life are contingent upon the health of community life. Dewey, for example, defined human freedom as "power-in-relation-to-others" (Cruz 1987:126).

This view of human beings as social beings led the Pragmatists to supplant the Utilitarians' central concern for individual self-interest and happiness with an alternative criterion of value—the common good (Bullert 1983:208). Whereas Utilitarian thinkers like Jeremy Bentham, John Stuart Mill, and Herbert Spencer had evaluated the merits of a economic process or of a social order on the basis of its consequences for the individual, the Pragmatists, instead, proposed that the litmus test of value be the consequences for both the communal whole and the individual. Indeed, they argued that the welfare of the individual is inextricable from the welfare of his or her society. John Dewey, for example, thought individual freedom and social welfare to be reciprocal concepts. Freedom, he argued, could exist only in a community. "We are bound together as parts of a whole and only as others are free, can anyone be free" (Dewey 1935:273).

Pragmatism pushed beyond the strict individualism of nineteenth-century liberalism and offered empowerment-oriented social workers, among many others, an inviting alternative—a commitment to community and individual fulfillment that refused to privilege one over the other. To achieve both, they argued, individuals, institutions, and communities must experiment, evaluate the consequences of their experimental actions, and then employ democratic decision making to decide what further experiments to do next. Their belief in action, experimentation, collective reflection concerning the outcomes of experiments, and the expansion of human interdependence as being necessary avenues to wisdom and freedom prefigured later empowerment thinking.

Du Bois and the Niagara Movement

Another major contribution to empowerment-based thinking and activity of early social work came from W. E. B. Du Bois. Du Bois, an African American scholar and political leader who founded the Niagara Movement in 1905, out of which grew the NAACP, conceived of and publicized the concept of "dual consciousness," the idea that in a vast and complex society such as that of the United States multiple subcultures of peoples sustain concurrently both identification with the encompassing cultural whole and separate identities that distinctively reflect their particular traditions and histories (Du Bois 1903, Boyte 1984:8, Marable 1986:55). Du Bois wrote and spoke extensively about the differences between African Americans' American consciousness and their "Negro" consciousness and about the profound tensions and strengths that accompany a lifetime of necessarily cultivating and juggling both.

His prescient understanding of both the anguish and the power of the "two-track" journey—psychological, spiritual, intellectual, cultural, and political—that African American individuals and their overall community travel constituted an original insight that myriad others have used subsequently in building various empowerment movements of people who are trying to develop positive identities, subcultural institutions, and decent living conditions in the midst of a society that is generally indifferent or hostile to them. Self-help, liberation, and client and consumer groups of every description owe an incalculable intellectual debt to the vision of Du Bois. He taught twentieth-century people in the United States that the survival and development of populations who are minorities within a larger culture require them concomitantly to both belong and be separate, to become recognized citizens and contributors to the larger whole while retaining a separate sense of worth and a distinctive communal subculture. Du Bois's nuanced analysis prepared members of twentieth-century empowerment movements for the complexities and difficulties that invariably follow when one sustains two sets of identities that at times cohere and at other times collide with each other.

Every form of consciousness bears the distinctive imprint of the context and era in which it evolved and of the unique configuration of cultural influences that commanded attention during its period of incubation. Empowerment visions of early social workers between 1893 and 1917, which will be detailed in the next chapter, are no exception. They are both outgrowths of and contributions to Progressivism's dialectic of thought and action that helped make the period such a vibrant and controversial quarter century.

FIGURE 3.1

INTELLECTUAL, RELIGIOUS AND POLITICAL INFLUENCES: 1893-1917

Populism

Social Gospel Movement

Unionism

Feminism

Pragmatism

W. E. B. Du Bois and the Niagara Movement

CHAPTER FOUR

The Early Period: Social Work's Visions of Empowerment, 1893–1917

> Individuals have wills and purposes of their own and are not fitted to play a passive part in the world; they deteriorate when they do.
>
> —Mary Richmond

Early Social Work's Visions of Empowerment

Professions, like social movements, do not begin at a single moment in history. Instead, over time, they gradually develop reasons for being, accrue members, establish an identity, develop alliances, and battle internally over basic directions to take and assumptions to make. Social work, bit by bit, became a profession during the last two decades of the nineteenth century and the first two decades of the twentieth, a period in the United States of the consolidation and regulation of old professions, such as medicine and law, and the elevation of voluntary civic services to the status of new professions, like nursing and librarianship (Abbott 1988, Garrison 1975, Larson 1977, Melosh 1982).

By 1917, the year in which a national vocational clearinghouse for social work positions, the National Social Workers' Exchange, was organized and the year in which Mary Richmond published *Social Diagnosis*, social work had evolved into a full-fledged professionalized occupation (Richmond 1917). By then, social work was equipped with all the usual trappings of a profession. It had its own knowledge base, ideology, organizational infrastructure, nomenclature, publications, educational sites and rites, and devaluing critics. One such critic was Abraham Flexner, the influential staff official of the Carnegie Foundation, whose "Flexner Report" of 1910 had been pivotal in the reorganization of the American medical profession and whose address in 1915 to the National Conference of Charities and Correction, "Is Social Work a Profession?" disparaged social work as being less than "professional in character and scientific in method" (Flexner 1915).

As cumulative, plural, and murky as the origins of social work are, this account of the empowerment visions that crystallized in early professional years will start at a particular historical moment, that of the economic depression that began in the winter of 1893. This severe economic shock lasted until 1897, swept away the jobs of an estimated 17–19 percent of the adult workforce, gave rise to Coxey's Army of unemployed workers who marched on Washington to demand relief and jobs, and led 750,000 workers to go on strike in 1894 in protest of wage cuts (Katz 1986:147–149).

The depression of 1893 completely overwhelmed the private charity organization societies, public relief organizations, immigrants' mutual aid societies, and charity efforts of churches and synagogues (Katz 1986:147–149). The severity and depth of the economic misery of 1893 through 1897 demolished any remaining legitimacy of the philanthropic approach known as scientific charity (Jimenez 1990:4). A Social Darwinist approach to alms perfected in the 1880s by charity organization society leaders, scientific charity emphasized the importance of systematic research into the present circumstances and past history of supplicants in order to distinguish in a rational fashion between the "deserving" and the "undeserving" poor.

Prior to 1893, charity organization societies viewed material aid as a debilitating force, to be thought of as a tool of last resort, that corroded the work ethic of the needy. Instead of cash or in-kind assistance, charity organization societies preferred to offer the poor the moral example and personal influence of friendly visitors.

The "charity bust" during the devastating winter of 1893 changed all that (Mandler 1990:25). Charities were besieged and inundated by jobless men and women and hungry families. Restrictions on the giving of material aid were relaxed, and the understanding on the part of charity leaders and workers of the environmental factors and contingencies that can push an individual or family over the line into poverty expanded dramatically. The vividness and massiveness of the impact of economic depression led many charity leaders and friendly visitors to distance themselves from moral explanations for poverty and embrace environmental explanations more closely than they ever had before. Like their settlement house contemporaries, charity organization personnel after 1893 began to attend carefully to the consequences for the poor of overcrowded housing, unemployment, industrial accidents, child abuse, child labor, and threats to infant and maternal health such as contaminated milk (Gordon 1988a).

As a result of this change in viewpoint, the proportion of private charities in the U.S. that disbursed cash and in-kind assistance increased from one-half to two-thirds during the 1890s (Mandler 1990:25). Josephine Shaw Lowell, the chief architect of the New York Charity Organization Society and a leading spokesperson of the scientific charity movement, reversed her position on the inadvisability of giving material aid to the poor and began working vigorously to distribute cash to poor families so as to get money into immediate circulation in poor neighborhoods (Germain and Hartman 1980:325).

The upsurge in demands made on charity organization societies during this depression led them to increase their professional staffs during the 1890s by as much as one-third and to plan systematic training for them (Wenocur and Reisch 1989:36). That planning process eventuated in the formation of formal training schools for social workers, beginning in 1898 with the Summer School in Applied Philanthropy established by the New York Charity Organization Society, which later became the New York School of Philanthropy and, much later, the Columbia University School of Social Work.

By 1917, New York, Boston, Philadelphia, Chicago, Cleveland, St. Louis, Richmond, and Houston each offered formal professional training schools in social work. Nineteen seventeen serves as a good ending marker for the first period of social work history since it was a year in which the U.S. entered World War I and, in so doing, effectively ended the Progressive era by redirecting resources and diverting energies towards the war and away from domestic concerns.

What conceptions of empowerment emerged from the fledgling profession of social work in the period between 1893 and 1917? What was the nature of the visions crafted by social workers of an empowerment bent in the Progressive era? These broad questions are best answered by examining three constituent elements of any social worker's vision: 1. the predominant metaphors one uses to characterize one's own approach to activity and agency as a professional, 2. the prevailing metaphors one chooses to characterize one's clients or constituents, and 3. the overarching conception one holds of the processes of change that social work attempts to further.

Early Social Workers' Self-Conceptions

Urban Interpreters Social workers of the early period who sought to assist clients with that which we now call self-empowerment thought about their own work in terms that are easily recognizable many decades later. Many early social workers, of both the settlement house and child welfare agency streams, perceived themselves to be urban mediators, "go-betweens" between clients and community (Richmond 1922:114), "interpreters" of disadvantaged individuals' and groups' expectations and hopes to mainstream institutions and vice versa (Addams 1910:167, Wald 1915:197), and "social adjusters" (Richmond 1922:114–118, Wald 1915:176).

A social adjuster worked on two planes at once: to help people adjust to their changing environments and to help environments adjust to the changing needs of individuals and groups (Richmond 1922:117–118). Indeed, one of the central reasons why Abraham Flexner's notorious denial of the professional status of social work at the 1915 National Conference of Charities and Correction drew so much attention for decades was that his characterization of the social worker as the "intelligence" that "mediates the intervention of the particular agent or agency best fitted to deal with the specific emergency" so closely squared with social workers' own view of their role and function (Flexner 1915:585, Germain and Gitterman 1980:351).

Unlike Flexner, however, many social workers of the period thought that significant skill, training, and judgment were required for the social worker to act as an effective liaison between the client and his or her society. Though social workers of the period were practicing five, six, and seven decades before the introduction of the language of empowerment, some, like Chicago's Edith Abbott, articulated in other words a direct early parallel to Ann Weick's contemporary "strengths perspective" (Weick 1986).

Abbott advocated that students first discover clients' strengths as well as their disabilities and then, with these strengths particularly in mind, link their clients with the neighbors, community institutions, social resources, and social reform movements that could help them and to whom they could, in turn, lend help and social evidence (Abbott 1942:44–80, 1943:350–356, Costin 1983a:107). These ideas, conceived by Abbott in the first two decades of the century and formalized by her in the 1920s at the University of Chicago, prefigured empowerment notions of social workers of the 1980s and 1990s.

Social work, in the early days, was understood by empowerment-oriented professionals as connecting work—labor that focused on assisting clients to reach out to groups and institutions around them that could provide immediate relief, short-term material aid, and, eventually, longer-term environmental changes. In the process, clients confirmed for themselves their own ability to survive and adapt in a difficult world. In a study of the Minneapolis Charity Organization Society between 1900 and 1930, renamed the Associated Charities/Family Welfare Association, Beverly Stadum found that agents there excelled at creating linkages between clients and sources of immediate and practical aid—the very reason why clients reported that they came to social workers in the first place (Stadum 1990:96).

Educators of Democrats   "Educator for democracy" was another common self-definition employed by social workers of the Progressive era who sought to extend the realms of social justice and find immediate relief for the miserable. Voiced most often by settlement house workers, but shared also by social workers in child welfare agencies, schools, hospitals, and courts, the theme of social worker as fosterer of democratic citizenship flowed directly out of Progressives' faith in representative democracy, rationality, social experimentation, an ever-broadening suffrage, and nonviolent, centripetal alternatives to despotism and revolution.

> As democracy modifies our conception of life, it constantly raises the value and function of each member of the community, however humble he may be. . . . We are gradually requiring of the educator that he shall free the powers of each man and connect him with the rest of life. We ask this not merely because it is the man's right to be thus connected, but because we have become convinced that the social order cannot afford to get along without his special contribution.

> It is at last on behalf of the average workingmen that our increasing democracy impels us to make a new demand upon the educator. As the political expression of democracy has claimed for the workingman the free right of citizenship, so a code of social ethics is now insisting that he shall be a conscious member of society, having some notion of his social and industrial value. (Addams 1902:178, 192)

Addams, here, was not simply making "a new demand" on educators in schools, she was also issuing a charge to social reformers and social workers who were attempting to make settlement houses crucibles of democracy. At Hull House in Chicago, she and her colleagues devised myriad educational forums for old people, new immigrants, young mothers, working men and women, as well as for children and adolescents. As was true in major settlement houses in dozens of cities, Hull House held adult education classes in spoken and written English, American history, American government, political economy, and journalism, creative writing, and expository writing (Addams 1910, Bryan and Davis 1990).

These courses were, as it has often been argued, ethnocentric attempts to Americanize and assimilate immigrants (Gans 1982, Davis 1967, Leiby 1978). However, at the same time, the courses were earnest efforts to equip new immigrants with the linguistic skills and historical, political, and economic knowledge that they would need to become citizens and then to make informed contributions in that role. At Hull House, Henry Street, Greenwich House, and many other settlements, social workers like Mary Simkhovitch believed that mass democracy, social equality, and domestic harmony would not accrue within the U.S. unless many reformers, among them social workers (whom she called "city workers"), succeeded as social educators and unless community residents who joined in settlement house activities took an ever larger and steadier role in the polity (Simkhovitch 1917, 1926, 1938).

Mary Parker Follett, Boston settler and neighborhood organizer, could not have agreed more. In discussing neighborhood organizations, she wrote that their aims and the aims of workers who helped form them were to "make a direct and continuous connection between our daily lives and needs and our government, to diminish race and class prejudices, to create a responsible citizenship, and to train and discipline the new democracy" (Follett 1918:217).

Caseworkers, too, saw themselves as nurturers of democrats in their daily work. Mary Richmond, for example, viewed this nurturing responsibility as having two prongs: caseworkers must themselves be reliably democratic in their beliefs and behavior and they must assist clients to achieve a "wider self" through the meaningfulness of the casework relationship, a bond intended to facilitate clients' widening connectedness and effectiveness within their own multitiered environments, meaning the family, community, society, and polity (Richmond 1922:153, 249, 260). Whenever possible, the caseworker should follow the lead of Anne Sullivan, who had assisted Helen Keller in becoming "a citizen of the world" (Richmond 1922:15).

Democracy, however, is not a form of organization but a daily habit of life. It is not enough for social workers to speak the language of democracy; they must have in their hearts its spiritual conviction of the infinite worth of our common humanity before they can be fit to do any form of social work whatsoever. (Richmond 1922:249)

Settlers Another common metaphor, or, in this case, a cluster of synonymous metaphors, emerged in the writings of leading practitioners who entered the field of social work through the settlement house door. They termed themselves "settlers," "residents," and "neighbors" (Addams 1910, Wald 1915, Simkhovitch 1917). Desiring to know a community and its inhabitants from within and having contempt for the model of maintaining social distance from the poor evolved by the agents and friendly visitors of the charity organization societies of the 1880s, settlement house workers "were to live in the neighborhood . . . identify ourselves with it socially, and, in brief, contribute to it our citizenship" (Wald 1915:8–9).

Through residence and active outreach, they sought friendship and personal acquaintance with the poor. "The settlements claimed to deal in brotherhood, not philanthropy; their spirit was fraternalistic rather than paternalistic," according to one major historian of the Progressive era, Clarke Chambers (1963:15). They enacted a vision of helping through intimate, reciprocal, and sustained personal contact with community residents, through commitment to the neighborhood twenty-four hours a day, and through the development of "local knowledge" of a community available only to those who have immersed themselves over time in the particularities of a time, place, and its people (Geertz 1983, Brieland 1990:134).

They understood settling to mean living in and helping out in improvised ways unimaginable by outsiders to the neighborhood or the settlement. That Jane Addams and Julia Lathrop of Hull House found themselves delivering a baby on a visit to a tenement house was unexpected only in an immediate sense (Brieland 1990:136). The act was an expected part of the repertoire of improvisations that settlers envisioned when they committed themselves to assisting their neighbors to cope with, manage, comprehend, and become more at home in an alien world.

Yet, furthering empowerment, settlers would have said had they used the phrase, involved more than residence, improvisation in emergencies, and helping neighbors adjust to difficult environments. They also viewed themselves as social reformers, as transformers of housing, schooling, workplaces, the Constitution, government, sanitation, health care, consumers' rights, and public spaces. The settlers of the three decades before World War I worked to make the social and physical environment of cities more habitable for poor and vulnerable people and to extend the realm of American social justice to include them. A partial list of Jane Addams's activities between 1902 and 1914, while she served as full-time head resident at Hull House, documents this settler's environmental focus and pursuit of a widened domain of social justice. Addams took major organizing responsibility for the national woman suffrage campaign, served as a member of a highly active and controversial Chicago School Board, took part in state and national campaigns to outlaw child labor, mediated labor disputes, negotiated the famous agreement between the Amalgamated Clothing Workers and Hart, Schaffner, and Marx, served as the first woman president of the National Conference of Charities and Correction, participated in the founding of the National Association for the Advancement of Colored People, helped to edit the national social work publications, *Charities* and its successor, the *Survey*, and assisted in the founding and creation of the platform of the Progressive party (Scott 1964:lxi).

Addams, of course, was the most famous of the settlers. Yet many others, less well known or now unknown, also engaged themselves in diverse and multiple reform movements at the local, state, national, and international levels. A list that includes the names of Grace Abbott, Sophonisba Breckinridge, Stanton Coit, Alice Hamilton, Florence Kelley, Julia Lathrop, Ellen Gates Starr, Vida Scudder, Mary Simkhovitch, Charles Stover, Graham Taylor, Lillian Wald, and Robert Woods is an abbreviated version of the honor role of settlers who brought their reformers' passions to bear on Progressive-era politics (Costin 1983b, Bryan and Davis 1990, Trolander 1987).

Settlers, it should be noted, were not the only social workers who took part in Progressive-era social reforms. Caseworkers did so as well, as Mary Richmond's life indicates. She started campaigns, while working full-time for charity organization societies, to establish sanitary reform laws in Baltimore, to prohibit child labor in Pennsylvania, and to enforce housing standards in New York (Pumphrey 1973:266). Yet, for Richmond and caseworkers like her who worked full-time in direct service with families and individuals, social reform and casework were different, though interdependent specializations within social work.

The other forms of social work, all of which interplay with case work, are three—group work, social reform, and social research. Case work seeks to effect better social relations by dealing with individuals one by one or within the intimate group of the family. But social work also achieves the same general ends in these other ways. . . . By a method different from that employed in either case or group work, though with the same end in view, social reform seeks to improve conditions in the mass, chiefly through social propaganda and social legislation. (Richmond 1922:223)

Richmond believed that it was caseworkers' duty to cooperate actively with social reform movements by gathering data on relevant topics on a case-by-case basis and, if they chose, to take part in social movements on their own time. However, she discouraged caseworkers from straying from their own focus on providing direct help to individuals and families since she perceived immediate one-on-one aid and the casework relationship as being necessary complements to environmental transformation that required full-time commitment to be effective.

No better advice could be given to family case workers, I believe, than to study and develop their work at its point of intersection with social research, with group activities and with social reform or mass betterment. This does not mean that they should drop their work or slight it in order to make special studies or to engage in legislative campaigns, but it does mean that they should be more scientifically productive than they now are, that they should be making social discoveries as a by-product of successful case work . . . and that they should be bearing faithful witness to the need of social reforms wherever their daily work reveals the need. They should supply the pertinent details necessary during the preliminary period of public education, and help later to make any new legislative measures workable by applying them in their case work. (Richmond 1922:225–226)

Early social workers who took an interest in helping clients or neighbors to expand their personal, interpersonal, and political capacities and choices thought of themselves as interpretive mediators between clients and their broader community and as educators of citizens for a broadening democracy. In addition, social workers of the settlement house wing of the early profession saw themselves as fellow citizens and neighbors of the residents who lived in the communities they were serving and as reformers of a society that was lagging inexcusably in its inclusion of immigrants, workers, children, the aged, the sick, and the poor into the American fold wherein, they believed, justice, liberty, and security inhered.

Conceptions of Clients

Closely related to the self-conceptions of early practitioners were their views of their clients or constituents within relationships that we would describe in contemporary terms as empowerment-oriented. Progressive-era social workers, whether settlers or workers in charity organizations, hospitals, schools, or courts, shared a double vision of clients or neighbors, one that continues to command respect from empowerment-based practitioners of the late twentieth century. They viewed clients or neighbors as, on the one hand, active agents of their own lives, working with the help of others on their own behalf. On the other hand, early social workers conceived of clients or neighbors as victims of social pathologies of long standing. These two visions hovered in uneasy and often confusing juxtaposition to one another in the Progressive years, just as they do contemporarily.

Active Citizens   The agency of clients and neighbors in the period between 1893 and 1917 was a given among those early social workers who sought to aid in the reversal of or, at least, the reduction of clients' and neighbors' marginality and relative powerlessness. Clients' or neighbors' role as active authors of their own life stories was described in different professional dialects, depending on the context of practice.

For Richmond, clients were "partners," fellow "participants" in a relation "in which she [the client] and the visitor [the social worker] together could share the responsibility of the successive steps to be taken" (Richmond 1922:170). For settlers like Jane Addams, Lillian Wald, and Florence Kelley, who was a dweller at Hull House and, later, the Henry Street Settlement and the founder and director of the National Consumers League, fellow residents in the community were neighboring "citizens" (Addams 1910:180), "workers" (Wald 1915:210), and "consumers" (Goldmark 1953). The settlers' neighbors were thought of, at one and the same time, as political members or prospective political members of a democracy, paid or unpaid laborers, and purchasers of goods and services. Each of these roles was characterized by activity and the taking of risks.

In addition, settlers conceived of their neighbors as bearers and creators of culture, both of American culture and ethnic cultures from their countries of origin. At major settlement houses in Boston, Chicago, New York, Philadelphia, and other cities, serious institutional commitments were made to the nurturance of neighborhood members' creation or performance of art, music, drama, literature, poetry, dance, and crafts (Addams 1910, Brieland 1990:35, Bryan and Davis 1990, Chambers 1963, Wald 1915, 1933).

The Neighborhood Playhouse of the Henry Street Settlement, for example, opened in 1915 in order to give Lower East Side New Yorkers an opportunity to perform in plays, learn more about music, poetry, and dance, and obtain training in the many dimensions of stage production—marketable skills in New York City (Wald 1915:185–186). The Neighborhood Playhouse seven decades later continues its Progressive-era tradition of fostering children's and adults' direct involvement in both the folk cultures and learned cultures of many countries, including but not confined to works from Western Europe and the United States.

Victims of Industrial Capitalism In contrast to their conceptions of clients or neighbors as active agents, whether partners, citizens, workers, consumers, or creators of culture, early social workers with empowerment inclinations also understood their clients or neighbors to be victims of urban forces that extended far beyond the reach of the neighborhood and dwarfed the resources of even the strongest of individuals. Price-fixing monopolies and trusts, urban congestion that spawned tuberculosis and family violence, economic depressions, industrial hazards, municipal corruption, low wages, excessive corporate profits, xenophobic immigration policies, and impure foods and drugs were among the long list of urban elements that early social workers considered to be systemic victimizers of their clients and constituents (Addams 1910, Costin 1983b, Wald 1915, 1933).

As an outgrowth of this viewpoint, some early social workers thought that the reduction of political and economic forms of victimization would come about most quickly through consumer boycotts of the products of offending companies and through legislative and regulatory attacks on the abuses that they, muckrakers, and photographers like Lewis Hine documented with care and poignancy. Through social research and social reform at the national, state, and local levels, they sought to use the revelations of journalism and official inquiries, the purchasing dollars of middle-class consumers, and the force of the state to delimit the power and license of institutions they deemed to be exploitative of the public and of the urban poor, such as railroad cartels, oil trusts, garment manufacturing companies that subcontracted to sweatshops, and meat packing companies.

Early social workers of the social reform wing, like Julia Lathrop, first director of the U.S. Children's Bureau, and Paul Kellogg, editor of the *Survey*, did not, for the most part, work at empowerment in a contemporary sense, meaning in a manner that involved disempowered people as direct participants in social reform movements. Instead, they sought to establish societal protections for vulnerable people through the abolition or regulation of practices and institutions that they considered to be unfair to millions of residents, workers, and consumers. Had they spoken in late twentieth-century terms, the Julia Lathrops and Paul Kelloggs of the Progressive era might well have said: "We prepare the ground for the later empowerment of vulnerable and marginal people by limiting now the prerogatives and excesses of the most egregious of the disempowering actors and forces."

Conceptions of Change Processes

Social Investigation   A third way to ascertain the core empowering visions of American social workers of the Progressive era is to examine their conceptions of key processes that, they believed, would bring about greater equity and justice. Social investigation, the foundation upon which social experimentation could be based, was one strongly preferred means to that end (Chambers 1963, 1986, Costin 1983b, Lubove 1975, Leiby 1978). The 107 publications of Edith Abbott, the renowned social work educator and social reformer, and the 66 publications and 21 pieces of formal testimony offered to Congressional Committees by her sister, the equally remarkable Grace Abbott, suggest the depth of Progressive-era social workers' faith in empirical inquiry as a route to social improvement (Costin 1983b:287–299).

The Abbott sisters were not anomalies, they were simply among the most prolific and talented of the social investigators within social work ranks of this period. They were joined by hundreds of other early social workers who, from their bases of operation in settlement houses, public and private child welfare agencies, government offices, the courts, hospitals, and schools, systematically gathered information on every imaginable topic and problem within the social environment of their clients, neighbors, patients, and students.

The first decades of curricula of influential schools of social work founded before World War I, from the most casework-oriented of schools to the most social reform-minded, reveal a sustained passion for knowledge-building and for basing practice on the careful accrual and use of data (Abbott 1943; Archival collections of the Boston School of Social Work, Bryn Mawr College School of Social Work and Social Research, New York School of Social Work [Columbia University], and the Pennsylvania School of Social Work [University of Pennsylvania]). The very bedrock of social casework, for Mary Richmond, was the worker's systematic analysis of the history and present circumstances and environment of a client and his or her family (Richmond 1917, Pumphrey 1973). Only upon that bedrock could the worker construct the "imaginative sympathy" for a client that Richmond thought to be the sine qua non of effective casework (Richmond 1922:23,106–7).

Linking of Local and Global Action A second approach to change favored by early social workers with an empowerment orientation was that of linking two foci—attending on a day-to-day basis to immediate local needs and, concomitantly, concentrating on longer-term social reforms in the regional, national, and international networks of which the neighborhood and locality were a but a small part. Catheryne Cooke Gilman, of the Northeast Neighborhood House in Minneapolis, issued the following charge to settlers: "Keep your fingers on the near things and eyes on the far things" (Chambers 1963:150). The social worker's job was one of local immersion in urgent matters and global citizenship concerning broader issues.

The biographies of salient leaders of early social work document this dual orientation (Minahan 1987:913–948). Jane Addams led both Hull House in Chicago and the Women's International League for Peace and Freedom. Janie Porter Barrett, a daughter of emancipated slaves, headed the Locust Street Social Settlement, one of the first settlements for blacks in the U.S., while she organized the Virginia State Federation of Colored Women's Clubs, an organization that created schools, vocational training programs, and rehabilitation centers for black girls and women throughout Virginia. Mary Simkhovitch headed Greenwich House while serving as an active member of the New York City Housing Authority, the New York State Board of Social Welfare, and the National Public Housing Conference. Lillian Wald directed the Henry Street Settlement, helped found the New York Child Labor Committee, and worked actively for the creation of the U.S. Children's Bureau, established in 1912. These leaders of early social work paid attention to both "near things and far." They would have endorsed and honored in practice Ann Hartman's present-day editorial conclusion that "Social workers must relate to both justice and care every day" (Hartman 1989:388).

FIGURE 4.1
SOCIAL WORK'S VISION OF EMPOWERMENT: 1983-1917

PROFESSIONAL'S SELF-CONCEPTION	METAPHORS FOR CLIENTS	CONCEPTIONS OF EMPOWERING CHANGE
Urban interpreters	Active citizens	Social investigation
Educators of democrats	Victims of industrial capitalism	Linking of local and global action
Settlers		

Empowering Aspects of Practice

What aspects of social work practice emerged in the period from 1893 through 1917 that contributed to the self-empowerment of vulnerable individuals and groups of that era? Four dimensions of practice that were designed to increase poor and stigmatized people's capacities to act on their own behalf and to obtain a fairer share of social justice and resources stand out in the historical record. They include the mobilization of immediate material aid in conjunction with the provision of psychological reassurance and support, the teaching of specific skills needed in survival and in the securement of well-being, the active enlistment of clients' or neighbors' participation and preferences in problem solving, and the public, educative, and advocative uses of the findings of social investigations.

None of these four aspects of early social work practice seems at all innovative or startling to the contemporary practitioner, given the long-standing familiarity and centrality of these strategies to effective social work practice. Nonetheless, for a society at the beginning of this century accustomed to addressing the poor with secular sermonizing and judgmental scrutiny intended to differentiate the low-down from the upright, these four contributions of early social workers were of major and lasting import. Each, in turn, merits a closer look.

Offering Concrete and Social Supports

Early social workers provided multiple kinds of immediate aid to individuals and families who came for help. Rent money, milk, diapers, food, bandages, medicine, nursing care, and obstetric help were among the most common requests met by Progressive-era social workers (Addams 1910, Gordon 1988a, 1988b, Leiby 1978, Richmond 1917, 1922, Stadum 1990, Wald 1915, 1933). They helped people obtain citizenship papers, lumber and volunteers for the repair of sagging steps, housing and jobs for newly arrived immigrants, false teeth, prosthetic devices, visiting nurse care for the homebound ill, summer camping for children, foster care placements for abused children, and separation and maintenance agreements for battered wives (Gordon 1988a:17, 281, Stadum 1990:91). Settlement houses also made available college extension courses, public baths, gymnasiums, theaters, public kitchens, meeting rooms, and swimming pools (Addams 1910, Brieland 1990:136, Garvin and Cox 1987:35, Wald 1915, 1933).

Social workers of the early period who offered this kaleidoscopic range of concrete help did so in the belief that immediate aids and services were necessary and justifiable in themselves, simply because clients or neighbors made evident their need for them. They thought, furthermore, that immediate help, when provided in the context of a respectful and supportive relationship, engendered hope and catalyzed physical and mental development, healing, rehabilitation, and self-respect (Addams 1910, Cannon 1952, Richmond 1917, 1922).

Whether in settlements, host settings like hospitals and schools, or family service agencies, early social workers consolidated "the psychological and material, the personal and social" (Gordon 1988b:157). In none of these realms did early social workers hold themselves "above" concrete service delivery. Nor did they overlook the import of helping to relieve intrapsychic or interpersonal pain. Nor did they excuse themselves from social reform activities related to their field of service.

Though different social work settings before World War I became clearly differentiated in professional emphases, skills, and strengths, no branch of social work thought of the human spirit as a disembodied entity. And no wing of social work in the early period elevated social change above the job of responding to the pressing immediate concerns of the persons, families, and groups who composed social work's clientele.

For example, settlement house workers excelled in social reform, community research and development, health care delivery, teaching and training with groups of adults and children, and the provision of emergency goods and services. However, they lagged far behind other social work venues in the development of effective methods of assessing and responding to emotional anguish and mental illness. Nonetheless, settlers, as generalists, recognized the importance of offering preventive and crisis responses to the spiritual and psychological aspects of their neighbors' poverty and social dislocation.

Hospital social workers, early in the first decade of the twentieth century, began developing major strengths in psychosocial assessment, casework, crisis intervention, information and referral work, and community assessment and outreach (Cannon 1952). In that same first, fertile decade of the twentieth century, founders of school social work started evolving expertise as family-school liaisons, caseworkers, and agents of institutional change within public school systems (Allen-Meares, Washington, and Welsh 1986, Radin 1989). Both hospital and school social workers, unlike their colleagues in settlements and charity organization societies, were new entrants into long established host organizations. As such, they necessarily and quickly became adept at intrainstitutional and interdisciplinary teamwork and consultation on such broad subjects as psychosocial development, family structures and dynamics, ethnic diversity, and community needs. Early hospital and school social workers, on the whole, were much less likely than settlers to take leadership in social reform campaigns that crosscut varied human needs and professional fields of practice. Nonetheless, they worked ardently for systemic change within their own respective worlds of public education and health care at the same time that they attempted to answer clients' urgent appeals for emotional support and material aid of every imaginable description (Allen-Meares, Washington, and Welsh 1986, Cannon 1952, Radin 1989).

Meanwhile, child welfare and family workers in urban charity organization societies concentrated on developing and applying the complex arts of psychosocial assessment and casework with impoverished individuals and their families. Interviewing, home visits, home studies, the counseling and placement of orphaned, unwanted, neglected, and abused children, and the emotional and material support of aged, widowed, abandoned, unemployed, battered, alcoholic, and disabled adults took up much of the time of generally overworked and understaffed charity organization society agencies (Gordon 1988a, 1988b, Stadum 1990). As compared with settlement house workers, their overall involvement with community development and social change campaigns were decidedly modest and episodic. However, child welfare leaders prior to World War I did take pains to document and make public the impact of poverty and illness on their clients and to pass on this information in a timely fashion to full-time reformers who took the lead in pressing for wide-ranging social and institutional reforms (Watson 1922).

In so doing, all of these workers established early in the profession's history the precedent of perceiving of a client or community resident as an environmentally embedded actor, rather than as a decontextualized psyche, a compartmentalized form of pathology, or a cause celebre (Germain and Gitterman 1980:347, Meyer 1973:271). Though some streams of social work have since strayed far from this precedent, others, among them practitioners invested in clients' self-empowerment, have hewed to it closely. They have done so not out of devotion to tradition or precedent, but rather because of their understanding that client empowerment builds upon clients' recognition of, trust in, and mobilization of their own internal resources in combination with those of their families, neighbors, friends, workmates, and fellow citizens (Goldstein 1990:271, Weick 1986:556–558, Weick et al. 1989:352–354).

Teaching Skills

A second aspect of early practice still relevant to contemporary practitioners who are applying an empowerment perspective is that of the teaching of specific skills to clients. Present-day empowerment theorists have stressed the importance of helping clients' learn practical, interpersonal, and political competencies for use at home, on the job, or in their community (Dodd and Gutierrez 1990:72–73, Kieffer 1984:27, Serrano-Garcia 1984:196, Staples 1990:38). Like-minded predecessors abounded in the Progressive era. Early social workers, in conjunction with public health nurses in New York City and Chicago at the turn of the century, created baby health stations at which they taught pregnant women and new mothers details about prenatal care, infant feeding, child development, an example that was replicated in many other states by the Children's Bureau after 1912 (Combs-Orme 1988:87). Housekeeping, cooking, and baking, highly marketable skills for new immigrants in the first two decades of the century, were taught at some casework agencies in New York (Richmond 1922:35).

Settlements of the Progressive era attracted immigrants to their English classes, preparatory workshops for citizenship tests, and vocational courses in tailoring, hatmaking, stage construction, practical nursing, and carpentry (Chambers 1963, Gans 1982, Leiby 1978, Lubove 1975, Wald 1915, 1933). The Cincinnati Social Experiment, organized by the National Social Unit Organization and led by Wilbur Phillips from 1915 to 1918, taught commuunity residents the mechanics of neighborhood organizing and of building federations of neighborhood groups (Franklin 1990:64, Garvin and Cox 1987:44, Lubove 1975:175–178).

Involving Clients as Participants

A third dimension of early social work practice that fostered empowerment was the conscious effort of some practitioners to involve clients actively in shaping the helping and problem-solving process. In the course of studying Mary Richmond's training notes and records from staff meetings of the Baltimore Charity Organization Society in the early 1890s and in interviewing a close colleague of Richmond's during the latter's Baltimore years, Muriel Pumphrey learned of Richmond's explicit emphasis on the central importance of caseworkers' encouragement of clients to think of alternate plans in addition to the first one discussed and to choose an option that seemed acceptable to them. Richmond also warned her staff repeatedly of the dangers of caseworkers' inadvertent use of patronizing mannerisms and language, usage that, she claimed, would sabotage completely clients' belief in their own significance as formative members of a working partnership with caseworkers (Pumphrey 1973:262).

In a similar vein, though in a distinctly different quarter of early social work, Mary Simkhovitch reflected retrospectively on the intention of the settlers at Greenwich House. "The House was never a building with a management, but a household of hospitable friends who stimulated the district to self-direction" (Simkhovitch 1938:155). The club movement within settlements, the formation of hundreds of organized groups of boys and girls for recreation, socialization, and the development of leaders, bore out Simkhovitch's claim. Boys and girls who participated in the groups elected their own leaders and selected their clubs' priorities. Some clubs in due course became interested in addressing social problems, such as the lack of a minimum wage, unemployment, the problems of immigrants, and housing conditions (Wald 1915:179–184).

Making Agency Data Publicly Useful

The public information campaign, a favorite Progressive-era endeavor, was a fourth building block added by early social workers to the foundation of empowering social work practice. Disseminating research findings to the public at large, to elected representatives of the public, and to administrators, lobbyists, judges, and regulators in the public domain was an ongoing project of many Progressive-era social workers (Muncy 1991). One early example of such work was the Immigrants' Protective League, founded by Grace Abbott and others in 1907. She and other settlement colleagues organized the Immigrants' Protective League to protect women and children immigrants from the particular forms of exploitation directed at them. The league was also created to counteract the anti-Semitism and anti-Catholic activities and influence of the Immigrant Restriction League (Costin 1983b). The Immigrants' Protective League provided information about housing, work, transportation, and immigration regulations to immigrants immediately upon their arrival in this country. The league's social workers guided newly arrived immigrants toward mutual aid societies, public help, and philanthropic resources and away from employers, landlords, pimps, and loan sharks notorious for their opportunistic exploitation of recent arrivals (Breckinridge 1921).

The representative public information specialist of the profession's early days was Paul Kellogg. After directing and publishing *The Pittsburgh Survey*, the first extensive community study in the United States and the first social survey of working conditions in the steel industry, he then edited from 1909 through 1952 the journal, the *Survey*. A publication intended to build an activist community of professional and lay social welfare leaders and philanthropic workers, the *Survey* was the most widely read and respected magazine on topics of social reform for social workers for more than three decades (Chambers 1971:40). The *Survey's* articles provided an informational base and political impetus for a wide variety of social movements. Kellogg and the *Survey's* writers reported on hundreds of social issues, among them lynchings, the conditions of many forms of industrial work, rural poverty, women's suffrage, the second-class status of American blacks, and the urgent need for a comprehensive social security and health care system.

The informational campaigns of the Children's Bureau were a third example of the outstanding quality and breadth of some early social workers' efforts to distribute essential information to the public in a systematic and timely manner. The reduction and prevention of infant mortality was the initial priority of the U.S. Children's Bureau. The bureau conducted infant mortality studies of more than 23,000 births in nine different communities between 1912 and 1920, using methodology that served as a basis for subsequent epidemiologic research (Combs-Orme 1988:86). The findings of these studies were used in lobbying and policy formulation during the decade of the 1920s. In addition, the Children's Bureau staff between 1914 and 1922 published and distributed more than 11 million copies of pamphlets in several languages for parents on health and parenting topics. The bureau also created study outlines on diverse child welfare subjects for use by local organizations that were planning educational programs for parents and future parents. In addition, the bureau held a series of conferences in eight cities of the United States to spread word of the findings from their infant mortality studies (Combs-Orme 1988:87, Costin 1983b).

FIGURE 4.2
EMPOWERING ASPECTS OF SOCIAL PRACTICE: 1893-1917

Offering concrete and social supports
Teaching skills needed in daily urban life
Involving clients as participants
Making agency data publicly useful

Clearly, the first era of practitioners and theorists contributed indispensable elements to the emergent empowerment tradition within the social work profession. However, one must take care to avoid the mistake of confounding a tributary with the larger river into which it flowed. At the same time that empowering aspects of practice were developing, so also were paternalistic ones.

Paternalistic Aspects of Practice

Paternalism is a system of relations, modeled on the parent-child template, in which those in authority act on behalf of other people without their permission to do so. Paternalists regulate the conduct of people subject to their authority through controlling the latter's access to desired resources and prerogatives. They do so by means of creating definitions of legitimate need and permissible behavior. Then, in the light of those definitions, a determination is made concerning the degree of fit between claimants' past and present conduct and that deemed acceptable by the authorities. Whether in a family, workplace, police precinct house, or social work agency, a paternalistic authority believes himself or herself to be acting in the best interest of the claimant, regardless of the claimant's view, much as a parent feels toward his or her young child.

"The folly of paternalism," Carolyn Swift has argued, is that it reduces the salience of the experience, wisdom, initiative, competencies, partnership, and participative commitment of the paternalist's subject in the process of defining and solving problems. Paternalism is, she believes, the antipodes of empowerment, since it undermines the agency and accountability of those seeking help or knowledge in the interests of sustaining the dominance of the expert (Swift 1984:xi).

That paternalistic social work was practiced in the earliest phase of the profession's history has been well documented. Historians and social work scholars who have studied case records from Progressive-era child welfare agencies have identified a common "drama" in which clients enacted "worthy" parts that they thought workers with middle-class prejudices would find credible (Katz 1990:227, Mandler 1990:15).

In many cases, men and women who sought material relief, advocacy, or protection initially hid their needs as adults behind those of their children, guessing, often accurately, that appealing for help with their children's poverty, vulnerability, or illness would constitute the path of least resistance and greatest moral magnetism (Gordon 1988a, Mandler 1990:22). Furthermore, the likelihood that an individual or family would be aided hinged in part on the degree of gratitude and deference expressed by the suppliant to the worker (Katz 1990:242). To earn the recorded attribution of "uncooperative" or "ungrateful" was to endanger one's status as a deserving recipient of help (Jones 1984, Stadum 1990:94–95, 1992).

At times paternalism took the form of conducting investigations against the stated will of the client. In her 1917 classic, *Social Diagnosis*, Mary Richmond brought forward and castigated detailed examples from case records of social workers who had ferreted out relatives, against clients' expressed wishes, for the purpose of reuniting families (Richmond 1917).

Casework was not alone in the early period in harboring paternalism. Settlements, also, made attempts to impose native-born, middle-class values and cultural habits on their diverse and yet-to-be-Americanized neighbors. Indeed, some historians have made the claim that, settlements, more so than child welfare agencies, sought to supplant neighbors' values and mores with a completely new set of values and goals—an assimilated, Protestant version (Gans 1982, Davis 1967, Mandler 1990:27)

Some paternalism crept into the fraternalism of settlements' youth clubs and classes in citizenship, cooking, American history, and parenting. Much of the time, the settler was simply a friendly neighbor; some of the time she or he was "a superior kind of neighbor" (Mandler 1990:25). Not given to overt preaching, like friendly visitors from charity organization societies of the 1880s and 1890s, settlers who were functioning in paternalistic and assimilationist modes cloaked their cultural conversion activities in metaphors of friendship, neighborliness, education, and preparation for leadership.

The paternalism of some caseworkers and settlers toward immigrants was woven into the unequal relationships that were created. In another form of paternalism, that of racism toward African Americans and Caribbean-Americans, the absence of relationships, rather than the quality of them, constituted the main problem.

Despite the sensitivity of a few casework agencies and settlements to the needs of blacks in the Progressive era, most served exclusively white clientele with exclusively white staffs, mobilizing black social workers and social reformers to form their own agencies, mutual aid societies, and settlements (Wenocur and Reisch 1989:259, Sterling 1984). Among the early leadership that arose was that of Eartha White in Jacksonville, Florida, who organized philanthropy there for African Americans, of Sarah Fernandis in Baltimore and Washington, D.C., who founded several settlements for blacks, and of Victoria Matthews in New York City, who created in 1897 the White Rose Industrial Association for young black working women and who helped found the National Association of Colored Women (Minahan 1987:913–948).

The prevalence of de facto and de jure segregation in the country in the years between 1893 and 1917 was mirrored in the institutional configurations, staffing policies, and client bases of social work. Like other professions of the period, social work, on the whole, had yet to realize that attacking the disfranchisement and poverty of black Americans was an integral part of its central charge.

The paternalism of early social work took other forms as well. In the major fight that took place in the second decade of the century over the wisdom of creating mothers' pensions, charity organization societies led the opposition to the pensions. Leaders of charity agencies believed that the creation of a publicly funded stipend for widowed, abandoned, or divorced mothers would transform charity into an entitlement (Katz 1986:127–128). Their opponents in the struggle were hoping for exactly that outcome.

In their vigorous opposition to child labor and child truancy, most social workers, whether social reformers, group workers, or caseworkers, failed to campaign with equal ardor for guaranteed benefits that would compensate poor families for the loss of wages that ending child labor entailed (Mandler 1990:27). The strength of early social work's child-saving impulse clouded many Progressive-era social workers' capacity for comprehending the historic need of many rural and urban families to rely upon child labor for survival. Over the overt and covert protests of families who depended upon both adults' and children's wages, the social work leaders of the period of every political persuasion placed a higher premium on ending child labor than on coordinating the abolition of that labor with the passage of income supports for families in which child laborers had been necessary contributors. It was a paternalism informed, on the one hand, by devotion to children and, on the other hand, by deafness to the pleas of the families directly affected.

The first phase of social work's development was tortuous and complicated, emerging as it did in a context of massive, rapid, and uneven changes. A nascent strain of social work practice devoted to the self-empowerment of clients took root between 1893 and 1917 in a cultural and professional soil steeped in paternalism, nativism, and racism. Nonetheless, the root proved tenacious.

CHAPTER FIVE

Wartime and the Interwar Years: Context and Influences, 1917–1945

It is no longer a question of whether it is *wrong* to try to make our fellow beings think and feel as we want them to. In the long run it is simply silly. The vital needs of their being will in the end determine what they shall feel and how they shall act. —Bertha C. Reynolds

The Context: 1917–1945

Throughout the Great War, the "roaring twenties," the most severe and sustained economic depression in American history, and World War II, social work continued to develop as a profession that harbored both empowering and paternalistic trends. Empowerment and paternalism evolved within social work amidst domestic and international troubles that would have been unimaginable to most native-born Americans prior to 1917. U.S. citizens had been long accustomed, after all, to the sustained hopefulness and insularity of the exceptionalist worldview, one anchored by the faith that God via natural law had ordained their homeland to be unlike any other in the world in its perfectibility and freedom from the contaminations of Old World tyranny (Ross 1991:22–50, 143–171).

Soon after President Wilson and the Congress jointly declared war on Germany in April of 1917, the horror of world war became much more than a removed regret, as it had been for many Americans in the first three years of the war while the U.S. maintained its neutrality. In place of prior aloofness, a preoccupying passion to retaliate against German submarine assaults on American sovereignty and shipping and to "make the world safe for democracy" consumed many Americans. The flames of their commitment and patriotism were fanned by a jingoistic press, government propaganda, reports from war correspondents at several fronts, and letters from some of the 4,355,000 American soldiers and sailors who took part in the carnage of trench warfare (Carruth 1979:450).

Lives, health, and property were not the only casualties of World War I. The American people's popular faith during the Progressive period in domestic reform, in social progress, and in the possibility of harmonious relations among people of differing ideologies, social classes, and nationalities within the world and the nation had been undermined seriously (Ross 1991:320–326). The savagery of the war, the impotency of rationality to counter the upsurge of imperialism and chauvinistic fervor, the demonic uses of science and technology, and the 1917 Sedition Act's repression of dissent in the United States— especially that expressed by socialists, anarchists, and pacifists—gave rise to profound anxiety and disillusionment with elected officials' capacity to make things right (Ross 1991:320–326). Small wonder that commitment to the public good waned also.

The era of the 1920s in the United States witnessed little popular interest in public welfare and social reform. To the contrary, it was a decade of retrenchment from the social gains of Progressivism. With the exception of the ratification of the Nineteenth Amendment, which granted nationwide woman suffrage in 1920, the twenties offered little for social workers who cared about removing social injustices and inequalities to cheer. In 1922, for example, the U.S. Supreme Court declared unconstitutional the federal regulation of child labor and the federal minimum wage laws, Progressive-era innovations that had taken decades of unremitting campaigning to win (Ehrenreich 1985:83).

The only major welfare movement of the twenties was that of welfare capitalism, large corporations' experiments with social insurance, fringe benefits, and the reduction of some hazards of industrial life (Katz 1986:186–190). These efforts were, at one and the same time, attempts to improve working conditions, reduce the appeal and membership of labor unions, obviate the need for governmental regulation of corporate and industrial affairs, and slow the spread of socialism.

Popular disinterest in the commonweal and preoccupation with private matters during the 1920s was also demonstrated by the emergence of the new culture of consumption following World War I (Benson 1986, Ewen 1976, Walkowitz 1990:1052). By 1923, 15 million cars were registered and 16 million telephones were installed in a country with 22 million households (Carruth 1979:455, 457). More than 2,500,000 American homes had radios by 1924, less than two years after New York City's WEAF broadcast the first commercially sponsored program in the United States (Carruth 1979:467, 463). The advertising and department store industries expanded exponentially and interrelatedly during this decade of proliferation in the ways to spend leisure hours and earnings (Benson 1986, Ewen 1976).

The rise of consumerism, privatism, and political apathy in the United States stood in stark contrast to the rapid spread of communism and socialism in Russia, Germany, Hungary, Finland, and other parts of Europe during the years of World War I and the period immediately following the Treaty of Versailles of 1919. The success of the Bolshevik Revolution in Russia of 1917 and the formation of the Third International and the Comintern in 1919, a Bolshevik mechanism for catalyzing proletarian revolutions throughout the world under Moscow's direction, inspired a series of strong reactions in the United States (Karger 1987:91–96).

The Red Scare of 1919 and 1920 was one response. In many states and localities, laws against advocating crimes or violence for purposes of political change were passed and used to harass and jail union leaders, pacifists, anarchists, and socialists (Ehrenreich 1985:47). Teachers and other public workers were, for the first time, required to take loyalty oaths. Hundreds of teachers were fired and aliens deported for being suspected of disloyalty (Chambers 1971:220, Ehrenreich 1985:47). The U.S. Attorney General, A. Mitchell Palmer, launched surprise raids on the homes, workplaces, and organizations of activists and radicals, arresting and jailing thousands of people, and confiscating their personal and organizational files.

The Palmer raids and other Red Scare tactics gave serious pause to many who had involved themselves in dissent and reform campaigns only a few years earlier. Expression of the desire for political change and the institution of social welfare measures, however modest, put one at risk of being considered a "red." The American Medical Association (A.M.A.), for example, which had endorsed national health insurance as late as 1916, changed its position and began denouncing the proposal as bolshevist (Ehrenreich 1985:48). Throughout the 1920s, the A.M.A. persistently labeled one of the few social reforms of the decade, the Sheppard-Towner Maternity and Infancy Act of 1921, the "prussianization" of American doctors (Muncy 1991:138).

Grace Abbott, Julia Lathrop, Florence Kelley, and Jane Addams were repeatedly charged in public speeches, editorials, and public hearings during the mid-1920s with being central actors in an international communist conspiracy (Muncy 1991:129).

Political reactionaryism during the post-World War I period also took the form of racism, especially in major cities of the North, to which millions of black men and women migrated during the war and 1920s in the hopes of finding jobs (Jones 1992). During what came to be known as the "Red Summer" of 1919, white rioters on Chicago's South Side initiated seven days of attacks on the black community. Twenty-three blacks and fifteen whites were killed, while five hundred others were injured and approximately one thousand people were left homeless (Shapiro 1988:150–151). In that same summer, a white mob lynched and burned a black man in Omaha, initiating violence that required the U.S. Army to intervene to end it. In Washington, D.C., in July of 1919, two hundred white sailors and marines attacked several black women and men, triggering three days of interracial violence that military units were called upon to stop (Shapiro 1988:154–155) During the 1920s, the Ku Klux Klan's resurgence in both the North and the South resulted in a wave of lynchings, whippings, brandings, tarrings, and other forms of violence against black citizens and, in some localities, against Jews and Catholics as well (Carruth 1979:458, Shapiro 1988:175–201).

Nativism also characterized the decade following World War I. The campaign during the war to foster national cohesion was called "100 percent Americanism" by Theodore Roosevelt. After the war, residual passions from wartime patriotism merged with long-standing xenophobia, anti-Semitism, and anti-Catholicism and newer hatreds of bolsheviks, anarchists, and Germans. One result was the notorious conviction of Sacco and Vanzetti in 1921 and their execution in 1927, despite international protests. Another was the Immigration Acts of 1921 and 1924, which introduced restrictive national quotas on immigration to the United States, favoring Northern and Western Europeans and discriminating against Asians, Africans, and southern and Central Europeans (Jenkins 1987:873). This system of national quotas that privileged Northern and Western European immigration lasted until 1965 and contributed to the scope of the later Holocaust by preventing the entry of thousands of people attempting to escape from Central and Eastern Europe in the 1930s and 40s.

The 1930s, of course, was the time of the Great Depression and of the New Deal created in response to that depression. On the eve of the stock market crash of October 1929, 60 percent of U.S. citizens had annual incomes lower than two thousand dollars, the estimated minimum needed in that year to supply the "basic necessities of life" (Carruth 1979:482). Things were to deteriorate quickly. In the spring of 1931, 16 percent of the labor force (8 million people) were unemployed (Wenocur and Reisch 1989:159). By 1932, 26 percent of the labor force (13 million people) were unemployed, and the total amount paid in wages was 60 percent less than that paid in 1929 (Carruth 1979:490, 492). The drought of 1934 drove many Midwestern farmers permanently off their lands and into a traveling limbo of hunger and rootlessness. In the first four years of the Great Depression, official unemployment rose from 3.2 percent to an astonishing 24.9 percent (Katz 1986:207). Unofficial estimates, which included people too discouraged to report their status to local or state labor officials, placed the unemployment figure in 1934 closer to a third of the adult employable population.

In responding to this monumental crisis, President Franklin Roosevelt, with Congressional approval, created thirty-three new federal governmental agencies, which employed 24,303 new federal employees (Carruth 1979:500, 502). The Federal Emergency Relief Administration funneled direct relief to the unemployed through state emergency relief agencies and local poor relief agencies. After the U.S. Supreme Court ruled in 1935 that the National Recovery Act, the foundation of the original New Deal, was unconstitutional in that it interfered with interstate commerce, the Roosevelt administration crafted the second New Deal.

Launched in 1935, the second New Deal did away with the emergency unemployment relief measures of the Federal Emergency Relief Association. Instead, the administration designed and secured Congressional approval of a permanent program for channeling relief to what were then called "broken families," the aged, and the disabled, authorized under the Social Security Act of 1935. For employable people, work relief programs were constructed under the Works Progress Administration (WPA), the Civilian Conservation Corps (CCC), and the National Youth Administration. Before the end of 1935, six hundred thousand people enrolled in the CCC. The WPA at its peak, in 1938, enrolled 3.3 million people, making it the largest single employer in the country (Leiby 1978:228).

While Franklin Roosevelt, his administration, and the American people grappled with the misery of the Depression, Europe experienced the rapid rise and consolidation of fascism, and Asia contended with Japanese aggression. Fewer than twenty years after the signing of the treaty ending World War I, Mussolini's forces had swallowed up Ethiopia and Hitler's army had invaded and occupied Austria and Czechoslovakia. With the German invasion of Poland in 1939, England and France declared war on the Axis, the coalition of Germany, Italy, and Japan. In 1941, Russia, after being invaded by German forces, joined the war on the side of the Allies, France and England. Japan's surprise bombing of Pearl Harbor brought the U.S. into World War II in December of 1941. For almost four years, the chief concern of the American government and people, along with its allies, was that of securing defeat of the Axis countries. When the Allied forces obtained unconditional surrenders in 1945, the costliest war and an entire era of unspeakable horror finally came to an end.

Influential Ideas, Beliefs, and Movements

Social workers during this turbulent three decades had a creative and diverse set of "instructors" to learn from on the subject of the impact of power and powerlessness on client welfare and on a professional's relationship and accountability to clients. One such teacher was Sigmund Freud.

Freudianism

Freud's work became rapidly influential in the interwar years in the thinking and action of social workers in general, among whom were those who were particularly invested in reducing client powerlessness and helplessness. Many scholars, of course, have documented the conservatizing effect of Freudianism on social casework and on the general direction of the overall social work profession during the interwar years (Axinn and Levin 1982, Ehrenreich 1985, Katz 1986, Leiby 1978, Lubove 1975, Trattner 1989). Some social workers during the 1920s who were captivated by their first exposure to Freudian thought helped promote individual pathology to the center of the profession's concerns and demote socioeconomic issues and campaigns for social justice to the margins. The inadequate and delayed response of the profession to the impoverishment and misery of millions of people during the initial phase of the Great Depression was, in part, a consequence of the lure of Freudianism, with its intrapsychic focus, for many social work practitioners, agencies, and schools.

However, a fuller rendering of the complex effects of Freud's thought on social work practice during the first three decades of its popularization in the United States, following Freud's visit to Clark University in 1909, requires further investigation of the uses of Freudian thought by practitioners working with stigmatized and disempowered groups and individuals. Freud's theoretical explication of the unconscious, of psychological defense mechanisms, and of the "talking cure," through which an individual's painful and self-defeating inner conflicts are relieved, modified, or resolved by being brought to consciousness through an exploratory talking relationship with a trusted and empathic practitioner, were invaluable contributions to the knowledge base and methodology of those social workers who were working with clients crippled by intrapsychic and interpersonal troubles.

At a time in the cultural history of the West when the lens of morality was the primary one through which behavior was viewed and understood, Freud introduced a second lens, that of psychology. His work, above all others, encouraged social workers and other professionals of the day to replace moral judgment with *verstehen*, Dilthey's concept of the approximate understanding and apprehension of the totality of another human being's inner experience. Freud's thesis that therapeutic revelation, interpretation, and alliance could lead to recovery and mastery catapulted the relationship between worker and client to the center of the social work stage of the 1920s. The building of relationships, rather than the evaluation of character or genetic makeup, became the accepted currency of the social work realm. It was a currency that could be circulated by clients as well as practitioners and by those on the margins as well as in the mainstream.

Both operationally and metaphorically, Freud's work suggested to his contemporaries that authentic and attuned human interconnection over time could result in the reversal of despair, self-destruction, hatred, and isolation, even among several categories of sufferers who had been deemed beyond help and hope by Freud's psychiatric predecessors. Freud and his followers helped clients achieve individual liberation from past traumas and present anguish. His was a message that emphasized not only the pathos of individual pathology but also the possibility of healing, recovery, and restoration. His work also created a focus in European and American thought on the dynamic aspects of human existence, on the developmental plasticity of human potential, especially when compared with his predecessors' concentration on the fixed qualities of individuals' character and genes (Allen

1935:698). Freud's emphasis on personal pathology has received thorough and excellent attention from historians of Freud's impact on social work. By contrast, the effects on the profession of his second emphasis—that of human reconstruction and plasticity—still await an evenhanded chronicle.

Marcus Garvey and Black Nationalism

In a wholly different vein, Marcus Garvey also was an important influence on social workers of an empowerment bent. Garvey articulated a cultural and nationalistic approach to promoting black liberation and undermining colonialism (Lewis 1988, Shapiro 1988, Solomon 1989). Having migrated from the Caribbean to Harlem, Garvey founded in the 1920s the Universal Negro Improvement Association, an organization that anchored a movement of African Americans who were in search of total emancipation from white domination. Through the creation of an ideology of black consciousness and pan-Africanism, together with a network of black-owned businesses such as Garvey's Black Star Line of steamships and Black Cross nurses, this leader sought to establish pride in and commitment to "Negritude," black cultural separatism and nationalism, and a back-to-Africa emigration. Malcolm X would become a direct political descendant of Marcus Garvey later in the century (Lewis 1988, Solomon 1989).

Though the social work profession of the 1920s was predominantly a white and middle-class occupation, it nonetheless had white and black members who paid close attention to the message of black consciousness and cultural self-determination that the charismatic and visionary Garvey preached in person and on radio. His explication of the nature of the damage done to blacks by white domination and of the daily costs for black people of an integrationist strategy became critical "texts" for social workers of the period who were seeking to comprehend the consciousness of the disempowered and of people attempting to release themselves from that condition.

Black Americans migrated in large numbers from rural areas of the South during World War I to take up jobs in industry opened to them for the first time. The wartime demand for the emergency production of uniforms, boots, steel, armament, planes, and ships forced the rapid desegregation of steel, auto, and armaments manufacturers. Black ghettos expanded rapidly in Detroit, Gary, Chicago, St. Louis, Cleveland, Cincinnati, Pittsburgh, Buffalo, New York City, Boston,

Philadelphia, New Haven, Trenton, Baltimore, Washington, D.C., and many smaller industrial cities during and after World War I (Jones 1992). Chicago, for example, saw its black population more than double between 1920 and 1930 (Katz 1986:175–176).

Whereas Progressive-era white social workers could more easily ignore the black poverty of Northern cities before the Great War, the increasing numbers of black poor men, women, and children after 1917 in the very cities in which social work had taken root made such denial increasingly difficult, both practically and morally. The more social agencies and social workers were confronted with black poverty, underemployment, and unemployment, the more curious some became about the messages of Garvey as well as that of Du Bois. The influence of both leaders was evident in the multiple discussions of Jim Crow laws and racism in *Social Work Today*, a journal of the Rank-and-File movement within social work from 1934 through 1942.

Existentialism

Existentialist philosophers and novelists also contributed significantly to the cultural bank of ideas and politics from which social workers drew in the interwar years. Heidegger's *Being and Time* (1927), Marcel's *Metaphysical Journal* (1927), Kafka's *The Castle* (1926) and *The Trial* (1925), Malraux's *Man's Fate* (1934), Camus's *The Myth of Sisyphus* (1942) and *The Stranger* (1942), and Sartre's *Nausea* (1938) and *Being and Nothingness* (1943) contributed to Western culture a growing consciousness of the contingency of human existence, of the burden of choice each individual faces in an often irrational world, and of the responsibility that individuals bear for creating new values and for taking action in the face of the absurd and of the incomprehensible.

Heidegger, Marcel, Kafka, Malraux, Camus, and Sartre, each in his own fashion, described a world devoid of meaning, freedom, and commitment and wrote of the necessity of filling such voids with the creative action and expression of individuals (Barnes 1962, 1978). During decades in which facism, Nazism, Stalinism, and the reign of apparatchiks took control of many domains of life in Eastern, Central, and Western Europe, European existentialists assailed the totalitarian tendencies of centralized bureaucracies and of collective movements and pointed to individual revolt and heroism as a necessary counterforce to authoritarianism and as an indispensable route to freedom and authenticity.

Social workers in the U.S. who were working with poor or stigmatized people during the period between the wars and who took particular interest in the question of how to help such people without in any way reducing their freedom or power found in existentialism a provocative and evocative philosophy that helped them to examine the intended and unintended tyranny that authorities, among them helping professionals, can introduce into the lives of individuals and families who are in their charge. Existentialist thought also assisted empowerment-oriented social workers in comprehending the despair, the cynicism, and the alienation that can follow from sustained experiences of helplessness and powerlessness. Finally, existentialism issued forth a beacon of hope to disempowered individuals and to those professionals working with them: if individuals can summon their own special strengths to resist, each in her or his own way, the brutality and banality that surround them, they will secure some measure of personal power and meaning and thereby reduce the isolation and anguish that characterizes a twentieth-century world that is, essentially, unfathomable. Both Freud and the German, Czech, and French existentialists considered the nurturance of human individuality, rather than collectivity, to be the primary antidote for humans' powerlessness. Some empowerment-based social workers of the Depression years followed this trajectory, a path that paralleled the earlier road chosen by nineteenth-century Transcendentalists.

Marxism and Socialism

By contrast, Marxists and socialists in the United States of the interwar years emphasized the liberating elements of collective action and the isolating dimensions of individualism. Few ideas and positions were shared by both American Marxists and socialists—the two groups fought bitterly and constantly during the interwar era just as they had before World War I (Cantor 1978). Nevertheless, they did agree that oppressed people would be well served by joining together to resist the encroachments of the owners and managers of industry and to create institutions of their own—like unions, credit banks, newspapers, and community centers—that would constitute counterinstitutions interruptive of the control of corporations, the banking establishment, and mainstream media.

The Congress of Industrial Organizations (CIO) was one outgrowth during the 1930s of a strong desire on the part of some left ward-looking Americans to perforate corporate domination over many things, including labor. The CIO was established as a federation of unions organized across whole industries instead of by craft as the American Federation of Labor (AFL) had been configured. Another concrete expression of leftist beliefs was the Unemployed Councils of America, a confederation of approximately twelve hundred local organizations organized by members of the Communist party in 1934 and 1935 to increase the militance of labor, to demonstrate for public works projects that would employ the unemployed, to obtain local relief programs and longer-term social insurance legislation, and to resist the evictions of unemployed tenants (Cantor 1978:120, Fisher 1980:98, 127).

The Catholic Worker Movement was a third form of activism that emerged from Depression-era dreams for a more collective and equitable society. Founded in 1937 by Dorothy Day and other Catholic trade unionists, the Catholic Worker Movement in the United States organized workers into unions that became part of the emergent CIO, created soup kitchens for feeding the poor, and sought to build a Christian socialist mass movement, using vehicles such as residential communes, reading and discussion groups, radical church congregations, and a network of newspapers, book stores, and food and craft cooperatives (Cort 1988).

A fourth initiative inspired during the interwar years by leftist conceptions of a more just society was the Industrial Areas Foundation (IAF) of Saul Alinsky. Influenced most deeply by his participation in the building of the CIO, Alinsky turned in the late 1930s from labor union organizing to community organizing, introducing a conflict approach that attempted to assist poor neighborhoods to transform themselves into "mass power organizations" (Alinsky 1946, 1971, Boyte 1984:129). Using IAF organizing in Chicago as a model, Alinsky-trained organizers responded to invitations from sponsoring committees in many parts of the country to assist poor communities to "organize themselves for power" (Boyte 1984:129). The organizers aided and abetted local efforts by reinforcing existing community organizations and indigenous community leadership, by creating adversaries that served to unite communities, by seeking out and winning multiple and visible confrontations, and by creating new organizations representative of several local groups (Alinsky 1946, 1971, Lyon 1987, Cortes 1984).

Although hundreds of other examples of activities during the interwar years that were informed by socialist or Marxist notions could be cited, it is the four already noted—the Congress of Industrial Organizations, the Unemployed Councils of America, the Catholic Worker Movement, and the Industrial Areas Foundation—that were most compelling to social workers of the period who made up the profession's "left wing" (Fisher 1980:66–172). These organizations actively sought on first the local and later the national level to reorder the power relations between leaders of corporations or governments, on the one hand, and line workers or community members, on the other. Each of these four organizations came into being for the explicit purposes of reducing the domination and power of "haves" and of expanding the share of power held by common people in everyday interactions and in institutional life. As a consequence, those social workers who held particular interest in the role of power and powerlessness in accelerating and subverting the processes of client recovery, development, and self-determination looked to the work of the CIO, the unemployed councils, the Catholic Workers Movement, and the Industrial Areas Foundation for illustrations of the paradoxes and contradictions embedded in the knotty dynamic of helping individuals and groups to empower themselves.

FIGURE 5.1
INFLUENTIAL IDEAS, BELIEFS, AND MOVEMENTS

Freudianism
Marcus Garvey and Black Nationalism
Existentialism
Marxism and Socialism

With the bombing of Pearl Harbor in December of 1941, the interwar period came to an abrupt and terrible end. Most social workers, like most Americans, joined the war effort as citizens or as soldiers. A small proportion of social workers, honoring their pacifist beliefs, conscientiously objected to U.S. involvement in World War II.

Social workers' conceptions of empowerment practice between 1917 and 1945 were crystallized amidst multiple contextual transformations and tumultuous cultural and political forces. Not surprisingly, their definitions of empowerment practice, which are characterized in chapter 6, evidenced their historical moment.

CHAPTER SIX

Wartime and Interwar Visions of Empowerment Practice, 1917–1945

If social case work . . . frees men from crippling accumulations of fear and hate so that they may have energy to use what intelligence they possess . . . it becomes not a luxury but a necessity in a time of social change. —Bertha C. Reynolds

What we want for our club members in the group work agencies, we want for ourselves. We know by experience that where autocracy can be banished, where each is freed from fear or sense of inferiority to make his contribution creatively to the group, there may spring up a wide expanding experience for us all. —Grace L. Coyle

Social Work's Visions of Empowerment: 1917–1945

Wars and economic devastation lend poignance and urgency to the exploration of the intertwined subjects of power and powerlessness. Unfortunately, the years between 1917 and 1945 provided ample opportunities for elected leaders and professionals to grapple with the related notions of empowerment and disempowerment. Social workers, some of whom were working directly with the swelling ranks of the displaced and the dispossessed at home and abroad, attempted to define roles for themselves that were properly responsive to the political, economic, and social dislocation swirling around them.

Social Workers' Self-Conceptions

Releasers of Clients' Potential Social workers who were particularly interested in the plight of the powerless during this period frequently referred to themselves as workers who were trying to release clients or constitutents from confining bonds—psychic, economic, environmental, legal, or physical—so that those people who sought social work assistance could live and work more freely and fully. The conception of social worker as she or he who aids another to release force, growth, will, energy, potential, power, talent, or capacities for human interconnection was in common circulation throughout the entire continuum of social work methods of the era. Caseworkers, group workers, community workers, and administrators alike worked toward the "emancipation of the personality" (Chambers 1963:100).

Social workers derived the language of release and emancipation from at least two distinct sources. Freud's project of freeing people from unconscious conflicts and from excessive repression of libidinal and aggressive drives was one major influence. The other was the Marxian and socialist commitment to the emancipation of the downtrodden (the proletariat) through the crystallization of class consciousness and participation in collective class struggle. Social workers between the wars practiced and wrote in a cultural climate suffused with the notions of both schools of thought, the one directed toward internal shackles, the other aimed at external chains.

Caseworkers, like Gordon Hamilton of the New York School of Social Work, helped shape the discourse of enfranchisement. "The test . . . of case work," she wrote, "is not only its pragmatic ability to help, but its power to liberate, enlarge, and socialize the human spirit" (Hamilton 1941:253).

She concerned herself with the spirit of workers as well as clients:

> It is not only clients who must be active on their own problems if they are to grow: as social workers, we must develop the sort of democratic technique which releases activity in ourselves and our fellows. . . . Professional social action . . . should mean the release of disciplined energies less complicated with hostility and aggression and so more susceptible to cooperative practices. (Hamilton 1937:170)

Another caseworker of the era, Virginia Robinson of the Pennsylvania School of Social Work, also thought that social work was an emancipationist project, but one constantly endangered by the tendency to control and manipulate clients.

> This approach to case work . . . brings out clearly the two contrasting and conflicting pulls which operate confusingly in all case work. One is the active, aggressive desire to help, to change, to reform, to control. . .

The other drive is the need to understand the client's very different reality which absorbs the worker through identification into the client's problem. (Robinson 1930:164)

Excellence in casework, Robinson taught, required the worker to stretch past both mental habits, that of controlling helpfulness and of identification with the client. Instead, the social worker would be effective only if he or she concentrated on the client's "growth process released in the relationship [with the caseworker]" (Robinson 1930:164).

Charlotte Towle, another caseworker of the era and a professor at the University of Chicago's School of Social Administration, joined in the emancipationist chorus in her claim that "it is their [caseworkers] primary concern to release the feeling necessary to enable the client to utilize these services and suggestions in a growth direction" (Towle 1936:320).

Group workers, too, saw themselves as unleashers of the human spirit. Grace Coyle, a theoretician of social group work who taught at the School of Applied Social Sciences at Western Reserve University, felt that "society must provide for its members opportunity for all kinds of experience that widens interest, develops latent capacities, increases knowledge of the world, encourages creative expression, brings forth intelligent, socially valuable human beings. The use of leisure for these purposes is one of the functions of the group worker" (Coyle 1937a:561).

Similarly, Mary Parker Follett, the former settlement house worker who became a scholar of organizational behavior and industrial relations, thought that leadership of groups, organizations, and political entities was a mission of liberation and enlivenment:

I think it was Emerson who told us of those who supply us with new powers out of the recesses of the spirit and urge us to new and unattempted performance. This is far more than imitating your leader. In this conception of Emerson's, what you receive from your leader does not come from him, but from the "recesses of the spirit." Whoever connects me with the hidden springs of all life, whoever increases the sense of life in me, he is my leader. (Follett 1928:294)

Katharine Lenroot, a social worker who served the U.S. Children's Bureau for thirty-seven years, succeeding Grace Abbott as its director in 1934, believed that the freeing of clients' individual capacities so diligently sought by social workers would only be meaningful if linked closely with efforts to unleash clients' social and political power. "Release of personal energy through favorable social environment and liberating human relationships must be accompanied by the development of power which comes from coordination of effort to achieve the general ends of the social group" (Lenroot 1935:58, 60).

Social workers with empowerment inclinations during and between the world wars clearly expected themselves to help uncork, open up, dislodge, unfreeze, unlock, and generally set free clients' motion, emotion, power, and intelligence. In the midst of this highly energetic pursuit, they also expected themselves to bear witness to the misery of the people with whom they worked directly. They thought that they should provide the public and its governments with testimony about the causes, contours, and range of social problems experienced by many of their clients, particularly those who were poor, sick, or physically dependent.

Witnesses Bearing witness, in its original, seventeenth-century meaning within Quaker meetings, meant breaking collective and individual meditative silence to testify about the spiritual truths that one's "inner light" illuminated. One had to both stand and speak the truth as it beamed out from the spirit within. In twentieth-century secular terms, bearing witness meant stepping forward to speak, testify, or write truths about issues and concerns that one had directly observed or taken part in.

It did not mean nor ever had meant speaking for other people whom one perceived as inarticulate, as Jacob Fisher claimed in *The Response of Social Work to the Depression* (1980:35). Instead, bearing witness was an enacted commitment to an issue that one was obligated to address professionally and ethically by virtue of one's own exposure to the subject. To bear witness was to express in the public realm one's knowledge obtained as a caseworker, group worker, or community worker. The phrase had no connotation of representing the voiceless or the absent. It was, rather, the communication of insights gained from one's direct connection to a public concern. Social workers from each methodological compartment of the profession shared the expectation that they should witness, meaning to furnish proof concerning the nature and consequences of rural and urban poverty, xenophobia and racism, unemployment, the absence of social insurance, and the presence of unregulated industry.

For example, the executive committee of the American Association of Social Workers (AASW), an organization of social work supervisors and agency executives, responded to the first year of the Great Depression with a formal statement, "The Responsibility and Contribution of Social Workers in Unemployment Crises" (AASW 1930). The AASW stated in that document that social workers were especially obligated in the midst of the unfolding crisis to "bear witness" to the effects of the economic depression on their clients (AASW 1930). It was not enough to serve clients or to encourage clients to bring forward their own stories, though both were crucial functions. In addition, social workers themselves should "speak truth to power," another Quaker concept and phrase.

Harriett Bartlett, a leader among hospital social workers, believed that medical social workers had a particular message to deliver to the larger society. To her way of thinking, hospital social workers possessed specialized information, by virtue of their professional responsibilities, organizational vantage points, and community involvement, that the public needed if it were to plan wisely for the common good and for the welfare of individuals within the polity.

> We must be careful to distinguish between action for which our skill and experience especially qualify us and that for which we are no better prepared than any intelligent citizen. As social case workers we are not experts in government, finance, insurance, and so on. There is, however, a special contribution to social planning which our experience qualifies us to make. We can and should present (though our statistics should be better) specific evidence of medical social need; we can demonstrate the importance and the appropriate methods of community organization to meet the need and of individualization within any broader social program which is to be developed. (Bartlett 1934:467)

Mary Young, a child welfare worker, thought along similar lines within her own specialization. Child welfare workers ought to testify because of their in-depth exposure to the deprivation of poor children and families.

> Since the number of children who come to the attention of skilled family workers is very small in comparison to the number which do not, it would be helpful to make available our fund of knowledge.

> I think we are not conscious enough of the wealth of material that our records hold.

We should coordinate and analyze our material. I do not mean only statistically, nor do I mean an enumeration of problems, but rather our contribution should contain much concerning culture or attitudes. (Young 1935:600)

Gordon Hamilton thought it a professional obligation "to support and promote mass measures for insurance, pensions, and the like . . . and to bear testimony in regard to the effects on people of tolerated political and economic systems" (quoted in Leighninger 1987:56–57). A specialist in family casework, Charlotte Carr held strong views on social workers' and social work agencies' obligations to bear witness to several forces that undermined families with whom she and her supervisees worked. She highlighted with persistent prescience the effects of work on family life.

But in my opinion our family agencies are only carrying on their fullest social obligation when they are able to give the public facts as to the general social—including industrial—conditions which they find in the course of their work.

It is my belief that our family societies are in a position to get information about the effect of industrial disease on family dependency which, if made public, would result in the passage of compensation laws to cover industrial diseases. If, for example, the number of cases of miner's asthma which come to family societies in coal mining communities in Pennsylvania were made public, . . . a real step would be taken toward making miner's asthma compensable in that state. (Carr 1930:734)

From the point of view of group worker Grace Coyle, caseworkers held an especially advantaged position for possessing and providing documentation of the harsh environments within which their clients dwelled.

It is obvious that the experience of the case worker is a rich mine of valuable information for those working for definite social improvement. He sees in concrete form, multiplied before his eyes, the effects of low wages, of unemployment, of bad housing, and he no longer regards them largely as the consequences of laziness or rum, as his predecessors did. . . . Case workers who realize the meaning in human life of the conditions of existence of their clients and who are able to portray those conditions vividly can be a powerful weapon in combating them, using their firsthand information in legislative committees or city councils or through the channels of organizations engaged to various programs of social action. (Coyle 1937b:566)

Dorothea de Schweinitz, a family caseworker and educator, concurred and emphasized the urgency of the imperative for social workers to bear witness, just as Progressive-era social workers had done earlier. In her charge to her colleagues in the heart of the Great Depression, de Schweinitz pointed out the need for bringing forward both quantitative and qualitative evidence of clients' misery.

> Now the community wants to have its information in degree and proportion. How low are low wages? How far do they fall short of maintaining health and providing a minimum standard of living? . . . How many old people need assistance? . . . The gripping story is needed as much as ever but it can be made doubly convincing when backed up by numbers. Family case workers and research workers can well combine efforts to reveal the evidence of suffering locked up in the files of family societies throughout the country. (de Schweinitz 1935:635–636)

Organizers For a vociferous and determined minority of social workers, during the 1930s, helping clients to release their own capacities and power and bearing witness in public arenas to clients' hardships were activities that they deemed necessary, yet insufficient in a time of profound poverty. Members of the Rank-and-File movement within social work from 1931 through 1936 thought that social workers owed much more to their clients and to their society.

Social workers, they believed, should become organizers, in the tradition of trade union organizing (Fisher 1936). They should organize several things: 1. themselves, into social work trade unions, 2. explicit social work support for the demands of organizations of the unemployed and also of Works Progress Administration workers, 3. alliances between social workers and labor union members, 4. mass political support for comprehensive social insurance, 5. ongoing collective advocacy for the abolition of discrimination against blacks and other minorities who were employees in public welfare departments, work relief jobs, or who were recipients of public assistance, and 6. their clients to secure just levels of public relief (Fisher 1980:238–239, Leighninger 1987:66–68).

Rank-and-Filers conceived of themselves as members of a mass movement rather than as members of a profession. Influenced by the views of such social workers as Mary van Kleeck, Jacob Fisher, Bertha

Reynolds, and Harry Lurie, Rank-and-Filers sought to radicalize social work colleagues in a leftward direction, one that would lead social workers to identify with disadvantaged and stigmatized people rather than with the middle class (Fisher 1980:237–240).

The movement's journal, *Social Work Today*, published from 1934 through 1942, reached approximately fifteen thousand readers during the peak of Rank-and-File influence in 1936. The majority of members were workers in public relief agencies in major cities of the East who had not trained in professional schools, although an influential minority were professionally trained (Wenocur and Reisch 1989:182–183). The movement's discussion clubs, journal, and practitioners' groups, and speeches at the National Conference of Social Work accelerated the social work profession's demands for social insurance and federal relief programs, especially in 1934 and 1935.

With the passage of the Social Security Act in 1935 and the studied indifference to social work demands by both major political parties during the presidential election campaign of 1936, the membership and sphere of influence of the Rank-and-File movement shrank rapidly (Leighninger 1987:67–68). For a quarter of a century, its particular themes slumbered in deep hibernation, only to be reawakened abruptly by the alarm bells of the 1960s.

Conceptions of Clients and Constituents

How were clients and constituents perceived by social workers practicing between 1917 and 1945 who dedicated themselves to helping stigmatized clients gain individual, interactive, and societal power (Pinderhughes 1989:109)? Two metaphors for clients prevailed—that of collaborator and member.

Clients as Collaborators The continuum of ways in which clients or constituents took an active part in planning and carrying out their own "release" from internal or external bonds was a favorite theme of social work literature during and between the wars. Despite bitter and prolonged disagreements over the operational meaning of the concept of client self-determination in the casework relationship, as in the intensive debates between representatives of the diagnostic and functional schools of casework, social workers of the era did manage to agree on one general point of practice—that clients' or constituents' active collaboration in the defining of problems to be solved, strengths to be capitalized upon, goals to be achieved, and steps to be taken was the sine qua non of effective casework, group work, or community work.

Gordon Hamilton, a theorist of the diagnostic or psychosocial perspective, spoke explicitly to the subject of client collaboration: "Case work, whether income be supplied or not, can only be a free will offering—an adventure in social participation. One cannot operate on a person to remove or engraft a relationship. Relationships are not taught, or forced, or directed, or managed—they are achieved" (Hamilton 1931:89).

For functional school theorists and practitioners, like Jessie Taft and Virginia Robinson, the partnership that clients and social workers developed began with the client's choice of the problem to work on (Dore 1990:364). "Starting where the client is," now an established if conceptually fuzzy principle of social work practice, was a contribution of functional casework theory. For functionalists like Taft, that phrase denoted the importance of acknowledging the client's definition of reality, especially of the problematic aspects of reality, and using that definition as the focus of the client and worker's collaboration (Dore 1990:364).

For some other social workers of the period, client collaboration in the process of problem definition was critical but far from unilateral. Bertha Reynolds, for example, an ardent believer in the centrality of client agency within the casework relationship, saw the client's definition of her or his "presenting problem" as an important starting place in a complex, diachronic process that interwove both the client's view of his or her need and the social worker's cumulative assessment of strengths and problems. The client specified a focus for their joint work that served as a springboard for the dialogic crystallization of other related foci, which the client may not have been aware of or able to address at the start of the process. "There would be [in an educational philosophy of case work] . . . a relationship in which counseling help is known to be available if, as, and when desired . . . proceeding always from the known (i.e., problems seen by the client) to the unknown (problems seen by the worker) but only as fast and as far as the client can go" (Reynolds 1934:70). Nonetheless, Reynolds thought that client collaboration entailed much say on the part of the client, including client determination of whether and when his or her connection to a social worker should begin and end.

> It [enlightened casework] assumes that the person who is having trouble with his adjustment to life is, nevertheless, a human being with every

human being's right to make his own mistakes. He may need only a little help or a great deal before his adjustment to his social milieu is again going to his satisfaction. It is his to decide where he will seek help, and if he can get it from his own friends so much the better. If he seeks, or comes by accident, into touch with a professional counselor in the art of living, the service should be more skillful than unprofessional help. . . . The problem is the client's and remains so. It is his to say when it is solved to his satisfaction (Reynolds 1934:35)

Group workers of the war and interwar years also had much to say about the salience of client collaboration with social workers, with fellow sufferers, and with fellow citizens in efforts on their own behalf. Grace Coyle discussed her observations of the intimacy of the interconnections between clients' self-help efforts and professionals' advocacy.

We see them [clients] not only as individuals, but, as Dollard says, as links in the cultural chain. . . . We and they are the conscious living edge of the stream of history. . . . And when we see them struggling with their situations in movements for better wages, for higher relief standards, for the right to organize, we understand better the historical significance of their efforts. We come to see that both they and we must find more adequate instruments for our purposes. At that point we shall stop bailing out the ocean with a teacup and turn our attention to harnessing the tides for the common good. (Coyle 1937b:567)

Some group workers of the period, like LeRoy Bowman, rejected altogether the conception of the group work client as collaborator in a therapeutic, socializing, or even a problem-solving process. In his view, clients in group work contexts were utilitarian collaborators in a social and political process. "Group work," he declared at the National Conference of Social Work of 1935, "is not a service to those who ask for help—it is the social mechanism perfectly competent people utilize to achieve their own ends" (quoted in Schwartz 1985:17).

In community work of the interwar and war years, social workers considered community residents to be the indispensable source of initiative, power, and imagination in any successful collaboration between professionals and citizens. Elizabeth McCord commented on professionals' ongoing reliance upon the continuing passion and involvement of residents in community development and organization.

There are forces within most communities that are continually active in behalf of people and, if they are not present, professional social workers will not be successful in injecting them. They can be imposed from outside for a time but the strength of a permanent program rests in large measure upon the conviction of lay people that it is necessary and desirable. (McCord 1937:588)

McCord's thinking reflected the earlier contributions of Eduard Lindeman, a man who was a formative force in shaping community social work of the era. Having derived his theory of community organization from his experiences as a rural organizer with independent farmers and in the YMCA movement, Lindeman, in 1921, published his most famous work, *The Community: An Introduction to the Study of Community Leadership and Organization* (Austin and Betten 1977:161, Leonard 1991). In that work, Lindeman conceived of community residents as "citizen participants" who express, cultivate, and spread a shared "consciousness of need" in close collaboration with a social work professional, whose primary responsibility is to reflect accurately and project to a broader audience the longings, observations, and activities of the residents (Lindeman 1921:14–15, 123–129). Lindeman's belief that the consciousness of constituents is the essential building block of community health and of democracy anticipated by four decades Paulo Freire's writings of the 1960s.

Clients as Members The term *client,* for some social workers of the period between 1917 and 1945, was an unacceptable one (Schwartz 1985:16–18). Group workers, on the whole, conceived of participants in the groups and clubs with which they worked to be *members,* rather than clients. To be a member was to be constitutive, essential, contributory, and deliberative. In the community centers, Jewish centers, "Y"s, and Townsend clubs of the 1930s in which group work was emerging as a bona fide professional specialization, participants were much more likely to be middle-class than were the far more desperate people who sought casework assistance in private or public agencies (Schwartz 1985:16–17).

As a consequence, many group workers embraced the concept of working with a membership, with its connotations of consolidating health, strength, activity, and democracy. In so doing, group workers distanced themselves from the older casework notion of serving a clientele, a heritage that implied a process of responding to dependency, emergency, disability, or illness. Grace Coyle helped lay the foundation of a group work method that perceived of participants as members. "By providing within the group-work agency for experience in group management, in co-operation for a common interest, in collective behavior, the agency can help its members to discover how to take their place in this organizational life of the community" (Coyle 1935:396). Striking the same theme, Bowman informed the National Conference of Social Work in 1935 that group workers "must help to relate the members of their groups (I did not say 'clients') to the national or mass concerns of the day" (Schwartz 1985:17).

Some community organizers within social work also thought of their constituents as members. Walter Pettit, for example, an educator and theorist of community organization in the interwar years, gave the following charge to social workers:

> The social worker's relation to his community is somewhat the same as the minister's to his parish. . . . It is necessary that a social worker be given the equipment to help him in the varied problems he is to meet as a leader in his community. . . . This must include an understanding of his relationship to his community . . . keeping his board, his committees, his membership in the closest relationship to his work. (Pettit 1925:581)

To comprehend fully the visions of social workers between 1917 and 1945 who are retrospectively identified in this discussion as empowerment-oriented, we must examine their assumptions concerning how individual, interactive, and societal change comes about. That understanding, when combined with a grasp of their views of themselves as facilitators of change and their metaphors for the people (clients, collaborators, or members) whom they assisted, will render their conceptions of social work practice more accessible to contemporary practitioners.

Conceptions of Change Processes

Stimulation Many a social worker of the period who worked to reduce the stigma and disadvantage of people who sought their help engaged in what they conceived of as a process of stimulation. Assuming, as they did, that people came to them with multiple inner strengths and potentialities, they sought to arouse, excite, actuate, and galvanize these capacities. Over and over again, they referred to their work as a project of stimulating individuals, groups, organizations, or communities to grow, develop, and overcome psychological, social,

and economic barriers and opposition. Social workers of the empowerment "stripe" saw change as a process that, on the one hand
involved the realization of untapped individual and collective potential, and, on the other hand, involved a sustained battle to keep more
privileged others from standing in the way of that realization. Client
self- empowerment, they thought, entailed both growth and the struggle to preserve the opportunity to grow. Their faith in the possibility
of human development was sobered by their knowledge of human
depravity and oppressiveness.

Bertha Reynolds, whose work as a caseworker, educator, and organizer spanned the entire historical period under discussion, captured
concisely a view of change processes that characterized the thinking
then among social workers like herself who envisioned a more just
world and a less paternalistic professional pursuit of that vision.

> Social work concerns itself with human beings where there is anything
> that hinders or thwarts their growth, their expanding consciousness,
> their increasing cooperation. . . . If we had remembered that "life is for
> growth" we should have made of our social services great cooperative
> projects in education through active participation of clients, as well as
> board and staff, in the study of the meaning of difficult life situations
> and a search for remedies. There would have been a linking up of com-
> munity work and case work. . . . There is an encouraging drawing
> together of social case work and social work with groups. Group work
> is finding that real leadership is based on the same principles as case
> work with individuals and demands the same ability to create confi-
> dence, to encourage free expression, and to stimulate energies.
> (Reynolds 1935:136–137, 146–147)

Similarly, Grace Coyle thought it the duty of group workers to spur
clients (members) on toward thought, activity, and collectivity on
their own behalf. Empowerment-oriented social workers of the era,
such as Coyle, abhorred passivity, resignation, and quietism, whether
on the part of clients or social workers. Down that path, she believed,
awaited inevitable despair, isolation, and defeat. Social workers
should prompt, encourage, goad, and urge clients to be fully engaged.
Parallel images emerged from the literature of this period of worker
and client's interactive animation, movement, and purposeful activity.

> His [the group worker's] problem lies chiefly in how to arouse the
> socially inert to a concern in public questions at the point nearest to

their already developed interests, and how to help those already aroused to intelligent and effective action along lines that seem to be socially desirable. The group worker cannot and should not determine those lines for his clientele, but like any good educator he can arouse interest and help people to think intelligently for themselves. In addition he, too, like the case worker, can use his own knowledge of the results of unemployment, low standards of living, bad housing, and so on, at many points where action is possible. (Coyle 1937b:567)

Social workers of an empowerment bent welcomed no sluggards into casework or group work ranks.

Neither did community social workers. Wayne McMillen, a community organizer and educator, thought that the community social worker's job was to "stimulate people to use their powers for the cooperative improvement of group life" (McMillen 1945:29–30). For McMillen, the central objective of community organization was "to help people find ways to give expression to these inherent desires to improve the environment in which they and their fellows must carry on their lives" (McMillen 1945:22).

Stimulation of clients or participants, for Mary Parker Follett, involved awakening people's recognition of their rights, needs, and capabilities and then helping them to organize expression of them. Her definitions of a leader's duties in relation to members of the organization or group for which he or she provides leadership were eloquent prefigurations of the explicit conception of empowerment that emerged much later among urban planners and social workers of the 1960s.

> I believe we shall soon think of the leader as one who can organize the experience of the group, make it all available and most effectively available, and thus get the full power of the group. It is by *organizing* experience that we tranform experience into power. And that is what experience is for, to be made into power. (Follett 1927:258)

A year later, in 1928, Follett further elaborated her Emersonian faith in the democratic leader as stimulator of popular purposive action. "I believe that the great leader . . . can arouse my latent possibilities, can reveal to me new powers in myself, can quicken and give direction to some force within me. There is energy, passion, unawakened life in us—those who call it forth are our leaders" (Follett 1928:293).

Stimulation of client or constituent growth and activism was one vital dimension of social work that sought to aid client self-empower ment in the years between 1917 and 1945. Demonstration of innova tive forms of collaboration between clients and professionals, both in the public and voluntary sectors, and of self-help community initia tives was another. The demonstration projects of the War on Poverty in the 1960s had distinctly recognizable antecedents in the decades immediately following World War I.

Demonstration Porter Lee, an educator and leading voice of the pro fession for three decades until his death in 1939, commented on the double opportunity that demonstration efforts provide members of affected neighborhoods. First, thought Lee, social experiments give community members a chance to communicate the relevance and acceptability of experimental services and projects before they become institutionalized. Community participants can signal acceptance of a program or service through their cooperation or indicate rejection through withholding or withdrawing their participation. Second, demonstration efforts allow community members to correct and redi rect the course of projects in their neighborhoods much more quickly than in programs already embedded in the institutional fabric of established agencies.

> The use of the demonstration is a method of long standing in social work which has recently come into more active use. The principle of the demonstration involves the establishment of a new service in a commu nity, sometimes carried on under more or less tentative administrative and financial auspices, until its permanent value is so apparent that it will be established by the community as a part of its permanent social equipment. . . . The value of the demonstration cannot be questioned. Properly used it insures earlier attention to community needs than would otherwise be given. It saves many communities the loss of time, money, and enthusiasm which the delays and mistakes of the trial-and error method of organization frequently involve. (Lee 1929:29)

One example of a demonstration project of the era that exemplified the responsiveness to client and community needs that Lee attributed to this experimental form of service was the Department of Child Plac ing for Negro Children in Chicago. Recognizing the open refusal of Chicago's white-run child welfare agencies to place black children into foster care and the absence of child-placing services within the black community, Edith Abbott and Sophonisba Breckinridge of the

University of Chicago's School of Social Administration created in 1928 a joint project with the city's largest nonsectarian child-placing agency.

The demonstration effort, which was staffed and run by the School of Social Administration, was intended to develop services that would protect black children from abuse and neglect. The resultant Department of Child Placing for Negro Children pioneered in Chicago several new forms of child welfare services, including foster family service for unmarried mothers and their babies, supportive services for families of origin as an alternative to child placements, the practice of paying higher rates to foster families that took in older and handicapped children, and the placement of children with serious behavioral difficulties (Stehno 1988:491). These innovations, which diverged dramatically from the prevailing practices of other Chicago child welfare agencies of the period, came about because of the attentiveness of the staff of the Department of Child Placing for Negro Children to the needs, resources, and preferences of Chicago's black community.

Social workers also engaged in demonstration efforts on a broader scale. In 1922, the Program for the Prevention of Delinquency of the Commonwealth Fund launched experiments throughout the United States that created systems of "visiting teachers," known today as school social workers (Ehrenreich 1985:70). Particularly concentrating on the early identification of developmental delays and of delinquency, school social workers tested the utility and feasibility of working with teachers in the early detection of children who were evidencing behavioral and emotional difficulties. This identification process was followed up by work with parents, the identified children, and the schools. The project introduced into the demonstration schools and their communities attention to normal child development, abnormal child development, and the prevention of delinquency (Ehrenreich 1985:70). After a designated number of years, the school social workers were moved to the next demonstration site in another city. As the demonstration teams departed, local boards of education took over responsibility for providing the system of school social workers in their respective cities.

In a related intiative, the Commonwealth Fund provided money in 1922 for the Committee for Mental Hygiene to create a five-year demonstration project that developed child guidance clinics in eight cities (Roberts and Kurtz 1987:82). Beginning in St. Louis, demonstration teams made up of psychiatrists, social workers, and psychologists worked with disturbed children and their families and trained local mental health personnel. After a few years, the child guidance team moved to the next demonstration city, leaving in its wake a center designed to be ongoing and self-supporting (Ehrenreich 1985:70).

Social workers who were invested in client self-empowerment envisioned desirable change as a process of stimulation and demonstration. Both activities, because they required concentrated collaborative involvement between professionals and clients, compelled social workers of the era to confront a major social and political conflict of the day, that which Eduard Lindeman identified as the conflict between democracy and "specialism" (Lindeman 1921:58, 173, Lubove 1975:179).

Reconciliation of Expert Wisdom and Public Wisdom In a world that World War I had attempted to make safe for democracy emerged a new danger, one less obvious than the militarism of Hitler, Mussolini, and Franco or the imperialism of the Austro-Hungarian and Turkish empires. The fresh threat to democracy within the U.S. following the Treaty of Versailles was the congealment of veneration of the expert—of the professional or scientist with specialized knowledge, technologies, and credentials. In facing crime, disease, and social conflicts of many kinds, governmental leaders, reflecting popular sentiments, turned increasingly to the social sciences, engineering, city planning, public administration, medicine, public health, nursing, law, and social work for answers. This proclivity following World War I to privilege the view of the specialist put at risk the "strong" democratic tradition within the country, the Jeffersonian, Jacksonian, and populist preference for locating ultimate decision making with those most directly affected by the decision to be made (Barber 1984). Within "strong democracy," specialists act as guides and consultants, rather than as decision makers. Within the emergent technocracy of the 1920s, in contrast, specialists were often called upon to act as sole or final arbiters (Ross 1991:397–407).

Social workers, like Lindeman, who were alert to the erosion of democratic processes that government and decision making by experts represented, thought that positive change on the individual, interpersonal, and societal levels would come about through the construction of conscious and careful relations between clients and professionals, between interest groups and specialists, and between communities and governmental experts. Both sides of the connections, thought Lindeman, needed to remain attentive to the contributions of each and the calculus of power retained by each (Lindeman 1921:58, 173). The relation would never be simple, but it would be both necessary and fruitful. Social workers of the era who took seriously the damage that unexamined professionalism could wreak on the self-determination of clients considered it their duty to help reconcile democratic rule with the authority of specialists in a manner that would leave democracy both intact and enriched. This process of reconciliation amounted to a third vision of a change process that, along with stimulation and demonstration, was important for social workers to engage in if they cared about enhancing, rather than compromising, client health, welfare, and power.

Just as Eduard Lindeman did for community social workers, Bertha Reynolds offered caseworkers a description of the balancing act that responsible social workers must sustain between the professional commitment to offering the finest possible service and the client's right and need to retain ultimate control over the course of his or her life and daily existence.

Reynolds valued as precious both social work expertise and client self-determination. She sought to place the one in the service of the other.

> Why, you ask, does it [assistance] need to be expert? Why not ask them what is the matter, and either fix it up or tell them you can't and send them home. Unfortunately, it is not as simple as that. The findings of psychology and psychiatry during the last quarter-century have confirmed what keen observers had noticed before without knowing the reasons: that often people do not know what is the matter; that, lacking knowledge of this, attempts to "fix it up" fail; and that people are not satisfied to be sent home without any better understanding of their situation or any gain in ability to cope with it. It is because feelings and desires buried beneath the surface of consciousness determine so largely what people do and how they cooperate with others that only a person who is expert enough to help these feelings to get to the surface can be very reliably useful in helping people in difficulty. . . . The findings of psychiatry and psychology, medicine, sociology, economics, and political science can now be applied to human problems in a consulting relationship which has been developed in a unique way in social casework. It differs from the relationship of psychiatrist and patient in that it does not assume that the person seeking help is sick and is placing himself in the hands of another for treatment, and it does not, or should not, ignore the social milieu to which the client is trying to adjust. It keeps the problem in the client's hands but diagnoses his difficulty with

it as a good teacher would diagnose a child's difficulty with reading or with learning to swim. (Reynolds 1935:141–142)

Mary Parker Follett, the former Boston settlement house worker turned political theorist, feared the consequences of the romanticization of either the expert or "the people." Both, she believed, had important and different kinds of knowledge. Neither could make wise decisions without the wisdom of the other. Her challenge to social workers and others who desired to salvage democracy was one of bringing experts' opinions to bear on popular judgment in such a way that the knowledge and values of each remained mutually accessible and indispensable (Follett 1924:3–30).

> To overemphasize the importance of the expert would be impossible, but after we have fully recognized his value to society, there still remains to be considered the legitimate relation between expert and people. . . . The community centre movement, the workmen's education movement, the cooperative movement . . . are not based on the assumption that the will of the people is "instinctively" good, and that our institutions exist merely to get at this will, to give it voice, etc. The essential aim of these, the most democratic movements we have, is to train ourselves, to learn how to use the work of experts, to find our will, to educate our will, to integrate our wills

> We need experts, we need accurate information, but the object is not to do away with *difference* but to do away with *muddle*. When for lack of facts you and I are responding to a different situation—you to the situation as you imagine it, I to the situation as I imagine it—we cannot of course come to agreement. What accurate information does is to clear the ground for genuine difference and therefore make possible, I do not say make sure, agreement. The object of accurate information is not to overcome difference but to give legitimate play to difference. (Follett 1924:4–6)

Meyer Schwartz restrospectively understood the purpose of these prescient social workers after World War I to be that of the "reconstruction of the small community" in a world that was increasingly global, specialized, and centralized. He characterized their pursuit as an all-inclusive "Deweyesque democratic process involving citizens and experts at the grassroots level" (Schwartz 1965:177). In the course of envisioning the restoration of small town life within the larger metropolis, they created forms of social work practice that helped to reduce the anonymity and vulnerability of clients who were experiencing the rapid bureaucratization of human services, public services, and their workplaces.

FIGURE 6.1
SOCIAL WORKS VISION OF EMPOWERMENT: 1917-1945

SOCIAL WORKERS' SELF-CONCEPTION	METAPHORS FOR CLIENT	CONCEPTION OF EMPOWERING CHANGE
Releasers of clients' potential	Collaborators	Stimulation
Witnesses	Members	Demonstrations
Organizers		Reconciliation of expert wisdom and public wisdom

---

Empowering Aspects of Social Work Practice

Social workers who embraced what we now call an empowerment orientation in the years between 1917 and 1945 converted the concept of client self-reliance within the profession from a moral directive to individuals into an economic charge to an entire society. In so doing, their demands and actions abolished within social work the atomistic idea that the burden of responsibility for providing economic security for families and individuals rests solely on the shoulders of each wage earner or job-seeker. They substituted, instead, the premise that economic security is a joint duty to be shared actively by the social order and the individuals who compose it. The social work client who sought economic aid or a job was transformed by the mid-1930s in most quarters of the profession from a charity case into a citizen.

Establishing Social Security

Client self-reliance had long been a goal of social work and of proto-social work since the founding of America's first charity organization society in Buffalo, New York in 1877. The precise meaning of that concept within philanthropy and social work had changed greatly over time. At one extreme, during the earliest phase of charity organization societies' existence, client self-reliance had meant the maintainance of complete economic and social independence by families and individuals. Eleemosynary and governmental supports were intended only for the impoverished aged, sick, blind, crippled, and orphaned. Everyone else was to survive on his or her wages and moral fiber. If the able-bodied individual slipped from the path of self-reliance, she or he was to be inspired by the moral suasion and example of friendly visitors and goaded into diligence by the denial of his or her requests for alms. In the incessant struggle for survival, only the morally and physically superior, those successful in sustaining economic self-reliance, deserved to live to an old age and reproduce the species.

This draconian view, systematized in the United States by William Graham Sumner of Yale University and popularized by many other social Darwinians, had been a widely held point of view throughout the middle and upper classes during the childhoods of most native-born social workers who were practicing in the interwar period. Fortunately, the concept of client self-reliance held a radically different meaning for most social workers and their professional organizations by the time of the Great Depression than it had for their charity organization precursors of the 1880s.

That client self-reliance was a social idea, one that could only be secured in a context that provided jobs, protection of employees' rights, and adequate economic insurance for times of involuntary joblessness, old age, childhood, sickness, and disability, was the public message of organized social work throughout the Depression. The insistent delivery of this message to elected officials, the media, and public commissions was an aspect of social work practice that assisted the pursuit of client self-empowerment as well as self-reliance.

Social workers communicated the idea of the interdependence of self-reliance and social security in several ways. As the desperation of the Depression accelerated, some social workers developed alliances for social action made up of clients, neighbors, and social workers. In Chicago in 1932, for example, a Workers' Committee on Unemployment was organized across the city, made up of fifty-seven local units, of which twenty-two were located in settlement houses and led by settlement members and staff. They formed self-help projects and lobbied legislators directly for unemployment relief (Chambers 1963:186–187). This activity was familiar to social workers who had organized clients in earlier decades to press for better wages, working conditions, and social insurance. Gertrude Wilson, for example, a leading group worker of the era, recalled having accompanied women workers in the 1920s from the silk mills of Allentown, Pennsylvania to Washington, D.C., to testify in favor of unemployment insurance (Wilson 1976:11).

In major cities throughout the United States, social workers who were members of the Rank-and-File movement collaborated with the work of unemployed councils. These groups of unemployed workers, approximately twelve hundred in number, engaged in mutual aid activities, blocked the evictions of jobless people who could not pay rent, and organized public demonstrations in support of unemployment relief and public jobs programs (Fisher 1980:127).

Many other social workers worked toward the passage of social security measures through their professional organizations. Porter Lee called for social workers to join in the larger effort to construct "economic security for all Americans" in an address to the American Association of Social Workers (AASW) in 1933 (Leighninger 1987:51). A year later, at its 1934 conference, the AASW formally called for a "permanent, comprehensive . . . adequate system of welfare services to insure ourselves, as a people, against the common hazards, of our economic and social life" (Leighninger 1987:52). That year the body proposed a long list of social reforms, among them state systems of unemployment insurance, extensions of federal employment projects, and the continued provision of federally supported direct relief at an adequate level. Even earlier, by 1931, participants at the National Conference of Social Work had come to similar conclusions (Wenocur and Reisch 1989:165–166).

Executives of large social work agencies that were swamped early in the Depression by the requests for material aid of unemployed people testified frequently in Washington and state capitols and lobbied in favor of immediate direct relief and long-term unemployment insurance. William Hodson, director of the New York City Welfare Council, wrote an open letter to President Hoover in 1931 in which he called for federal grants-in-aid to supplement local relief. Many administrators documented the inadequacy of local relief, the rising levels of unemployment, and the daily misery experienced by their clients at public hearings and forums. Agency and professional leaders like Helen Hall, director of the Henry Street Settlement, Samuel Goldsmith, the head of the Chicago Jewish Charities, and Grace Abbott, the director of the U.S. Children's Bureau, documented the extremity of need at the U.S. Senate hearings on unemployment between 1930 and 1933 (Leighninger 1987:55).

The *Survey* published and endorsed throughout the 1920s and 1930s the findings and proposals for model labor legislation and social insurance of the American Association for Labor Legislation (AALL). *Social Work Today,* from its first issue in March of 1934, focused on the urgency of creating a social welfare system that would allow Americans the opportunity to be economically secure.

Conducting and publicizing research on pressing social problems was another way in which social workers spread the word about the urgency of establishing social entitlements if clients were ever to achieve independence from charity, hunger, and premature death. Among the organizations run by social workers during the 1920s and 1930s that researched the problems shared by many and then proposed social strategies concocted in the light of that research, two stand out for their persistence and foresight. The National Federation of Settlements (NFS) was one, the U.S. Children's Bureau the other.

From 1920 through 1922, NFS investigated the state of urban housing across the country and followed up its study with a formal call for housing commissions at each level of government (Chambers 1963:135). Later in the decade, NFS, under the leadership of Helen Hall, studied in 1928 and 1929 the human costs of unemployment (Wenocur and Reisch 1989:161). The results of this study were published in 1931 as *Case Studies of Unemployment* (Hall 1931).

Similarly, the Children's Bureau regularly studied and disseminated data on infant mortality and morbidity and new mothers' health levels throughout the 1920s and 1930s (Combs-Orme 1988:90–96, Muncy 1991:93–157). It excelled in its ability and commitment to make its findings and recommendations as accessible to rural families as to urban ones. The bureau also worked hard to distribute its data in many forms of publication, some written specifically for pregnant women and new parents, others for administrators and legislators, still others for the press (Combs-Orme 1988).

Demanding, alongside their clients, the creation of a welfare state in the U.S. was one aspect of empowerment-based social work, as we now call it. A second dimension, closely related to the first, was the establishment by social workers of two federal precedents for categorizing infants and their mothers as social resources, people whose health constituted an intimate imperative of the public good as well as of the individual family's welfare. The Children's Bureau in both regards was the hero of the piece.

Attending to Maternal and Child Health Care

Two former Hull House workers, Julia Lathrop and Grace Abbott, engineered the passage of the Sheppard-Towner Maternity and Infancy Act of 1921 (Muncy 1991:93). This law, a major triumph for social feminism of the era, created a partnership between the federal government and the states dedicated to educating women, particularly in rural areas, about prenatal care and providing resources for prenatal and infancy care (Combs-Orme 1988:90). The act called for individual states to create plans for the work and for the Children's Bureau to approve of and help fund those plans.

Congress failed to renew Sheppard-Towner, which lapsed in 1928. In the seven years of its implementation, Grace Abbott reported, the Maternity and Infancy Act was responsible for a long list of precedent-setting accomplishments (Abbott 1931). State child hygiene bureaus were created in twenty-eight states; 1,594 permanent and local prenatal, child health, or combination prenatal and child health clinics were founded; birth and death registration was made systematic in a wider geographic area; 183,252 well-baby visits, known then as "health conferences," were recorded; 3,131,966 home visits were made by public health nurses and social workers; 22,020,489 health pamphlets and other pieces of literature were distributed. Between 1925 and the end of 1928, 700,000 pregnant women and 4 million infants were seen by state personnel under the Sheppard-Towner Act (Abbott 1931, Combs-Orme 1988:90). For one all-too-brief period, health care for infants and their mothers was a right.

For another, even briefer period, that precedent was reestablished for the wives and infants of noncommissioned servicemen in the armed forces during World War II. Troubled by the inadequacy of obstetrical, pediatric, and hospital services near military bases within the United States, Katharine Lenroot, director of the Children's Bureau in 1943, convinced Congress to pass and fund the Emergency Maternal and Infant Care program (EMIC). This act provided free prenatal, obstetrical, postnatal, pediatric, and other related services to servicemen's wives and infants. The act mandated social services as an essential part of the health program. EMIC served 1.25 million mothers and 230,000 infants before it was discontinued in 1945 (Combs-Orme 1988:92).

Building African American Schools of Social Work

A third expression of the empowerment tradition within social work between 1917 and 1945 was the formation by black social workers of two schools of social work within black-run universities. Founded in 1920 to educate black social work professionals during an era when many white-run schools refused to do so, the Atlanta School of Social Work encouraged its students and graduates to focus their talents particularly on the numerous unserved and underserved black communities in urban and rural America (B. B. Solomon 1985:226–227). Howard University followed suit in 1936 with a comparable mission.

The creation of both of these schools constituted an act of self-empowerment in two senses. First, the founding of the schools immediately expanded the resources and opportunities available to black men and women whose race prevented them from being considered by or admitted into many of the white-run schools of social work of the era. Black Americans who figured in the establishment of the schools thereby demonstrated their rejection of white efforts to maintain a segregated profession. By building these graduate schools, black founders and black students of the programs transformed the powerlessness of those categorically excluded from white institutions into the strength of those who were able to pursue their chosen vocational goals despite Jim Crowism.

Second, Atlanta and Howard's schools of social work provided educational laboratories in which the particular needs, problems, and desires of urban and rural black individuals and communities could be discussed and explored in unparalleled depth. Given that the student bodies and faculties for the most part had been raised in neighborhoods that were exclusively or predominantly black, they brought decades of direct experience to bear on the formulation of approaches with which to serve and organize black communities. At a time when few white-run schools of social work were interested in investigating the particularized economic, political, and psychosocial concerns of black America, Atlanta and Howard's graduate programs made that the second half of their mission (Ross 1978).

Normalizing Social Services

A fourth aspect of empowerment concretized within social work between 1917 and 1945 was the practice of locating social services alongside the daily path of people's routines so that service delivery was maximally accessible as well as minimally intrusive and stigmatizing for them (Hartman 1986:90). Bertha Reynolds created such a service in her work at the Personal Service Department of the United Seamen's Service of the National Maritime Union from 1943 through 1948 (Reynolds 1963:242–259, 1951).

In setting up shop at the union hall, United Seamen's Service and Reynolds helped to normalize the crisis intervention, alcoholism counseling, information and referral work, all-around casework, and material relief that seamen sought. Seamen were, as a consequence, able to keep their primary identities as sailors in the Merchant Marine and as members of their union intact while relating to social workers like Reynolds. It was a model of installing social work services in the union hall and workplace that was replicated in many other unions after World War II.

As was true in the prior phase of social work's evolution in the U.S., movement within the profession toward dignifying and enfranchising the role and status of clients was a salient but secondary theme between 1917 and 1945. It constituted a forceful countercurrent that was erosive of yet subordinate to the pronounced paternalism of the profession and the era.

FIGURE 6.2
EMPOWERING ASPECTS OF SOCIAL PRACTICE: 1917-1945

Establishing Social Security
Attending to maternal and child health care
Building African American schools of social work
Normalizing social services

Paternalistic Aspects of Social Work Practice

Social work, like every other profession in the United States following World War I, was influenced profoundly by the disillusionment with politics and social reform movements that the Great War bequeathed in its failure to make the world safe for democracy or for much else. In their despair, many Americans lost faith in the promise of Progressive politics and turned instead to a new church, that of scientism.

Scientism was an intellectual and political movement that was "the result . . . of an effort to make good on the positivist demand that only natural science provided certain knowledge and conferred the power of prediction and control" (Ross 1991:390). Science, under scientism, became defined solely by its method. The methods of the natural sciences were made the standards by which the social sciences in the U.S., unlike Europe, were practiced (Ross 1991:390).

Social sciences and applied social sciences would now serve as America's salvation in matters of governance and in the resolution of social problems but only if these fields employed the methods of the natural sciences exclusively and rigorously. No longer would theology, history, literature, and philosophy be considered proper guides for those conducting domestic and world affairs. Economics, sociology, political science, psychology, and social planning would take their place, *provided* that they followed the same scientific principles employed so successfully by Mendel in explaining genetic hybridization, by Pasteur in advancing the germ theory and discovering the anthrax and rabies vaccines, and by Koch in finding the bacterial cause of tuberculosis. Then, and only then, might the U.S. and other nations solve the problems of recurrent wars, chronic poverty, hunger, and interracial and ethnic conflicts. Not politics, with its disorderly passions, tensions, and sentiments, but science, with its dispassionate powers of observation, measurement, prediction, and control, would rule the day, the country, the academy, and the professions.

Small wonder that the enthronement of the scientific expert within the broader culture of the U.S. following World War I reinforced the existing paternalism within social work. At a time when knowledge and expertise came to be thought of as the sole preserve of people who studied problems through the lens of science, it was predictable that the people who most directly suffered those problems were discounted as interested parties and therefore suspect as sources of knowledge and insight. Clients, in other words, came to be seen as good sources of data but not as reliable actors with whom to consult in the process of making sense of the data which they offered and embodied.

Professionalism, for many social workers, became a conscious quest in the 1920s for a more scientific practice. Regrettably, it devolved into a generally scientistic quest instead. To be *scientistic*, as opposed to *scientific*, is to make two fundamental mistakes. First, one selects investigative methods on the basis of the level of legitimacy they hold in prestigious sciences rather than choosing methods on the basis of the nature of the particular problem to be studied and of the particular context in which the problem is lodged. Second, when one is acting scientistically, one reifies the theory and hypotheses that one is using, that is, one falls into the trap of treating these abstractions as if they were real.

Had the social work search for professionalism in the 1920s been an authentically scientific one, social workers would have developed an idiomatic epistemology, range of methods, and cluster of conceptual paradigms that would have emerged organically from their exploration of the particular situations their clients lived and worked within and the particular challenges and problems these clients encountered. The preponderance of social work's tools, questions, and criteria for discovering and verifying truths would have been, in short, homegrown, though fertilized with selections of the most resonant ideas and approaches from a wide variety of disciplines, professions, and traditions.

Social workers who were interested in crafting a science of social work would not have attempted, as often happened, to imitate wholesale the approaches of other disciplines. Instead of looking to others outside of social work for a definitive delineation of heuristic social work methodology and knowledge, they would have directed their primary gaze to the collaborative work that they were performing with clients, members, and communities. It was in these relationships, activities, and settings that the scientific "treasures" lay hidden, waiting to be discovered by those practitioners who had the wisdom to derive practice methods and knowledge from systematic reflection on accumulated daily excavations into the meaning of continuity and change in human behavior, institutions, attitudes, feelings, and affiliations.

Unfortunately, many in the profession mistrusted their own capacity to create a science and art of social work. Hampered by the underconfidence historically characteristic of those in newer and predominantly female professions, many social workers turned for methodology and theoretical grounding to those applied scientists, the psychiatrists and other physicians, whose prestige was most pronounced and whose work brought them into regular contact with caseworkers, the social workers who made up by the vast majority of practitioners of the period.

With medical science invoked as a template in the 1920s, the "medical model" infiltrated the practice of social work, particularly within its psychiatric wing. The multiple causes and consequences of this infil tration have been analyzed extensively over the past three decades and do not require recapitulation here. Only the paternalistic effects of the medical model on social work during the period beteen 1917 and 1945 are relevant to this discussion. As Charlotte Towle, Carol Meyer, Carel Germain, and Ann Weick, among many others, have pointed out, the model predisposes practitioners to think of clients as being clusters of symptoms—as being decontextualized bearers of a defect or a disease (Germain 1970:11–22, Germain and Gitterman 1980:52, Meyer 1970:110–113, Towle 1969:209–234, Weick 1986:554–555). This reductive tendency is also a dualistic one that "makes it possible to diagnose and treat diseases as though they have no connection with the human being in whom the symptoms are expressed" (Weick 1986:554). The physician (or social worker who employs the physician's model) launches a campaign against the disease as if it were a foreign agent occupying the body of the patient. The patient is thus viewed unconsciously as the terrain upon which the medical battle is waged. Or, to switch to another metaphor altogether, physician is protagonist, illness is antagonist, patient is stage on which the drama unfolds. Whether considered battleground or stage, the patient devolves into a passive and onlooking object, rather than a subject acting in concert with the doctor (or social worker) on his or her own behalf.

The widespread modeling of social casework on medicine's approach to patients and disease enhanced paternalistic proclivities that were already extant in the field before Freudian and Rankian thought entranced many in casework and group work during the 1920s and 1930s. The damage done to client dignity and autonomy by the introduction of the medical model into social work was then compounded by the mimicking, on the part of some influential psychiatric social workers, of the relationships that Freud and his disciples had created with upper-middle-class patients in the more authoritarian cultures of turn-of-the-century Vienna, Berlin, and Prague (Bettelheim 1990:3–13). In aping indiscriminately the Freudian posture of the intentionally distanced healer, some psychiatric social workers ignored wholly the worlds of difference between their own milieux, clientele, and purposes and those of Freud, Adler, and Jung. In so doing, they subjected their social work clients to a caricatured version of a paternalism that was both out-of-date and out of context.

Another, older, aspect of paternalism within social work evident during these years was the coercion of clients by some social caseworkers, coercion effected through the withholding of material relief and in-kind supports as punishment for noncompliance with case-workers' directives. Historian Linda Gordon and her team of histori-cal researchers studied the case records kept from 1880 to 1960 by three Boston child welfare agencies and found clear examples of such official cruelty in the records of the years from 1917 through 1945.

Among them was the case of Mabel in 1924. Mabel was a child who had been hospitalized with "tuberculosis of the spine." After she was released from the hospital, her family was supposed to keep her in a "Bradford frame" to correct curvature of the spine. When the caseworker from the Massachusetts Society for the Prevention of Cru-elty to Children (MSPCC) found out that the family was not keeping Mabel in the frame, she stopped supplying the free milk that MSPCC had been providing the family. The worker noted in the record, "The family are clever enough to pretend to cooperate . . . and then they do as they please" (Gordon 1988a:141).

In another case cited by Gordon, a mother in 1943, having left her abusive husband, created a child care arrangement that drew disap-proval from her MSPCC worker. The mother worked in a cafe from 4 P.M. to 3 A.M. A babysitter stayed with her three children until 11 P.M., leaving the children by themselves until the mother could return from her shift. Instead of helping the woman find and pay for supplemental babysitting for the hours between 11 P.M. and the moth-er's return home or assisting her to find a day job, the worker scolded her and noted in the record that "Mo's place is at home" (Gordon 1988a:149–150).

Paternalism, alas, was also no stranger to the domain of social group work in this era. Perhaps its most virulent expression was the settlement house movement's version of the broader "Americaniza-tion" movement that took place during the mid-1920s in the U.S. The Americanization movement that stretched from the 1890s through the mid-1920s in settlement houses across the country was designed ini-tially to make adjustment to America easier for new immigrants and to educate native-born neighbors of the settlements about the diverse contributions to America that immigrants were bringing (Karger 1987:92–93).

By the early 1920s, however, the Americanization movement in set-tlements no longer connoted the reverence for pluralism and the exchange of cultural gifts and ideas that Jane Addams and others had envisioned when they launched the movement thirty years earlier (Addams 1910, 1930). Infected with the venom of the nation's "100 percent Americanism" campaign during and following World War I, the settlements' Americanization work, in many places, took on the character of a crusade to make immigrants safe for the American democracy and as much like their native-born neighbors as possible. In studying the records of Minneapolis social settlements, Howard Karger found a pattern evident after 1917 of mean-spirited conde-scension and intolerant paternalism toward immigrants. One illustra-tion follows, taken from a published letter of Margaret Chapman, the head resident of Wells Memorial House in Minneapolis, to a Russian neighbor who had returned to Russia after the 1917 revolution:

> The most offensive and dangerous thing with which this nation is con-fronted, is the wicked disloyalty of those who have come from foreign parts, only to abuse our institutions and to seek to disrupt our nation-al family life. . . . The best possible [response] is not to interne them, or to place limitations upon their movements but, to ship them back to the countries from whence they came. . . . We have been altogether too lenient, and too soft and gentle, in dealing with the traitor within our gates. We shall do so no more we hope. (Karger 1987:93–94)

FIGURE 6.3
PATERNALISTIC ASPECTS OF SOCIAL WORK PRACTICE: 1917-1945

Scientism
Coercive Case Work
Americanization Movement in Settlement Houses

Paternalistic social work in the U.S. from 1917 through 1945, like its rival, the empowerment tradition, spoke in the idiom of its time and place. Both traditions lived on after 1945 in forms easily recog-nizable to their friends and foes from earlier days, even as they dressed in the garments of a new era.

CHAPTER SEVEN

Recent Practice:
Context and Influences,
1945–1994

If the building of a bridge does not enrich the awareness of those who work on it, then that bridge ought not to be built and the citizens can go on swimming across the river or going by boat . . . so that the bridge in whole and in part can be taken up and conceived, and the responsibility for it assumed by the citizen.   —Frantz Fanon

Democratization and empowerment both refer to gaining control over the conditions of our lives. The manner in which feminists employ the term "empowerment" best captures the duality of this process: the assertion of individuality within a united group. . . . Like knitting, empowering requires an even tension to balance the closeness and the separateness: if the links are too loose, the shape collapses; if they are too tight, the flexibility of the whole diminishes.   —Joan Pennell

The flowering of the empowerment tradition within the United States since 1945 is an outgrowth of both homegrown and imported seed implanted into local soil beds. The soil was fully ready, prepared as it had been by cultivators who were steeped in the oral and written traditions that gave rise to contemporary strains of empowerment practice.

In order to trace and comprehend the development of empowerment thinking and action within the social work profession of the U.S. of the late twentieth century, one must first appreciate the nature of the times and places within which the broad social campaigns for human liberation eventually sprang up, campaigns that inspired social work's visions and versions of empowerment. The contemporary portion of the narrative begins with the close of World War II.

The Context: Since 1945

Booming economic and technological expansiveness characterized the U.S. during the decades immediately following World War II despite labor unrest, housing shortages, and rising inflation. The "GI Bill of Rights" (the Servicemen's Readjustment Act of 1944) was one demonstration of the bullish optimism of the period. The GI bill paid for the tuition fees, books, and living expenses for up to four years of education for World War II veterans and, later, for Korean War (1952) and Vietnam War (1966) veterans (Morris 1976:835). By 1947, more than 1 million former servicemen were enrolled in college out of the country's total of 2.5 million college students (Carruth 1979:557).

The Employment Act of 1946 declared that the federal government's continuing policy was to be henceforth the promotion of maximal employment, production, and purchasing power (Morris 1976:514). That aggressive stance reverberated throughout the nation's commercial and industrial circles. Six million cars and trucks were manufactured in the U.S. in 1949, a new high for the industry (Carruth 1979:565). Aggregate salaries and wages in 1949 were also the highest in American history as was agricultural productivity (Carruth 1979:565). 6.2 million refrigerators, 14.6 million radios, 7.4 million television sets, and $33.6 billion of new residential and business construction were built in 1950 alone (Morris 1976:729, 731).

In 1951, the employment of women in the United States reached its highest point in American history, higher even than during the "Rosie, the Riveter" days of World War II (Carruth 1979:573). That statistical zenith was achieved in spite of the forced termination of 2,100,000 women from manufacturing jobs at the end of the war (Ferree and Hess 1985:4–5). Women, who had been welcomed as productive substitutes in the industrial work force during wartime, suddenly were required to return to underpaid women's work in offices, schools, private residences, and hospitals and unpaid work in their own homes after 1945. Resegregation of the work force by gender kept pace with the rapid expansion of the U.S. work force after the war (Kessler-Harris 1982).

The postwar bullishness of American industrial magnates, commercial leaders, and consumers was shared by U.S. foreign policy makers. Confident of America's emergent status as a world leader, the Truman administration undertook global initiatives in international relief work and economic investment and reconstruction in portions of Western Europe and Asia decimated by World War II.

Through the Displaced Persons Act of 1948, approximately 220,000 people uprooted by the war were admitted to the U.S., provided that they had sponsors in America. In 1953, another 205,000 were allowed in as refugees (Jenkins 1987:873). Many European Jews and other survivors of the Nazi Holocaust were among the influx of persons admitted to the U.S. in 1948 and 1952.   Meanwhile,   in 1947, Secretary of State George C. Marshall urged the U.S. and Europe to undertake a coordinated effort to foster European recovery after World War II. The Marshall Plan disbursed more than $12 billion in American aid between 1948 and 1951 for the rebuilding of European nations' economies (Levey and Greenhall 1983:519–520). The U.S. also administered and financed the restoration of Japanese industry and commerce during its postwar occupation of Japan.

In stark contrast to the domestic and international exuberance of U.S. economic planners of the postwar period was the country's fearful and repressive approach to pluralism of thought and expression among its own citizens. Indeed, the postwar era proved to be a temporary debacle for First Amendment freedoms. Beginning in 1947, the U.S. House Un-American Activities Committee conducted a prolonged series of investigations of alleged communist influence in government, the motion picture industry, labor unions, and schools (Ehrenreich 1985:140).

Despite recent victory over fascist forces in war and economic buoyancy at home in the postwar peace, insecurity about the stability of capitalism and democracy and dread of communist infiltration became a preoccupation of many governmental officials. Perhaps the nineteenth-century American presumption about its own exceptional purity as a nation free from European "contaminants" had residual consequences in the mid-twentieth century. If the country's mythology had, for more than a century, considered national strength to be a function of isolation and independence, then involvement in a more interdependent global economy and polity could breed self-doubt and a sense of vulnerability. McCarthyism was the work of people profoundly unsure of America's internal cohesion and power. McCarthyites were so unsure of America's strength, in fact, that they judged the country's historic penchant for pluralism of thought, expression, and taste as evidence of internal political deterioration and disloyalty. In abandoning "From many, one" (*E pluribus unum*) as the republic's watchword, spokespersons of McCarthyism sought to persuade the nation to draw its strength from forced conformity rather than diversity. Tragically and ironically, the freedom to read shrank at the very time—in 1950—that Americans' capability to read accelerated. In that year, illiteracy in the U.S. dropped to a historic low of 3.2 percent of the adult population, which constituted a commendable 16.8 percent decrease in illiteracy over eighty years and a 1 percent decline in American illiteracy in just one decade (Carruth 1979:571). Meanwhile, also in 1950, McCarthyism penetrated the daily decisions of both the staffs and the clientele of publishing houses, universities, libraries, and bookstores when J. Edgar Hoover, director of the Federal Bureau of Investigation, announced the start of a campaign to identify the fifty-five thousand communists and five hundred thousand fellow travelers who he thought were active in the U.S. Soon thereafter, Senator Joseph McCarthy mobilized the Senate to appoint a special investigating committee to explore allegations of communist activity within the State Department. Further, Congress passed into law, over President Truman's veto, the Internal Security Act, which authorized the detention without a trial of suspected dissidents and established a system of detention centers for detaining such suspects (Carruth 1979:568, Ehrenreich 1985:140–141).

Immigration policy constructed in the McCarthy era resonated with the general fear of communist insurgence from within and suffusion from without . The McCarran-Walter Act of 1952, passed over the veto of President Truman, generally retained the quota system based on maximum immigration of 1924, a criterion that privileged Northern and Western Europeans over immigrants from most other parts of the world. The 1952 law also banned the immigration of homosexuals, "subversives," and other social and political undesirables. The attorney general was empowered to deport immigrants who were affiliated with "communist and communist-front" organizations, whether or not they had already acquired U.S. citizenship (Morris 1976:658).

While the search for internal enemies preoccupied some, many southern black tenant farmers concerned themselves with their very economic survival. They faced a new threat posed by the mechanization of cotton farming, which had been introduced commercially in the early 1940s. Spurred by hunger and joblessness at home and the promise of greater economic opportunity in World War II's defense industries in northern cities, five million black Americans between 1940 and 1970 moved from the rural South to the urban North and Midwest in the hopes of securing a living in industrial work (Jones 1992:233–265, Lemann 1991:6).

Similarly, Appalachian white migrants, searching for relief from intensifying rural poverty, acclerated their movement to the Midwest during World War II and the balance of the 1940s. Between 1940 and 1970, 3.2 million Appalachians moved out of Kentucky, Tennessee, Missouri, and West Virginia, primarily to industrial cities of the Midwest (Jones 1992:227). Unlike their black counterparts, white migrants who found industrial jobs in the 1940s were not, on the whole, displaced by the automation and consolidation of firms in the mid-1950s (Jones 1992:238). By contrast, black people who found factory work were the first to be displaced by the restructuring of industries, which commenced in the 1950s. Prolonged unemployment and underemployment followed.

Given the general prosperity of the United States during the 1950s and 1960s, American poverty—urban and rural—seemed particularly disconcerting, once Michael Harrington's bestseller, *The Other America*, first drew the public's attention to this previously "invisible" subject (1962). Since 1945, the domestic gaze of the general public and media, prior to the publication of Harrington's alarm, had been fixed not on the socioeconomic casualties of postwar capitalism in the U.S., but, instead, on the apparent upward mobility and accrued economic gains of "average" households. Between 1952 and 1972 in the U.S., median family income nearly doubled, from $8,881 to $16,102, in inflation-adjusted 1977 dollars. In that same twenty years, the percentage of families making more than $25,000 a year increased more than 600 percent, from 3.2 percent to 20.5 percent of all American families (Edsall and Edsall 1991:95). As of 1972, 99.4 percent of American households had refrigerators, 99 percent had electric or gas cooking ranges, 94 percent had vacuum cleaners, 80 percent had washing machines, 51 percent had clothes dryers (Morris 1976:731).

General prosperity notwithstanding, poverty continued to plague urban and rural families. Impoverished children, in particular, captured a large share of public concern during the early 1960s as President Kennedy's New Frontier, *The Other America*, civil rights activities, and student activists heightened awareness of the gaps between the comfortable and the disadvantaged in America and of the necessity for expanded citizen participation in combating rural and urban misery in the midst of surrounding plenty. Departing dramatically from the oblivion of the Eisenhower administration to disadvantaged individuals and groups, the Kennedy administration initiated a series of programs designed to relieve the burdens of the poorest and most disabled in America. For example, public welfare amendments of

1961 and 1962 to the Social Security Act and community mental health legislation of 1963 sought to assist poor and ill people with material and social supports. This legislation also embedded the concept of citizen participation in federal expectations and mandates. Furthermore, the New Frontier's investment in the arts, higher education, the Peace Corps, and Latin America through the Alliance for Progress reversed a contempt for cultural diversity and international intellectual exchange that was a central feature of McCarthyism.

Following Kennedy's assassination in November 1963, President Johnson quickly pushed through the Congress a sweeping Civil Rights Act. The presidential campaign of 1964 further highlighted the plight of economically disadvantaged and politically marginal communities. Building on the model of New York City's Mobilization for Youth (MFY), started in 1957 at the Henry Street Settlement, the newly elected Lyndon Johnson and a U.S. Congress dominated by Democrats launched their national "War on Poverty" and "Great Society" programs with the Economic Opportunity Act of 1964. That law incorporated MFY's plan of saving impoverished urban children by mobilizing the entire community as well as the youth of the neighborhood. The War on Poverty, like its template, MFY, sought to empower communities through invigorating and coordinating adults' energies and talent in the battle to salvage their children and teenagers from delinquency, premature parenthood, and adulthood spent in continuing poverty (Moynihan 1969:38–73). The Office of Economic Opportunity (OEO), the central administrative apparatus of the antipoverty campaign, funded and legitimated only those initiatives that attempted to "mobilize communities to help themselves and to democratize the delivery of services" (Hoffman 1989:81). OEO, in short, made the empowerment philosophy of social movements of the 1960s into federal policy.

But the sweeping Great Society policies were to be short-lived. Urban riots of the mid- and late-1960s rapidly eroded popular support for the federal antipoverty campaign and the assassinations of Malcolm X in 1965 and of Martin Luther King and Robert Kennedy in 1968 savaged the leadership identified with both the grassroots and official assaults on poverty. The costly and demoralizing war in Vietnam and the 1968 and 1972 presidential victories of Richard Nixon foreshortened the federal government's campaign against poverty (Edsall and Edsall 1991:101). With the abrupt end of the twenty-year trend in expanding family income in 1973, the popularity of federal spending for poor people was relegated to a few isolated pockets of the voting public.

Suddenly, between 1973 and 1975, the steady economic growth that had buoyed American coffers, self-conceptions, and hopes since World War II came to a halt. Hourly earnings, which previously had increased every year since 1951, declined in real, inflation-adjusted dollars in 1973, 1974, and 1975. Weekly earnings and median family income also shrank between 1973 and 1975 (Edsall and Edsall 1991:105). Meanwhile, welfare rolls expanded by more than one million families, and the food stamp program quadrupled between 1970 and 1975 (Edsall and Edsall 1991:106).

Compounding this troubled economic scenario was the soaring crime rate. Between 1970 and 1975 alone, all reported crime in the U.S. increased by 39.4 percent, reported violent crime increased by 40.9 percent (Edsall and Edsall 1991:112). The generosity of taxpayers of the 1960s toward the economically disadvantaged turned, by the mid-1970s, into self-protective stinginess. Taxpayers had seen their earnings in real dollars decline at the same time that federal expenditures for Aid for Dependent Children and food stamps had multiplied. Adding insult to injury, the physical danger and violence faced by American adults and children was at an all-time high.

Small wonder that by 1978, the War on Poverty was replaced by a popular war on taxes. California's Proposition 13 was the opening round of the tax revolt. That referendum measure, passed in June 1978, fixed property taxes at 1 percent of actual value, barred any new tax increases, and rolled back real estate assessments to the levels of 1976 (Edsall and Edsall 1991:18). The victory of Proposition 13 inspired a cascade of referenda on tax cuts and tax limitations in eighteen states between 1978 and 1982. At least seven states passed such measures, which were attacks on government spending as well as anti-tax campaigns (Edsall and Edsall 1991:131). The days of broad public support for federally funded interventions against poverty, hunger, and discrimination were clearly past.

In their stead came the revolution of Presidents Reagan and Bush. During the 1980s and early 1990s, the ascendance of Republican conservative populism and the virtual collapse of Democratic New Deal liberalism was an outgrowth of a complicated "chain reaction" that had begun with the large migration of black Americans to the North that reconfigured both northern and southern race relations (Edsall and Edsall 1991:3–31). White ethnic voters in the North and West and lower-income whites in the South, who came to be known as

"Reagan Democrats," began abandoning the Democratic Party as it increasingly committed itself, during the years of the Lyndon Johnson presidency, to a federal program of governmental legal and economic supports and incentives for historically disadvantaged minorities.

As many policy analysts have documented, Reagan and Bush's success in reordering American domestic priorities has been thorough. Twelve years of Republican rule shifted the American tax burden downward, redistributed American wealth upward, and slashed social spending for regulatory efforts, education, Aid for Dependent Children, Supplemental Security Income, food stamps, housing subsidies, Medicaid, job training, and many other means-tested programs (Berman 1990, Edsall and Edsall 1991:137–153, Katz 1993, Palmer, Smeeding, and Torrey 1988, Wilson 1987).

During the decade of the 1980s, the average after-tax income of the richest 1 percent of Americans grew by a remarkable 87.3 percent, from $213,416 to $399,697 (stated in terms of 1990 dollars). The next richest layer of Americans, those in the top 5 percent of earners, saw their after-tax income between 1980 and 1990 grow by 50.8 percent, from $100,209 to $151,132. Meanwhile, the 15.8 percent increase in the average after-tax income of all Americans between 1980 and 1990, from $27,484 in 1980 to $31,840 in 1990, seems modest by comparison. During that same decade, the Reagan-Bush administrations saw to it that the poorest Americans' after-tax income dropped by 10.3 percent, from $4,785 in 1980 to $4,295 in 1990 (in 1990 dollars) (Edsall and Edsall 1991:220). The "trickle-down" approach to ensuring domestic well-being of Presidents Reagan and Bush would be more accurately characterized as a "let them eat cake" strategy. The first decade of Reagan and Bush leadership successfully consolidated the economic privilege of the wealthiest Americans and further intensified the economic desperation and marginality of people in the bottom six income deciles of the U.S. population. While United States' dollars, produce, and products succeeded far beyond George Marshall's wildest dreams in assisting countries like Germany, France, and Japan to rebuild themselves, America failed strikingly in its efforts to untangle the Gordian knots of its own continuing racism and intractable poverty, a poverty that haunts urban, suburban, and rural areas and communities of every skin color.

The early 1990s, prior to the defeat of George Bush in November of 1992, presented a particularly unappetizing menu of domestic con cerns to the American citizenry. A sustained economic recession, mas sive public debt, skeletal public services and social service programs, and an increasing incidence of homelessness and pauperization haunted the land. The Supreme Court and Department of Justice, under Reagan and Bush, had succeeded in shrinking the civil rights of women, people of color, and immigrants in the arenas of employment, housing, and schooling. They had diminished women's and girls' reproductive rights and reduced legal protections for detainees and prisoners that had been previously ensured by the writ of habeas corpus. Furthermore, demagogic intensification of racial polarization and of the scapegoating of people on welfare and of gays and lesbians was evident in the presidential campaigns run by the Republicans in 1988 and 1992.

The Democratic victory of 1992 promises to put at least a temporary halt to some dimensions of the "new class war" that was waged against poor and working-class Americans from 1981 through 1992 (Piven and Cloward 1982). Yet, at the time of this writing, it is far too early to tell if the Clinton administration will have the necessary vision, will, and clout to fulfill its promise to end the politics of class, gender, and racial division and to make more equitable Americans' access to jobs, housing, education, and safety.

In historical moments of guarded optimism, like those immediately following the election of Clinton, the inspiration of empowerment ideas, beliefs, and movements constitutes a vital fillip to national officials who intend to "do the right thing," but whose poll-conscious pragmatism sometimes dilutes the steadiness of that intention. Particularly after three presidential administrations in which leaders at the federal level have cloaked their social Darwinian policy wolves in the sheepskin of Bush-Kemp "empowerment strategies," it behooves social workers to distinguish clearly between bona fide empowerment efforts and those that are thinly enshrouded attempts to transfer, under the name of empowerment, the collective responsibility for ensuring the common good and righting the most egregious wrongs to society's most vulnerable members.

The presidential election of 1992 intensified the debate about remedies for the so-called "underclass." In their bid for reelection, Bush and Quayle ascribed responsibility for extreme economic poverty to the moral impoverishment of the poor and to the Great Society programs of the 1960s, which, in their view, have created a welfare caste and culture. Single women who raise babies alone, outside of mar riage, bring poverty onto their own heads, the Republican ticket argued. Men who fail to marry and support the women they impregnate cause intergenerational desperation and marginality. The corrosion of "family values," insisted Bush and Quayle, caused the riot in South-Central Los Angeles in April of 1992. It is self-evident, they said, that single mothers cannot raise decent and upwardly mobile children, especially if the children are boys. Only two-parent families blessed by marriage can do so, in their view. Poverty, argued Bush and Quayle, stems from deficient individual and subcultural values and corresponding behaviors that fail to conform with the prevailing norms of the Christian home and capitalist workplace.

The proper remedy is to "reform" welfare by making people work for their welfare checks and by removing families from the rolls whose adults prove too irresponsible to secure steady jobs. The empowerment strategy articulated in the reelection campaign of Bush and Quayle had only two elements: 1. stimulating poor people to "better themselves" through the threat of economic punishment if they do not remove themselves from welfare and 2. reducing the tax obligations of private companies if they move to the poorest neighborhoods—to "enterprise zones."

In neither dimension of their plan was the public asked to invest in the "human capital" of disempowered communities. Nor was a remedy proposed for the poverty of people who are working full-time. Nor was an adequate response offered for the vacuum of jobs that pay a livable wage in communities long ago abandoned by employers whose economic interests and cultural biases took them far away to suburban sites clustered near federally funded circumferential highways. Nor was a solution formulated for bringing neglected and underfunded public schooling in the poorest areas closer to the quality of that offered in middle and upper-middle-class neighborhoods and of that required by late-twentieth-century employers. Finally, their approach to empowerment neglected altogether ways of stanching the flood of drug-related violence and illness in America's cities. That incursion, which Cornel West has termed the "gangsterization of inner-city black neighborhoods," has turned numerous peaceful black neighborhoods throughout the nation into war zones (West 1993). Far from being arenas attractive to businesses that seek both profits and the economic revival of a neighborhood, they appeal only to highly specialized entrepreneurs—those who profit directly and immediately from the sale of automatic and semiautomatic weapons, sex, heroin, and crack-cocaine.

Any ennobling human initiative is vulnerable to debasement. Empowerment is no exception. Consequently, to help distinguish between the sleight of hand named empowerment by Republican strategists of 1991 and 1992 and the authentic empowerment movements long rooted in American culture, it is important to retrace the recent history of activity on the part of those who have known powerlessness first-hand and, as a result, labor mightily and collectively for its extinction.

Influential Ideas, Beliefs, and Movements: 1945–1993

The contemporary language of empowerment within social work has sprung most directly from the civil rights, black power, and feminist movements, three sustained initiatives that were themselves syncretic fusions of autochthonous longings and internationally derived visions. We turn first to the international inspirations for empowerment thinking and action in U.S. social movements and social work since 1945 and then to domestic social formations that directly fueled the empowerment "wing" of the profession.

World War II brought a dramatic end to the political isolation of citizens of the United States. The concerns and allegiances of people and countries in Asia, Africa, Latin America, and Europe became part of the foreground of common considerations during the war itself and remained a heightened part of the backdrop of American consciousness in the Truman era. Between 1945 and 1952, news of displaced persons and refugees, the Holocaust, the Marshall Plan, the U.S. occupation of Japan, and the cold war became daily fare in local newspapers, radio broadcasts, and moviehouse newsreels across the country. In almost no time, television would add to this unprecedented availability of world news. Debate about global issues was no longer the rarified discourse of the diplomatic corps, intellectuals, and international bankers. The role of the United States in world affairs and the impact on the U.S. of transformations on other continents had become matters of popular interest.

Gandhi

One of the topics that captured the public's imagination in the years immediately following the war was the movement to end British rule on the Indian subcontinent. The Indian liberation movement led by Gandhi received major play in American newspapers, newsreels, radio broadcasts, and the emergent medium of television. Some Americans and some social workers who had long been troubled by the impact of colonialism, imperialism, and racism on the peoples of colonized regions followed the Gandhian revolutionary movement with particular interest, judging from the attentiveness to the campaign for a liberated India of Paul Kellogg's *Survey Graphic*, a monthly magazine for social workers and other social reformers who were interested in global social welfare subjects. In 1947, for example, the *Survey Graphic* devoted four of its ninety-six feature articles (4.2 percent) to coverage of the emergence and meaning of an independent India (*Survey Graphic* 1947). During 1949, the first year in which the former *Survey Midmonthly*, a domestically focused periodical for social workers, was merged with the former *Survey Graphic* to form the *Survey*, articles on the needs of liberated India and the assassinated Gandhi's legacy there again constituted 4 percent of the whole, a significant figure for a magazine charged with coverage of all domestic and worldwide issues of interest to American social workers (*Survey* 1949).

Social workers had special reason to take interest in Gandhian approaches to liberation. The Indian independence campaign placed Gandhi's concept of *Hind Swaraj*, the self-determination of the Indian people, at its epicenter of tenets (Jesudasan 1984). Similarly, the profession of social work, since the time of Jane Addams, had considered the honoring and reinforcing of client self-determination to be at its professional core of practice principles and had grappled in each era for an operational definition of that ideal (Freedberg 1989). Gandhi offered some guidance on the subject with his published description of *Hind Swaraj*, a conception that he first committed to writing in 1910:

> It is *Swaraj* when we learn to rule ourselves. It is, therefore, in the palm of our hands. Do not consider this *Swaraj* to be like a dream. There is no idea of sitting still. The *Swaraj* that I wish to picture is such that, after we have once realized it, we shall endeavour to the end of our lifetime to persuade others to do likewise. But such *Swaraj* has to be experienced, by each one for himself. One drowning man will never save another. Slaves ourselves, it would be a mere pretension to think of freeing others. . . . It lies with us to bring about such a state of things. (Gandhi 1932: 39–40)

For Gandhi and his many millions of followers, *Hind Swaraj* was a historically relative term that meant, according to Jesudasan, a Gandhian scholar, 1. personal and political self-rule, 2. systematic passive resistance to colonial rule, 3. *Swadeshi*, that is, multiform reliance on indigenous products, culture, and leadership and rejection of dependence on foreign resources, 4. a sense of duty as being the supreme guide in all matters, 5. governmental forms that evolve through experimentation, trial, and error, and 6. an active, ever-vigilant citizenry (Jesudasan 1984:52–68). In Gandhi's words, originally written in 1925, "Real *Swaraj* will come not by the acquisition of authority by a few, but by the acquisition of the capacity by all to resist authority when it is abused. In other words, *Swaraj* is to be attained by educating the masses to a sense of their capacity to regulate and control authority" (Gandhi 1958:26:50).

Gandhi's indirect influence on empowerment approaches to social work practice of the past fifty years has been incalculably large, especially since his nonviolent conceptions of social and spiritual transformation inspired the political vision and methods of Martin Luther King. Gandhi's examination of colonialism, dependence, independence, and interdependence in all dimensions of living has provided crucial concepts and caveats for many post-Gandhian social workers.

Chinese Consciousness-Raising

Other revolutionary movements of the postwar period also made contributions to the thinking and strategic repertoire of social workers in the United States who have sought to assist client self-empowerment. The Maoist use of consciousness-raising in the Red Army mobilizations of the 1920s and 1930s, repeated later during the Cultural Revolution's "speaking bitterness" campaign, taught Westerners about an important technique. Mitchell defined consciousness-raising, in the course of examining its impact on the contemporary women's movement, "The process of transforming the hidden, individual fears of women into a shared awareness of the meaning of them as social problems, the release of anger, anxiety, the struggle of proclaiming the painful and transforming it into the political—this process is consciousness-raising" (Mitchell 1971:61). The ironic and perverse use of this technique by Maoists to repress dissent and pluralism in China since 1949 has not taken away from the potency of the exported process of consciousness-raising in many other parts of the world, including the self-help and liberation movements of the United States since the early 1960s.

African Independence Movements

African liberation campaigns during the quarter century following World War II also yielded a host of theories central to the development of empowerment-based social work practice. Revolutionaries such as Fanon, Memmi, and Nkrumah surveyed the complex psychological, social, cultural, economic, and political terrain of subjugation and racism under colonialism (Solomon 1989:154). The writings and chronicled examples of prominent African leaders of the 1950s, 1960s, and early 1970s became required reading for architects and followers of several American political movements: civil rights, black power, student activists, and women. Members of those movements, in turn, ensured that the thoughts, language, and imagery of Fanon, Memmi, and Nkrumah made their way into the discourse of social workers who worked with historically disadvantaged groups and individuals (Gran 1983:150–153, Solomon 1989:153–154).

Freire

Latin American theorists also contributed salient analyses of the nature of the relations between the developed and underdeveloped worlds during the postwar period. Among them, Freire stands out as one whose thoughts have particular appeal and utility among empowerment-oriented social workers. His concept of *conscientization* continues to inform community-based health, education, and social service projects of many descriptions (Freire 1986). The Sayville Project in New York State, for example, was created as a Freire-inspired model of an aftercare and advocacy program for mentally ill adults who have been deinstitutionalized from state mental hospitals (Rose and Black 1985). For Freire, *conscientization* is a process "in which men, not as recipients, but as knowing subjects, achieve a deepening awareness of the sociological reality which shapes their lives and their capacity to transform that reality" (Silva 1979:56). The client as "knowing subject" has been a matter of deep interest to empowerment-based social work practitioners since the founding of Hull House and the infancy of social casework. Freire's writings and the experiments that embody his writings have helped to crystallize and direct that interest.

The Civil Rights and Black Power Movements

Extensive cross-fertilization took place in the postwar period between Third World liberation movements and the U.S. civil rights and black power movements (Garrow 1986, 1989). Empowerment-based social work in the U.S. is a direct beneficiary of both international anticolonialist work and domestic black liberation activity. The latter, in particular, has had a profound effect on the social work profession's conceptions of power, justice, self-determination, equity, and the normative relationship between a worker and his or her client. The story of that influence begins during World War II.

The March on Washington movement of 1941, conceived of and led by A. Philip Randolph, head of the Brotherhood of Sleeping Car Porters, was an all-black effort to build, in Randolph's words, "faith and confidence of the Negro people in their own power for self-liberation" (Solomon 1989:11). Articulating demands for fair employment practices, the march was a nonviolent and mass demonstration that foreshadowed both subsequent marches on Washington by civil rights groups and a host of nonviolent strategies of resistance to segregationist law.

The momentum of the March on Washington movement inspired a subgroup of the Fellowship of Reconciliation to become an independent organization known as the Congress of Racial Equality (CORE) in Chicago in 1942 (Garrow 1989). CORE melded CIO sit-down techniques of the 1930s with direct-action approaches of Gandhian resistance (Solomon 1989:12). It sought to call attention to the forms of racial segregation that blocked black Americans from finding work, housing, transportation, education, public accommodations, and economic security. During and after World War II, CORE dramatized through direct action the unfair treatment of black men and women who were serving their country's cause both in the armed services and at home. CORE's Freedom Rides of the 1940s, for example, underscored the unavailability of citizenship rights to blacks. CORE's protests, together with the legal, educational, and economic advocacy of the National Association for the Advancement of Colored People (NAACP) and the Urban League, sustained the campaign for racial and economic justice for African Americans throughout the war and the McCarthy era. That was an artful and major accomplishment, given that domestic dissent was treated as categorically suspect by numerous national, state, and local authorities during those years.

The better-known portion of the history of the twentieth-century movement for equal rights and economic justice of black Americans took place during the 1950s and 1960s. The Montgomery Improvement Association institutionalized Rosa Park's courage with the famous bus boycott of 1955. Martin Luther King, directly informed by the writings of Thoreau, Du Bois, and Gandhi, helped found the Southern Christian Leadership Council (SCLC) in Atlanta in 1957, the organization that launched, refined, and made internationally renowned a strategy of civil disobedience to racial segregation and discrimination (Garrow 1989). In the course of leading that organization and the larger movement of which it became a part, King, in Boyte's words, "held forth the belief that ordinary people could take their lives in their own hands" (Boyte 1984:12). King "considered the civil rights movement's greatest achievement to be what . . . [he] called the 'new sense of somebodyness' " that it instilled in its participants (Boyte 1984:12).

Throughout this period, the work of CORE, the Montgomery Improvement Association, and SCLC was aided by the Highlander Folk School of Monteagle, Tennessee. Myles Horton founded the Highlander Folk School in 1932, using as an explicit model the settlement house movement's work in citizenship training and cultural preservation, which he had observed firsthand as a student at Union Theological Seminary in New York City in the 1920s. The Highlander Folk School and its Citizenship School Program prepared hundreds of volunteers from civil rights groups of the South to "teach the unschooled and disenfranchised in their communities to read and write and understand their State constitution in order to pass voter registration tests, to become " 'first-class citizens' " (Horton 1989:xi). The school was thought by John Dewey, on the one hand, to be "one of the most important social-educational projects in America" and by the Georgia Commission on Education, on the other, to be "the Communist Training School."

The courts of the state of Tennessee took the same view as the Georgia Commission on Education and, in 1961, closed down the Highlander Folk School, revoked its charter, and confiscated its property. The courts of Tennessee ruled that Highlander's populism violated McCarthy-era state laws that prohibited the teaching, publication, and export across state lines of ideas that advocated the violation of existing state and federal laws. Nonetheless, in its three decades of existence, Highlander staff members had assisted small farmers in

Tennessee, Alabama, and Virginia in forming a National Farmers Union, had trained volunteers in the skills of building unions and self-help movements, and had developed an adult and student leadership education program that trained core members of the emergent civil rights movement (Horton 1989:3, Morris 1991:2–6). In Horton's words, "It's a matter of having a concept of education that is yeasty, one that will multiply itself" (Morris 1991:35).

"Yeastiness" was fully evident in the efforts of the civil rights movement of the 1960s to educate the public. In 1960, under the SCLC's sponsorship, the Student Nonviolent Coordinating Committee (SNCC) was formed and immediately instituted a campaign of face-to-face nonviolent confrontations with local and state authorities and businesses, resulting in mass arrests of SNCC demonstrators (Evans 1979, Garrow 1986). CORE, meanwhile, brought back its Freedom Rides. The Freedom Summer of 1964 saw thousands of northern college students join southern black organizers and students in the work of voter registration, literacy training, and the building of housing and health clinics in the Deep South (Solomon 1989).

Meanwhile, in the North, the Nation of Islam under the leadership of Elijah Muhammad and Malcolm X, the founder of the Organization of Afro-American Unity, articulated a message and strategy of black nationalism and separatism. Following in the tradition of Garvey, Malcolm X believed that efforts to achieve integration had only diluted and divided black people's individual and collective strength and betrayed their interests in the United States (Solomon 1989). By 1966, both CORE and SNCC changed from integrationist to separatist organizations that were pursuing the tack of black nationalism (Solomon 1989:14). Followers of Malcolm X publicly denigrated the efforts of integrationists like King and groups inspired by King, Du Bois, and others who had advocated nonviolence as an overarching approach to ending the oppression of black Americans.

Conversely, King, Whitney M. Young, who was head of the National Urban League and the National Association of Social Workers at the time of his unfortunate death, and other advocates of nonviolence condemned the calls to violence and separatism of Malcolm X, Stokely Carmichael, and others. They believed that black violence would escalate white unofficial and official violence against blacks and that black separatism would leave the black community without sufficient material resources to survive and thrive. Though the assassinations of Malcolm X and Martin Luther King silenced their dialogue, the debate between integrationists and separatists continued.

Social work professionals listened, observed, read about, discussed, and, in some cases, directly participated in civil rights and black liberation activities. The profession's graduate school professoriat, the leaders of its national organizations, and the editors of social work newsletters, journals, and books, by 1969, were much affected by the national debate on racial discrimination in the U.S., by the assassination in 1968 of Martin Luther King, and by the urban riots that erupted after his killing. The profession's educational and agency-based leadership and membership actively explored the multilayered implications for social work and for the country as a whole of ethnic and racial divisions.

In the seven years between January 1962 and December 1968, fifteen feature essays were published on the topic of racism and its effects on people and institutions within the United States in *Social Work*, the social work journal with the widest readership of the period. During the next seven years of publication, *Social Work* featured thirty-seven articles on the nature, impact, and implications for social work of racism, a representation that constituted a 247 percent increase over the prior period in attentiveness to the subject (*Social Work* 1962–1974). A similar increase in social workers' concentration on racism was evident in the *Encyclopedia of Social Work*. The fifteenth edition, published by the National Association of Social Workers in 1965, included four major discussions of race and racial discrimination (Lurie 1965). The sixteenth and seventeenth editions of the *Encyclopedia of Social Work*, published in 1971 and 1977 respectively, each more than quintupled the number of articles and pages that its 1965 antecedent had devoted to the topic (Morris 1971, Turner 1977).

Much as the popularization of Freud in the 1920s and of Marx in the 1930s had catalyzed the reconfiguration of practice methods and practice theories within the profession, so the public debate about black movement themes and demands transfigured entire segments of social work practice, education, and thought by the mid-1970s. By the time Barbara Bryant Solomon implanted in an explicit way the language and concepts of empowerment into the profession's discussions, social work's "soil" had been plowed and readied for her ideas by the social and cultural turbulence of two decades.

"Maximal Feasible Participation"

Also serving to prepare the ground of the social work profession for the 1970's strain of ideas about empowerment-based practice with historically disempowered people was the federal government's response to the civil rights and black power movements of the 1960s. "Maximum feasible participation," a mandate of the Economic Opportunity Act of 1965, was interpreted by the director of the Office of Economic Opportunity, Sargent Shriver, to mean that the poor for whom Community Action Programs were created had to have a direct and active role in planning and shaping the services that were to be offered if such services were to be approved and funded (Ehrenreich 1985:169–171, Moynihan 1969:89–91).

Ehrenreich has argued that this power-sharing arrangement became rapidly elevated into an ideology that dovetailed nicely with the preexisting goals and beliefs of black nationalists and civil rights activists. Black liberationists' desires for community control of local institutions and programs sprang from decades of having little or no voice in the running of schools, hospitals, governmental offices, and businesses in their communities (Ehrenreich 1985:171). "Maximum feasible participation" as an approach welled up from civil rights marches, settlement houses, the streets of organized poor neighbor-hoods, and campuses into government circles. In the words of Senator Moynihan, who was a White House insider at the time, "Community action with citizen participation was a coherent and powerful idea working its way into national policy" (Moynihan 1969:xvi).

Liberation Theology

Another wellspring from which contemporary empowerment-based social work practice has drawn ideas and inspiration is liberation the-ology. A movement of radical Catholic and Protestant theologians and activists, liberation theology congealed in the late 1960s, cat-alyzed by the writings of the Jewish theologian, Martin Buber, and Pope John XXIII's *Pacem in Terris* of 1963. Liberation theology pri-marily took root in Latin America and Western Europe, where its cen-tral focus was and continues to be centered on improving the lot of the poor through the illumination of and elimination of class injustice. The seminal work of the movement, *A Theology of Liberation*, writ-ten in 1973 by the Peruvian, Gustavo Gutierrez, made a Christian socialist argument that "Christ must save bodies as well as souls" (Cort 1988:311, Gutierrez 1973, Smith 1991).

Liberation theologians have pointed persistently to the collusive relations among the church, the state, and the wealthy in maintaining forms of private ownership that leave most people poor in most of the world. Gutierrez and others have called for the active participation of the poor, in collaboration with other Catholic faithful, in redistributing economic and political resources in an equitable pattern that would be in closer keeping with Jesus' intention (Gutierrez 1973, Smith 1991). By 1986, even the National Conference of Catholic Bishops in the United States, a group not known historically for its liberalism, let alone its radicalism, reflected the influence of liberation theology in its pathbreaking pastoral message, *Economic Justice for All: Catholic Social Teaching and the U.S. Economy*. The bishops' message called "for the U.S. to launch a worldwide campaign for justice and economic rights" (Cort 1988:311, National Conference of Catholic Bishops 1986).

The commitment of liberation theology to assisting poor people in tranforming their own conditions, with the help of allies in powerful institutions, is a mission of empowerment that has reinforced American social work's long-standing devotion to the same purpose. Liberation theology has helped sharpen the profession's understanding of the centrality of the poor in initiating and sustaining processes that will transform poverty into a condition of adequacy and equity and has heightened the profession's awareness of the intransigence of the institutional obstacles that stand in the way.

The New Left

The New Left also was a major donor to the substance and form of empowerment-based social work in the postwar era. Its core idea, the notion that "participatory democracy" constitutes an indispensable complement to representative democracy, was articulated first in *The Port Huron Statement* of 1962, the manifesto of the Students for a Democratic Society (SDS) (Miller 1987:13, 142, Students for a Democratic Society 1964). That document stated that participatory democracy was a condition in which and a process through which "the individual share in those social decisions affecting the quality and direction of his life. . . . We seek the establishment of a democracy of individual participation" (Miller 1987:142). For Tom Hayden, a leader of SDS and a key author of *The Port Huron Statement*, participatory democracy meant:

> Number one, *action*; we believed in action. . . . Active participation. Citizenship. Making history. . . . Secondly, we were very directly influenced by the civil rights movement in its student phase, which believed that by personally committing yourself and taking risks, you could enter history and try to change it after a hundred years of segregration. . . . Voting was not enough. . . . [It was important] as an end in itself, to make the human being whole by becoming an actor in history instead of just a passive object. Not only as an end in itself, but as a means to change. (Miller 1987:144)

Participatory democracy as an idea and a practice sprang from three different sources. It came from the tradition of civic republicanism, with its orderly, face-to-face decision making and communalism, handed down from Aristotle through Jefferson to Dewey. Participatory democracy also reflected the Quakers' stress on direct, moral witnessing of injustice and on the immediacy of the imperative of building a "redemptive community" that engages all its members in the individual and collective pursuit of peace and justice on earth. Third, the New Left inherited the existentialists' mistrust of centralization and bureaucracy and their glorification of individual heroism and direct action in the face of authoritarian rule (Miller 1987:145–147, Breines 1982:16, 46).

Out of this complex set of ideas grew SDS's Economic Research and Action Project (ERAP) in 1964 and 1965. ERAP was a cluster of community development initiatives staffed by SDS members in the ghettos of northern cities. Employing the example of the Student Nonviolent Coordinating Committee's organizing, SDS workers in ERAP attempted to organize poor people to resist particular forms of racism and economic injustice. Many members of the social work profession observed these efforts and began to replicate them and write about them in professional publications of the late 1960s. Empowerment-oriented social workers resonated with the salient features of ERAP, which Breines has captured in a few words, "Dramatically, the search for community and agency come together in this short period; acting on one's own behalf, creating meaningful political activity in both a public and private sense" (Breines 1982:97).

The Self-Help Movement

Similarly, social work's interest in empowerment has been fueled by the self-help movement, an efflorescence of mutual aid groups that witnessed a renaissance in the United States during the 1970s and 1980s (Gartner and Riessman 1984, Levin, Katz, and Holst 1979, Katz and Bender 1976, Lyon 1987, Riessman 1986:54–58). The self-help ethos has been characterized as a prefiguration of the empowerment orientation (Riessman 1986:59–60). The self-help movement emphasizes identification with underdogs, mistrust of experts, hierarchies, and of large institutions, cooperative and voluntary participation in mutual aid groups of people who are confronting commonly shared conditions or problems, the importance of gaining control over one's own life, and a strong preference for the flow of initiative, resources, and ideas from the bottom upward (Riessman 1986:53–63). Thousands of consumer groups, neighborhood organizations, and mutual aid networks have formed that incorporate this self-help ethos. A stunning array of informal and formal associations has evolved in the contemporary U.S., from support groups for people with severe physical disabilities to organizations of teenagers with braces on their teeth.

Obviously, the relationship of social work as a profession to self-help groups is necessarily complicated. The very inspiration for some self-help organizations has sprung from members' bad experiences with professionals, among them social workers. Some self-help groups shun all professional contact, others seek out professional consultants whose role the group carefully delimits ahead of time, still others rely on professionals to serve as ongoing staff members (Gitterman and Shulman 1986, Silverman 1987, Simon 1990).

Nonetheless, despite the inherent tensions between social work and the self-help movement, empowerment-based social workers have derived much from observing the latter's emphasis on "interdependence rather than on dependence" and on its forms of self-reliance that, paradoxically, congregate rather than isolate members (Riessman 1986:62). The "self" of the self-help movement connotes a three-tiered reservoir composed of one's own indigenous strengths, those of the immediate group of supporters that one is part of in a face-to-face sense, and those of the larger community of fellow "survivors" who know firsthand the nature of the trauma that one has undergone and the daily processes of recovery and transcendence that one must mount (Riessman 1986: 60–62).

This complex interpretation of mutual aid of the self-help movement served to reinforce, for group workers within the profession of social work, a long-standing conviction that the small group is "the cornerstone of democracy" (Gitterman 1992). Early group work had learned, from the progressive education movement led by Dewey and from its own social experimentation in the settlement house and recreation movements, that active membership in groups and organizations, together with social action, schools democrats and anchors democracies (Gitterman and Shulman 1986, Gitterman 1992). The self-help movement confirmed and updated this founding premise of group work.

Feminism

Feminism, like the civil rights, black power, and self-help movements, rapidly expanded the conceptual, methodological, and relational universe of empowerment-based social work of the 1970s and 1980s. Empowerment-based social work derived different things from each of the three major strains of feminism in the United States.

Radical feminism, beginning in the mid-1960s, contributed an analytic lens that revealed multiple forms of women's subordination to men within the gendered constructions of the family, the economy, schooling, the government, sexuality, communication, religion, and the workplace (Baines, Evans, and Neysmith 1991, Donovan 1990, Ferree and Hess 1985, Katzenstein and Mueller 1987). Radical feminists also created thousands of examples of consciousness-raising groups, self-help efforts, newspapers, and community-based initiatives to provide to women and girls education, health care, job training, sports programs, and protection from rape and battering (Freeman 1975, Marieskind 1976:27–32). Lesbian feminists, a vigorous and vocal constituency within radical feminism, contributed in major ways to the leadership and staffing of many of these efforts.

Liberal feminism developed a critique of the discriminatory aspect of laws, judicial decisions, bureaucratic regulations, and workplace and educational policies and set in motion a series of sustained campaigns to reform them (Freeman 1975, Ferree and Hess 1985, Gelb 1987). Feminists with a liberal philosophy created national, statewide, and local organizations and publications for lobbying, for advocating, and for educating men and women about the kinds of social, political, and institutional changes that are needed to bring about a nonsexist society. The Equal Rights Amendment, wage and salary equity, reproductive rights, reforms in social security, and child care were among liberal feminism's central foci during the 1970s and 1980s.

Meanwhile, socialist feminism brought forward analyses of the interrelationships of oppressions linked to gender, race, and class. Like radical feminism, it popularized in American terms the Maoist device of consciousness-raising to identify the ways in which politics shaped personal as well as public life. This stream of feminism created many community-based organizations that focused particularly on the health, housing, and job needs of poor women. Socialist feminist groups, in particular, entered into local political coalitions with labor unions, black and Latino movement groups, tenant rights organizations, and full employment groups (Evans 1979, Ferree and Hess 1985, Abramovitz 1988).

All three forms of feminism have, like nineteenth-century forms of populism, concerned themselves with empowerment. Elizabeth Minnich views both feminism and populism as "movements of anger that affirm what has been violated and, in that affirmation, claim worth for what has been devalued and so open up thought about as well as action for strong, positive values (Minnich 1986:192).

Feminism, then, has helped social workers to mobilize the self-respect and anger of individuals who, together, constituted communities of devalued sufferers. It has helped professionals appreciate the centrality, the legitimacy, and the potency of the vision and action of those who have known firsthand and begun to reject a disempowered condition.

Gay and Lesbian Liberation

Social workers' knowledge of the forms of disempowerment that constrain and stunt the lives, the rights, and the possibilities of their clients also has been expanded by exposure to the lesbian and gay liberation movements. Lesbian liberation, an outgrowth of radical feminism of the 1960s, created a vocabulary, discourse, and constellation of organizations by the mid-1970s that confronted mainstream America and social work with evidence of the pervasiveness of heterosexist domination. Similarly and separately, the gay rights movement, an heir to the militancy and liberationist spirit of the New Left and of the women's movement, consolidated in the wake of the Stonewall Rebellion of June 1969 (Adam 1987). Previously hidden communities of gay men and bisexual people formed consciousness-raising groups, collectives, newspapers, journals, presses, free universities, psychotherapy and law practices, consulting firms, and advocacy organizations (Adam 1987:76).

Gay and lesbian activists and writers initiated inquiry into the broad subject of the consequences for human beings of "closeting" entire parts of their identity. Sustained advocacy led to the removal, in 1973, of homosexuality from the American Psychiatric Association's official list of mental disorders (Bayer 1981). With the onset of the AIDS epidemic, gays and lesbians formed many advocacy, lobbying, public education, and support groups with and for gay, bisexual, and heterosexual people infected with the virus. The Gay Men's Health Center of New York City, like its counterparts in many other cities, devised indispensable social supports for men, women, and children afflicted with AIDS. Since Stonewall, homophobia of thought, word, deed, law, and institutional regulation has become a topic that is compelling to many empowerment-oriented social workers who are seeking to comprehend more fully and compassionately a caricatured and despised group.

The Disability Rights Movement

Similarly, since 1970, a movement of people with disabilities has stretched the sensitivities and sensibilities of many social workers. Believing that "disabled people should be integrated into society and participate with the same rights as everyone else," members of organizations such as the Disabled Peoples' International have retrieved persons with physical and mental disabilities from the condition of being pitiable unfortunates to being those who are "citizens with rights" (Driedger 1989:3–4, 94). Three branches of this movement have developed during the past two decades: an independent living branch, consumer groups, and self-help organizations (Driedger 1989:3–4). In an otherwise bleak era for social movement successes at the national level, the movement of people with disabilities in the U.S. has gained significant ground with the passage of the landmark Americans with Disabilities Act of 1990.

The movement of persons with disabilities has educated social workers about the impact of various forms of physical and mental impairment on individuals' daily lives and those of their families. Disability movement activists and writers have exposed interested social workers to numerous innovative forms of self-help and advocacy that people with disabilities have undertaken and have highlighted the multiplicity of physical, attitudinal, and institutional barriers that still impede their full citizenship. Social workers have learned from disability movement theorists about the social construction of disability, a process that makes it probable that most persons who have some form of discernible impairment become marginal members of society and culture (Oliver 1990).

FIGURE 7.1
INFLUENTIAL IDEAS, BELIEF, AND MOVEMENTS: 1945-1994

Gandhi
Chinese Consciousness-Raising
African Independence Movements
Freire
Civil Rights and Black Power Movements
"Maximal Feasible Participation"
Liberation Theology
New Left
Self-Help Movement
Feminism
Gay and Lesbian Liberation
Disability Rights Movement

The period of 1945 through the early 1990s—a time of the demise of colonialist empires and the rise of national independence movements and multinational economics—has been an especially fertile one for the generation of ideas, beliefs, and social movements that cast empowerment in contemporary terms. The visions of social workers who are drawn to notions of empowerment have been broadened by the accrued knowledge base provided by this complex body of philosophies, symbols, belief systems, and recorded experiences of grassroots campaigns. The next chapter turns to those social work visions.

CHAPTER EIGHT

Recent Visions of Empowerment Practice, 1945–1994

Empowerment refers to a process whereby persons who belong to a stigmatized social category throughout their lives can be assisted to develop and increase skills in the exercise of interpersonal influence and the performance of valued social roles. —Barbara Bryant Solomon

Empowerment is a process of increasing personal, interpersonal, or political power so that individuals can take action to improve their life situations. —Lorraine Gutierrez

Social Work's Visions of Empowerment: 1945–1994

Social workers with an empowerment perspective have promoted, during the postwar period, the self-determination and interests of clients and community members in a wide variety of ways. In doing so, they have encoded in their language and symbols the spirit and imperatives of many of the influential movements and beliefs of their time.

Social work approaches of an empowerment orientation now constitute a dense and diverse thicket. Despite its complicated nature, however, it is a thicket with a discernable pattern.

Social Workers' Self-Conceptions

Social workers of an empowerment bent in the postwar period have conceived of themselves in one of four ways in relation to clients' own efforts to gain greater mastery over their everyday affairs: as nurturers, facilitators, mobilizers, or social reformers. Those four identifications, each of which will be detailed below, have helped social workers shape their particular approaches to empowerment. Amid the dispersed heterogeneity of American social work since 1945, social workers' self-conceptions of their primary responsibility to clients have served as ballast in attempts to navigate among the many interventive paradigms that currently proliferate.

Social Workers as Nurturers Social workers dedicated to client empowerment have sought over the past five decades to nurture the self-empowerment of clients in a variety of ways. Some have targeted clients' self-esteem, others clients' identity and consciousness. Still others have focused primarily on the technical repertoire of clients and communities. Virtually all empowerment theorists, except for those of the mobilizing branch, have understood the relationship between a social worker and his or her client or client group to be the primary site in which the nurturance of clients' efforts at empowerment takes place, viewing that relationship as a restorative and generative bond that serves as a template for other key relationships. Many within the "nurturer" strain of empowerment-based practice have combined the work of nourishing client self-esteem with the projects of fostering positive identification with a shared community and of building skills needed in securing some measure of safety, comfort, and fulfillment in everyday life at work, at home, and in one's neighborhood.

The pioneer of empowerment theory among social workers, Barbara Bryant Solomon, for example, viewed professionals' nurturance of client self-esteem as a prerequisite to sustained empowerment endeavors. She considered the provision of material relief to poor people to be a crucial activity but, nevertheless, one distinctly secondary in importance to the erasure of the sense of helplessness that dispirits people accustomed to a stigmatized and marginal condition. Her emphasis on matters of the spirit echoes in American terms the chief priority of Frantz Fanon, which was captured earlier in this volume in an epigraph to chapter 7.

> Ironically, the provision of resources may be least helpful in achieving the goal of empowerment if such provision only serves to reinforce a sense of powerlessness and dependency. . . . The *resource consultant* role . . . involves linking clients to resources in a manner that enhances their self-esteem as well as their problem-solving capacities. (Solomon 1976:346–347)

Similarly, Elaine Pinderhughes has constructed a notion of empowerment that stresses the salience of strengthening two dimensions of clients' self-respect: their personal self-conception and their collective sense of self. "Empowerment requires the use of strategies that enable clients to experience themselves as competent, valuable, and worthwhile both as individuals and as members of their cultural group" (Pinderhughes 1989:111).

Pinderhughes's contemporary emphasis on nurturing clients' sense of self-worth honors and extends a long tradition of empowerment-based social work. Her work resonates, for example, with that of Ross, who held that a social worker who is a community worker must be an enabler and social therapist, one who engages "in a process by which a community identifies its needs or objectives, orders (or ranks) these needs and objectives, develops the confidence and will to work at these needs or objectives" (Ross 1955:39). Ross, like Pinderhughes in the late 1980s, found the expansion of client and community self-assurance through participation in problem definition and problem solving to be the linchpin of subsequent individual and community development. His conception of the enabler and social therapist was derived from the example of community development workers in Africa, Latin America, and Asia of the 1940s and 1950s, who sought to speed the peaceful transformation of Third World villages into self-reliant communities through encouraging citizen self-confidence and participation (Lappin 1985:62). The inspiration for Pinderhughes's theoretical contributions came from a source closer to home, her own agency-based practice in the U.S. with poor and working-class African American, white, and Hispanic clients.

Germain and Gitterman, architects of the ecological perspective of social work practice, explicitly share with Solomon, Ross, and Pinderhughes their emphasis on nurturing client self-esteem as a salient dimension of empowering social work practice (Germain and Gitterman 1987:491–492). "Self-esteem and the sense of identity may be individual, familial, or tribal—and may be attached to a community as well—but respect for one's self and/or one's group seems to be a universal concern" (Germain 1985:39, 1979).

Fostering people's sense of self-worth is a mandatory part of practice for others, as well, who have made useful contributions to the emergent theory base of empowerment-oriented social work. Weick, creator of the "strengths perspective," gives high priority to "giving people confidence to proceed with the difficult choices in their lives" (Weick et al. 1989:353). Social workers who are able to nurture clients' confidence in their own wisdom, Weick and Loren Pope argue, are those whose own practice wisdom springs from "interior ways of knowing" and who are therefore able to recognize the inner wisdom of clients (Weick and Pope 1988:16).

Members of historically denigrated groups, especially, have decades of direct experience in not being believed, in having their views of reality discounted by authorities whose own experiential truths are often discrepant wholly or in part from those of people who have grown up on the margins of society. Without a fundamental and daily commitment to honoring the verity of clients' definitions of their own experience, authorities—whether social workers, nurses, physicians, teachers, judges, police officers, or politicians—can easily and unwittingly reinforce the self-hatred and self-doubt of members of vulnerable groups simply by failing to take seriously the latter's conceptions of themselves and of their situation.

For example, chronically mentally ill people are particularly susceptible to having their confidence undermined by authorities who question the legitimacy of their worldview. Tobias has written that the role of "validator" is often the primary responsibility of the social worker who seeks to build the confidence of chronically mentally ill clients and thereby start or further the empowerment process. For him, "the function of the validator is to confirm, legitimize, substantiate, or verify the feelings, ideas, values, or beliefs of . . . that client's system (Tobias 1990:357).

Tobias clearly believes that the nature of the client-worker relationship is primal in either increasing or decreasing a client's confidence and, therefore, his or her ability to proceed with self-empowering steps. So also do Dodd and Gutierrez, who argue that the client-worker bond has the signal capacity to generate, implant, and realize within the dyad a client's faith in herself or himself as an effective actor. From that dyadic source, often a corrective and restorative experience for a client who has known little self-respect or social honor previously, springs a more broadly encompassing trust in one's general efficacy and import.

> Workers can also facilitate empowerment by assisting the client to *experience a sense of personal power within the helping relationship.* This technique is based on the assumption that the experience of power within the intervention can be generalized to feelings of power in the larger social environment. (Dodd and Gutierrez 1990:69–70)

Building individuals' sense of personal power and mastery in daily relationships and tasks is also integral to the empowerment vision of

Hegar. In her work on empowerment-based practice with children, Hegar defines empowering practice as that which helps them "build a sense of efficacy and control" (Hegar 1989:378–379). Children, she writes, gain a grasp of their own strength and capabilities mimetically, through observing and imitating self-assured and effective adults around them. Regrettably, one must note, the inverse is true, as well.

> It is consistent with the first principle [the premise that children make emotional gains through association with empowered adults] to infer that foster children are helped toward empowerment when they observe their parents, foster parents, or respected social workers being assertive and confident of their own efficacy. (Hegar 1989:379)

Closely linked to the nurturance of self-esteem, which is the indispensable sense of being effective and worthy in one's own immediate universe, is the enhancement of clients' consciousness of their own identity as individuals and historical actors, as members of families, groups, and communities, and, sadly, as objects of stigma and oppression. Social workers of an empowerment orientation have given considerable thought to the work of speeding the client's replacement of despised and ambivalent identities with authentically affirming ones. How are social workers to do this?

One approach is that of Hartman and Laird, who have advocated extensive exploration with clients of the stories, metaphors, and rituals of their families that characterize the meaningful links between people and generations (Hartman and Laird 1987:587). They have been joined in this conviction by Weick, who has encouraged social workers to assist clients in learning to "describe, name, pool, and honor their own stories" (Weick 1990). By articulating and rearticulating to others their own narratives and interpretations of their lives, clients "take back the power" of constructing their own multiple identities (Weick 1990). Goldstein has agreed and emphasized the centrality of humanistic social workers' appreciating, in a multilayered manner, clients' accounts of their own life dramas. He writes:

> When we peel back the layers of theory, technique, style and other characteristics that give the change experience its character and movement, what we find is two or more human beings engaged in conversation. . . . If all goes well, a relationship will grow out of this conversation. . . . If we put aside our cherished theories and other presumptive notions about the human state and listen carefully to how people frame and define their own lives, we might truly learn something about the

meaning of strength . . . . The most reliable text cannot be found in the universal and abstract features of theory; rather, it is contained within the stories our clients tell us about their individual lives. (Goldstein 1990:273–274)

Still more illumination of the empowerment-oriented social worker's obligation to nurture the client's quest for comprehensive understanding of the nature of her or his past and present identities is found in the work of Rose. He writes that the "first principle" of what he terms the "advocacy/empowerment" approach is "contextualization."

Contextualization means acknowledging the social being of the client. . . . This orientation . . . assumes that workers have the possibility of helping people to learn of their social historical existence and its influence in shaping their experiences and perceptions of themselves as dynamic dimensions of a larger social contextual/ideologically constructed universe. (Rose 1990b:46)

Helping clients to comprehend the complex nature of their own identity, including those psychological aspects that have been formed through identification with the aggressor (or oppressor) and that lead them unconsciously to collude in the creation of relationships in which both dominating and submissive power relations are embedded, is a key aspect of the social worker's job. Human liberation and empowerment hinge, suggests Lichtenberg, on the victim's understanding of the active and passive parts which he or she has played in the "victim-aggressor syndrome" (Lichtenberg 1990).

Attending to the client's consolidation of a psychologically informed and historically rooted identity is also fundamental to the empowerment approach of Hegar. She urges social workers to recognize that "children derive a sense of mastery" from consolidating their own identity (Hegar 1989:379). For Hegar, mastery is "a feeling of accomplishment and control" that is indispensable to empowerment (Hegar 1989:379).

Nurturing clients' and colleagues' efforts to recognize and grapple with the ongoing tensions between one's overall identity as an individual and one's identity as a member of a collectivity—whether a voluntary or involuntary member—is part of Pennell's charge to empowerment-oriented social work. In studying the democratic configurations and contortions of the battered women's movements in Canada and the U.S., Pennell has concluded that social workers would be well-advised to remind themselves and their clients of the incessant juggle of identities that self-empowerment entails.

> [To move] beyond the conventional process of empowerment, that is, from granting power to the membership, to the feminist process of empowerment, where power originates within the membership. . . . On the one hand, individuals are to assert their autonomy and, on the other hand, they are to merge into a collectivity. . . . Over time, though, they have also increasingly recognized that, without affirming differences, merger disempowers. (Pennell 1990:195)

Also among those who identify themselves with the "nurturer's" approach to empowerment-based practice are those social work theorists and practitioners who have stressed the professional responsibility of facilitating clients' acquisition of skills. This perspective is an especially familiar one within social work, invoking as it does at least two important traditions: that of group work's emphasis on helping clients develop social skills and that of social worker-as-technical assistant, which dominated the rational planning stream of community organizers' thinking in the 1940s and 1950s.

Group worker Coyle placed the nurturance of the sophistication of clients' social skills at the heart of her charge to social workers. "But it is not too much to hope that group workers—along with other professional workers also dealing with personal relations—may be among those who can help in the replacing of the social skills necessary in the present distracted state of the world" (Coyle 1947:97). Coyle meant by the term *social skills* many things. She referred to the skills of exploring individual and group preferences, of communication, of debate, of compromise, of self-government, of resisting illegitimate authority, of program and organizational planning, of representation, of consensus building, and of democratic leadership in small and large groups (Coyle 1947).

Prior to the 1960s, community organizers, guided by the theoretical work of Dunham, concerned themselves with helping client organizations and communities become more proficient in the administration, planning, and assessment of local needs and resources, in the coordination of programs and services, and in the evaluation of the effects of community programs (Gilbert and Specht 1987:610–613). Dunham's work accented social work planners' responsibility for teaching the leadership of community organizations such competencies as the development of program proposals, grant applications, program evaluations, and practice-based research (Dunham 1948, 1958, Dunham and Harper 1959).

Empowerment theorists within social work, since the mid-1970s, have constructed their practice approaches in the reflected light of both traditions: group workers' earlier focus on building democratic skills and community organizers' prior concentration on enhancing community proficiencies in the establishment of programs and services. Solomon's strategies of empowerment, for example, have incorporated an emphasis on the social worker's "teacher/trainer role," a role enacted preferably in an informal group setting that least resembles traditional contexts of formal instruction (Solomon 1976:350–352). Social workers, in Solomon's approach, impart as teachers and trainers whatever information, knowledge, and skills that a client asks for, desires, or appears to need in the course of persevering in daily life. Each client would require a particularized set of skills. One might need to know how to obtain scarce resources from complicated bureaucracies, another, public speaking skills, and another, detailed knowledge of his or her strengths and varieties of self-sabotage.

Helping clients refine, update, and employ in a situationally adept fashion their survival and coping skills is also important in Gitterman and Germain's conception of social work's multiple responsibilities in relation to clients from historically disenfranchised groups. They view social workers as educators, in part, as people responsible for making sure that clients know how to negotiate as well as to change their environment. If clients are to negotiate deftly their physical and social environments, they, like anyone else, need to know: 1. their organizational and social entitlements as citizens and as people with special needs, 2. the art of framing their needs so as to fall within the established service definitions of social and public agencies, 3. organizational procedures relevant to their use of desired programs and services, 4. service organizations' formal and informal support systems and decision-making processes, 5. ways of calling upon and extending their own social networks, and 6. the skills of using fully municipal and county resources, such as transportational and health care systems, school and college networks, libraries, museums, and public concerts (Gitterman and Germain 1981:45–48).

Promoting competence in clients is, for Maluccio, the aim of social work (Maluccio 1979b, 1981). Competence is, in his view, skill in living derived from accruing and interpreting life experience. Skill in living incorporates a broad range of components, including, among many other forms of competence, skill in parenting, skill in communicating, skill in comprehending the stated and unstated meanings of another person, and skill in surviving stigma and poverty (Maluccio 1979a, 1979b, 1981).

Even more recently, others have added to the social work profession's thinking on the topic of assisting clients with the acquisition of skills. Kopp, for example, has encouraged social workers who are dedicated to client self-empowerment to teach clients the skills of self-observation, self-recording, and self-monitoring through the use of self-anchored scales, diaries and logs, and checklists. These skills, suggests Kopp, aid clients in bringing forward information vital to differential assessments, in learning about the contextual dimensions of their problems, in expanding their self-awareness, and in enhancing their involvement in and degree of control over therapeutic and problem-solving processes (Kopp 1989:278–279).

Similarly, Ivanoff, Smyth, and Blythe have been building empirically based empowerment strategies that highlight the importance of teaching women clients social skills that will assist them in the reduction of self-blame, in the assumption of direct responsibility for effecting personal and contextual change, in the development of group consciousness, and in the expansion of self-efficacy (Ivanoff, Smyth, and Blythe 1992:4–5). Ivanoff has also rooted in an empowerment approach her consultation and research with police officers who have survived violent encounters. In that work, she emphasizes the transmission of such skills as the capacity to inventory one's own feeling states and those of fellow officers in the wake of a traumatic event and to solicit actively solace and help from peer support networks and informed professionals when post-traumatic stress accumulates (Ivanoff 1991).

The interdependence of the link between skill and power is traced in the thinking about empowerment of Weil and Kruzich. They credit feminist theory with reconceptualizing "power as shared," with postulating the indispensability of clients' attempts to imagine the transformation of their immediate environments, and with highlighting the range of skills needed in effecting environmental transformation (Weil and Kruzich 1990:1–2). By their definition, empowerment is a notion that "connotes actualizing the latent powers that an individual or group possesses, or enabling them to use their capacities and power more effectively" (Weil and Kruzich 1990:1). They remind social work practitioners that clients with good self-esteem who are lacking in such necessary skills as planning, leadership, and decision making are as remote from empowerment and effectiveness as are clients who are technically skilled in planning and problem solving yet unaware of their personal worth and subgroup identities.

To nurture client self-empowerment, in short, is to couple a client's pursuit of enhanced personal and social power with three interactive processes. One seeks to help his or her client cultivate and acquire a firm sense of self-worth, an identity as a critically conscious and dignified member of a historically stigmatized group, and a set of daily living and working skills that enable the person to survive and then, hopefully, to thrive with a greater portion of authority, satisfaction, and community than previously.

Social Workers as Facilitators Another self-conception commonly held by contemporary social workers who are involved in empowerment work is that of the facilitator—one who makes the pathway to greater power and efficacy easier for clients, members, and constituents. Facilitation becomes necessary because, as Solomon made evident almost two decades ago, sustained powerlessness damages many people's ability to take good care of and empower themselves. In her words: "Individuals and groups in black communities [and, by extension, in other collectively and historically stigmatized groups] have been subjected to negative valuations from the larger society to such an extent that powerlessness in the group is pervasive and crippling" (Solomon 1976:12).

Solomon assigns a complex duty to social workers who want to further clients' chances to heal from the multiple wounds inflicted by stigma and deprivation and to realize personal and communal power. They must facilitate clients' identification and transcendence of three kinds of "indirect power blocks" to the problem solving of members of historically stigmatized groups: 1. those that dwarf the development of individuals' personal resources, such as cognitive skills and self-confidence, 2. those that diminish the development of skills needed in interpersonal and technical domains, and 3. those that shrink people's efficacy as social actors (Solomon 1976:17–18).

Additionally, Solomon charged social workers with a second major obligation, that of making it easier for clients to challenge the three "direct power blocks" to problem solving in impoverished or denigrated populations: 1. insufficient local health and mental health services that result in substandard health for individuals and the community, 2. constricted opportunities for education, continuing education, and staff development, and 3. the denial of the full range of valued social roles or of the material bases needed to sustain those roles (Solomon 1976:17–18).

Third, if social workers are to facilitate meaningfully the empowerment of historically oppressed persons and groups, they must continually reassess the force of clients' strengths in relation to both indirect and direct power blocks. The social work assessment process is conducted, of course, in close and ongoing partnership with the client and with reference to a broad social and historical framework of analysis. The client is both the primary interested party and the key informant who provides information and clues to the social worker that are indispensable to an unfolding and accurate appraisal of the ever-changing calculus of the clients' capabilities, inabilities, resources, and contextual hurdles.

At about the same time as Solomon, Schwartz conceived of social work as a facilitating project, one that entailed both expediting and mediating responsibilities. Social workers have three aims: 1. to build "not harmony but interaction" among the many domains in which people live out their lives, 2. to inspire clients to invest in and take greater charge of institutions in which they have a part, and 3. to motivate institutions to take a deeper interest in clients' needs and contributions (Schwartz 1976:183–184).

Schwartz's approach required social workers to accelerate interactions that heighten clients' awareness of their own interests, sharpen their negotiating and navigating capacities, and expand institutional responsiveness to clients' expressed needs. His call for the professional facilitation of interactions between clients and the systems in which they are embedded was a charge to social workers to advance, quicken, and generally push forward the communication, collaboration, and confrontation between individual clients or client groups and the institutions that compose their social and economic universe. Schwartz's work asks social workers to expedite the recognition on the part of both clients and the institutions accountable to clients of their reciprocal relations as stakeholders in each other.

A more recent view of facilitation that conceives of empowerment as both an end and a means is the "membership perspective" of Falck (1988). He maintains that the purpose of social work practice "is to render professional aid in the management of membership" (Falck 1988:56). By membership, Falck means a complex process that has four ongoing tiers for each person. They include physical functioning, social interaction and belonging, attaching meanings to one's own behavior and that of others, and the intrapsychic process of internalizing object relations (Falck 1988:35–45). From his perspective, both clients and social workers are members of "helping situations" (Falck 1988:4).

Falck is a contributor to the empowerment tradition of social work practice in that he defines social work as the art of facilitating clients' supervision of their own varieties of membership in the physical, social, symbolic, and psychological worlds. His seven practice principles require social workers and clients to share the same conditions, rights, and requirements of membership in helping situations and relationships, despite the necessary differences in roles between social workers and clients (Falck 1988:70). Falck's work falls within the facilitator strain of empowerment practice by virtue of its stress on social workers' obligation to smooth and advance the client's execution of the captaincy of his or her own cluster of memberships.

Facilitators sharpen the acuity of clients' recognition of desirable opportunities and resources within the complex organizations and social processes that envelop their communities. They also sponsor and support client efforts to acquire the competencies and strategic footholds with which to gain a fair share of those opportunities and resources. Additionally, facilitators encourage institutional leaders to take seriously the claims and talents of members of historically stigmatized people's groups.

Social Workers as Mobilizers A third definition of the chief responsibility of the empowerment-based social worker—one that was especially influential during the late 1960s and 1970s—was that of the "mobilizer" of resources, rights, and rage. To mobilize was to animate one's client group to advocate for itself collectively and, at the same time, to advocate as vigorously as possible for that group's interest. Breaking away from the earlier nurturing and facilitating inclinations within social work and community organization, empowerment theorists like Grosser borrowed from the example of radical lawyers of the early 1960s professional stances that were significantly more direct, militant, and adversarial than those characterized by caseworkers, group workers, or community organizers of the enabling or technical assistant branch. For Grosser, "the worker is not an enabler, broker, expert, consultant, guide, or social therapist. He is in fact a partisan in a social conflict, and his expertise is available exclusively to serve the client interests. The impartiality of the enabler and the function-alism of the broker are absent here" (Grosser 1965:17–18). Crafts-men of the mobilization approach, like Grosser and Brager, adopted the Hobbesian premise that sustained opposition, conflict, and jock-eying for power among incompatible interests constitute common social relations of the human condition rather than exceptional ones. Consequently, they maintained, historically disempowered groups needed to become energetic and knowledgeable partisans on their own behalf if they were ever to gain an equitable share of social jus-tice and resources among the competing political and economic con-stituencies of the United States. The job of the social worker was that of the "political tactician" who assists client groups in becoming effective political forces (Brager 1968:5–15).

For the mobilization stream of empowerment-based social work, nurturing the development of clients' skills and empowered identities was a woefully insufficient charge. Instead of merely providing tech-nical assistance and inculcating political and social skills, they believed that professionals who were committed to empowerment should be focusing on the "transfer of skills" to clients and client groups so that the latter would be free of the former as soon as pos-sible (Hoffman 1989:83). In the words of Hoffman, a political theo-rist who has analyzed at length the activist movements in medicine and urban planning, "The problem," for professional activists of the 1960s and early 1970s, "was not delinquent professions but profes-sionalism per se. . . . The activist role was to mobilize communities to help themselves and to democratize the delivery of services" (Hoff-man 1989:81).

From the transfer of skills would flow community mobilization and mass organization. From community mobilization and mass organization would flow the transfer of power and social functions to the people and communities most directly affected by them. Only then would the debilitating and disempowering dependencies on social workers and other professionals and bureaucrats end at last (Grosser 1973, Grosser and Mondros 1985:169–173, Hoffman 1989:81–106). This view, which captured perfectly the ideals, the optimism, and the militance of its times, also made good sense to many clients, former clients, welfare recipients, and community resi-dents whose experiences with social workers, public servants, and health care professionals had been demoralizing, at best, and inca-pacitating, at worst.

Social Workers as Social and Organizational Reformers The fourth and last approach to aiding client empowerment that has been advocated by social workers since 1945 is that of social reform. Theories of social change, and of its cognate, organizational change, have found adherents among each of the three other branches of empowerment practice already discussed. Indeed, those who have advocated social and organizational reform as primary responsibilities of social work practitioners have, in most cases, required social workers also to nurture, facilitate, or mobilize clients' pursuit of empowerment. The reverse has been equally common. Theorists of empowerment through nurture, facilitation, or mobilization have woven social and organizational change into the battery of their expectations for social workers and their clients or constituents.

Among the nurturers of client empowerment efforts who consider social reform a central part of their mission are practitioners who have adopted the ecological perspective of Germain and Gitterman. The authors of this approach have stressed the transactional nature of clients' relations to the contexts of their everyday lives and have highlighted the responsibility of social workers to make environments suitable and just places for human development and expression. "Empowerment emphasizes efforts—jointly with clients where possible—to remove environmental obstacles and stressors and to increase the environment's responsiveness to clients' needs, rights, and goals, particularly for excluded or vulnerable groups" (Germain and Gitterman 1987:496). Central to the ecological perspective is the concept of human beings' "niche," which is the "status occupied in the social structure by a particular group or individual and is related to issues of power and oppression" (Germain 1985:45). Social workers' recognition of the niches that their clients inhabit in a sociopolitical sense compel them, as practitioners invested in client empowerment, to use the leverage of their professional associations, political coalitions, access to the media, and individual citizenship to improve social policies that affect their clients (Germain 1985:45).

Theorists who propose that professionals facilitate client self-empowerment efforts have also incorporated social reform into the heart of their vision of social work practice. Falck presented an eloquent argument concerning the organic relation of social reform to the overall membership perspective of social work practice. Since, like themselves, their clients and client groups are members of society and communities, "justice rather than charity is the key term. Social justice addresses those qualitative and quantitative goods to which members are entitled because they are members" (Falck 1988:55, 63, 192). For Falck and other professional facilitators who are invested in their clients' obtaining fair shares in the commonwealth, social workers and their clients are all bound, by virtue of their shared membership in society and in a helping relation, to work for social reform that will treat all members more equitably.

Most mobilizers of clients and client groups' self-empowerment have also considered social reform a necessary part of social work practice. Brager, for example, a former leader of Mobilization for Youth and a theorist of the mobilization school of social work, considered the role of the social reformer to be interdependent with that of the "political tactician" in his promotion of a social work practice based on advocacy (Brager 1968:5–15). Grosser, by contrast, privileged the partisan advocate's role above all others in empowerment work and viewed even social reform as a potentially diluent activity. He cautioned that social workers' investment in social reform should be contingent upon and secondary to the imperatives of adversarial partisanship in support of one's declared constituency. Grosser worried that the alliances and tradeoffs that are the predictable concomitants of long-term social reform work might well intrude upon the vigor and concentration of the partisan advocate's loyalty to his or her charge. "If advocacy is compromised in the interests of social reform . . . it is no longer advocacy" (Grosser 1973:199).

Nonetheless, empowerment theorists and practitioners, with Grosser as a notable exception, have been in general agreement since 1945 about the continuing import of social workers' joining with each other and with their clients in pressing and pushing governments, schools, health and mental health institutions, corporations, and professions to reduce their collaboration in the perpetuation of American patterns of inequity and injustice. The prevailing view of social workers dedicated to empowerment is that they will be directly responsible for participating in the reform of U.S. institutions, economic policies, and political processes as long as discrimination, poverty, violence, and sickness persist in affecting historically marginal groups disproportionately. Social and organizational reform, in other words, will not be disappearing anytime soon from the primary agenda of empowerment-directed social workers. They are necessary, long-term, companion activities to the shorter-term work of helping people transform their immediate situations.

Differences in emphases, rather than in kind, distinguish the mutually compatible interventive stances of the nurturing and facilitating approaches to empowerment-based social work. By contrast, leaders of the mobilizing school, the only outlier among the various identities, carved out their conception of mobilization in explicit contradistinction to the multiple interventive stances of contemporaneous caseworkers, group workers, administrators, and community organizers of an "enabling" orientation (Lappin 1985:76–82). The mobilizers rejected traditional social work roles and relationships with clients that involved sustained helping, enabling, supporting, facilitating, and mediating roles, viewing them as, generally speaking, paternalistic and irrelevant to the main problem of people's political and economic disenfranchisement. They endorsed, instead, a conception of social work as partisan political work and advocacy in partnership with clients of historically marginalized groups and communities (Lappin 1985:76–85). The history of empowerment-based social work since 1945, is, in short a schismatic one. Despite their shared commitment to social reform work as a continuing requirement of all social workers in a society that remains markedly unjust, empowerment-oriented nurturers and facilitators have occupied one empowerment "tent" and mobilizers quite another.

Empowerment Views of Clients

Having inspected the varied conceptions of social workers' responsibilities in supporting clients' quests for empowerment, we turn now to empowerment theorists' most prominent metaphors for the clients who are the protagonists of their vision. Three metaphors for clients and their activities stand out in the social work literature published since 1945 that emphasizes empowerment.

Clients as Causal Agents   The first is that of the client as "causal force" or "causal agent." Solomon, in her groundbreaking discussion of the process of engaging black client systems, found fundamental the ongoing activity of "establishing the client as causal agent in achieving a solution to the presenting problem" (Solomon 1976:315). The client, in this view, is the primary mover, the determiner of whether or not an issue in her or his life will be addressed, corrected, or resolved with or without the help of a social work professional.

This conception of the client as arbiter—as the authority concerning the key questions as to whether a partnership and contract will be formed and sustained between a client and a worker and as to whether work will take place toward a chosen goal—is shared by Rothman. In his effort to "untangle the knot of client self-determination," Rothman specifies the many ways in which the client acts as the primary cause of engagement, treatment progress, failure, attenuation, interruption, or termination of the working relationship with a professional. He reminded practitioners of the potency of the "veto power" held by clients, who can withdraw altogether or remain physically present but emotionally disengaged from their work with professionals (Rothman 1989:610).

The client's self-determination, in short, takes many forms at many points of the helping, healing, and change process. A client's multiple "veto powers" determine the extent to which she or he will authentically cooperate with a social worker and the extent to which and ways in which she or he will permit self-empowerment activities to be witnessed, guided, and aided by a professional.

The writing of Schwartz evidences a similar view of the client as causal agent.

> The worker-client relationship was one in which the client was not an object at all, but a dynamic force with a will and energy of his own. The client did not hold still to be examined, labeled, and treated, and the engagement was not between a detached expert and malleable entity— between fixer and fixed, teacher and taught, changer and changed. The person in need retained the ultimate power—using it both consciously and unconsciously—to accept help or reject it, and much of the impetus for change came from the client. Thus, even as the worker strove to "enable" his client, he was himself being enabled by the latter's own motives and energies (Schwartz 1976:173)

The client, for Schwartz, was the prime mover of or chief obstacle to work in progress.

Clients as Healers A second leading social work metaphor for a client who is involved in the empowerment process has been the conception of the "healer," a person who is using his or her own internal resources and those of the social work professional to restore himself or herself to fuller functioning and happiness. Weick's work, in particular, has been instrumental in articulating and promoting this conception. She posits that "all human beings have the capacity and therefore the power to make themselves whole" (Weick 1986:556). Some people, because of trauma, illness, or ignorance, need help with self-healing. The job of the social worker, for Weick, is to support that all-important process (Weick 1986:556).

Weick's characterization of the client as self-healer is reinforced by her conception of the social worker as midwife to the client's restorative processes. Her view places a premium on the client's capacity for rejuvenation and rehabilitation and presumes the organicity of humans' search for health.

It is a point of view held by other scholars, as well, among them Katz. In extensive studies of "self-care" as an emerging social movement, Katz and his colleagues have analyzed the upsurge over the past quarter century in citizen interest in maximal health and in "*self* as a resource for growth, fulfillment, and expanded creativity" (Levin, Katz, and Holst 1979:81). The popularity within social work circles of "wellness" programs for senior citizens, employees, union members, adolescents, and women and of "recovery" or "recovering" groups for people grappling with a wide range of addictions and behavioral disorders documents the continuing power and appeal of approaches that portray clients as people in the process of self-restoration.

For some empowerment theorists since 1945, clients are causal forces, for others, they are self-restorers, for still others, clients are "survivors."

Clients as Survivors The concept of survivorship has received significant attention from scholars, humanists, theologians, and human service and health care professionals since 1945, in large part because of the massive numbers of persons who lived through the random and calculated violence, slaughter, dislocation, and deprivation of war, death camps, prison camps, and displaced persons camps of World War II and its aftermath. Relying on the insights of Frankl, Weisel, Bettelheim, Lifton, Kai Erikson, and others, many social workers have studied and assisted "the survivor of a catastrophe caused by other human beings [who] can no longer look at other people and their institutions with innocence" (Getzel and Masters 1985:13, Frankl 1984, Weisel 1982a, 1982b, Bettelheim 1979, Lifton 1970, Erikson 1976). For example, Getzel and Masters, in their work with support groups for families of homicide victims, have grappled with the many feeling states—the generalized and specific rage, hopelessness, vengefulness, depression, sense of abandonment, mourning, anguish, sense of impotence, and isolation—that survivors often harbor (Getzel and Masters 1985:11–16).

Similarly, other empowerment-oriented social workers who work with many different sorts of vulnerable populations have embraced the concept of survivorship (Gitterman 1991:5). Social work with orphans, foster care children, abused and sexually abused adults and children, widows and widowers, amputees, people with AIDS, prisoners, veterans of war, and a host of other types of clients who have endured major losses, traumas, and stigmas has impressed upon the profession the salience and utility of the survivor's identity and capacity for providing mutual aid to others in a similar situation (Gitterman 1991). Hundreds of groups and organizations in the self-help movement have also fueled professional and popular understanding of survivorship (Gartner and Riessman 1977, 1984, Katz and Bender 1976, Silverman 1980, 1987). So also has the emergence of the interest in the post-traumatic stress disorder (ptsd), a diagnosis and condition inspired initially by emergent awareness of the trauma to civilians and military personnel of the war in Vietnam (McCann and Perlman 1990). Since the early 1970s, when the disorder was named and framed, it has been applied in work with diverse kinds of trauma survivors, such as individuals who have endured fires, earthquakes, domestic abuse, torture, rape, kidnapping, and imprisonment (McCann and Perlman 1990).

Feminism has also added to the body of knowledge about clients as survivors. Jalna Hanmer and Daphne Statham, two feminist social workers in Great Britain, have explicated their strong scholarly disapproval of practice approaches that view women clients primarily as societal and familial victims. Instead, Hanmer and Statham encourage social workers to see women clients as survivors of multiple historical and cultural forces and institutions that have been generally centered on the priorities of men. To conceptualize women clients as survivors rather than victims is, they suggest, to view them as active, resilient, and enduring actors on their own behalf rather than as sorry objects of other people's words or actions. To survive is to carry on and to find ways to manage one's own life, relationships, responsibilities, problems, and illnesses with the guidance and support of carefully selected others (Hanmer and Statham 1989:83–98).

> The survival behavior of women is crucial in creating and maintaining a sense of self and self-worth that enables women to continue to meet or alter the demands made upon them. . . . Women are survivors, not merely victims upon whom the world acts. In the act of survival lies a reassessment of self-worth and a reintegration of self-identity.

Survival involves more than perseverance or living a life of quiet desperation; it means assertion, however unobtrusively this may be expressed. Survival means taking on what has to be confronted, preferably in your time, on your grounds, around your issue. Women social workers are involved in these processes as well as clients. (Hanmer and Statham 1989:96–97)

Analysis of the visions of empowerment that have guided social work practitioners in the decades since World War II requires more than an understanding of practitioners' characterizations of their own responsibilities in the empowerment process and of their prevailing metaphors for clients and client groups. In addition, professionals' underlying assumptions concerning the processes of psychological, cultural, organizational, and social change that bring about client empowerment must be understood if their vision is to be fully portrayed.

Conceptions of Change Processes

Having examined the four prevailing self-conceptions of empowerment-directed social workers and the three dominant metaphors with which they have characterized clients as actors, we turn now to the three modal premises about the nature of empowering change that surface in the social work literature since 1945. The change process for some has been essentially discordant, for others, primarily adaptive, and for still others, principally catalytic.

Empowering change has been, for one significant segment of the profession, necessarily contentious and adversarial in nature in any circumstance in which some individuals and groups control substantially more resources, privileges, and powers than do other individuals and groups. Change, from this perspective, has been a social rather than a psychosocial construct. The job of the social worker, in this view, has been to mobilize people to consolidate and sustain conflict vertically in the social structure, that is, upward against people and institutions that dominate important aspects of their lives.

Conflict, according to proponents of this perspective, will remain an essential constant, long after a formerly disempowered group achieves a stronger footing in its community. The reason for the constancy of conflict is the institutionalized nature of injustice and inequity in the United States, a state of affairs that tends to tilt the economic and political "playing field" in favor of the historic "haves" and that tends to destabilize the gains of historically disadvantaged persons and groups (Alinsky 1946, 1971, Brager and Purcell 1967, Brager and Specht 1973, Grosser 1973). Marxian and Gramscian conceptions of social class, class warfare, class consciousness and solidarity, the historical dialectic, and the hegemonic force of ruling ideas provided the metaphysical and political ideas that gave rise to this view of the change process (Barrett 1991, Gramsci 1990, McLellan 1983, Marx 1988, Mills 1967, Tucker 1978).

Other social workers have viewed empowering change as being a reciprocal and systemic process of ongoing adaptation. People adapt to their environments in order to survive and anchor themselves in ever-changing terrain. Meanwhile, those same persons and groups work to reconfigure their environments to respond more fully to their interests and needs. Environments are modified incrementally or, on occasion, massively by people's making institutional innovations and concerted demands on authorities and social institutions for greater health, security, and equity (Germain and Gitterman 1980, 1987, Gitterman 1991:15–260.)

A third conception of the nature of empowerment is also discernible in the social work literature—that empowering change is, essentially, a matter of the activation of extant properties or attributes of clients and communities. Empowerment comes primarily through the unleashing of horizontal activity on one's own behalf (Brager and Specht 1973:19–20, Warren 1978:331). Horizontal activity is that which takes place on one's own socioeconomic and political level, within the circles of power and influence to which one has direct access and with which one has considerable familiarity. Horizontal activity helps people to "overcome fatalistic apathy . . . and [helps] instill *Gemeinschaft*-like conditions of mutual assistance and collective action" (Lyon 1987:116). Relationships with neighbors, peers, or fellow sufferers that help heal personal and collective wounds, pool resources, and build on the strengths of individuals and the community in the course of finding solutions to long-standing problems are emphasized more than are conflicts with holders of power or adaptations made between persons and their environments.

Change as Conflict   Grosser was one prominent articulator of the conflict vision of empowerment. Rejecting the view that social inequities are unintentional and that "the system" is, broadly speaking, constructive, he argued that "inequities are . . . often created by intentional, knowing acts on the part of individuals and institutions"

(Grosser 1973:12). He saw "both worker and client as suffering from the effects of existing social arrangements" and perceived "an individual's inability to cope . . . as a function of social disorganization" (Grosser 1973:13).

Consequently, he thought that the fitting reactions to inequity on the part of social work were "partisanship, advocacy, social brokerage, clients as policymakers, and accountability through public ownership of welfare organizations" (Grosser 1973:13). For Grosser, vulnerable people's poverty and marginality were a result of the choices and acts of those institutional leaders who consciously sought to ensure the security and wealth of some at the expense of many others. What is the only adequate response to these outrages? Not education, or persuasion, but power—"sufficient power to overcome a condition willfully created by society" (Grosser 1973:12).

A more recent version of the conflict view of empowerment has been put forward by Gould. In considering social work with women, she maintains that a feminist approach to social work "must conclude that conflict is an inherent feature of institutional reorganization, and, therefore, it is fundamental to the person-environment interaction" (Gould 1987:349). Gould highlights the utility of conceiving of society as a prolonged contest among groups with divergent and, often, opposing aims (Gould 1987:348). She recommends that social workers, in their efforts to join women clients in removing structural barriers for women in society, adopt the conflict model's view of conflict "as a regenerative social force" (Gould 1987:349).

Furthermore, she argues, the constructive aspects of conflict at the intrapersonal, interpersonal, institutional, intergroup, and societal level merit significant attention in the preparation of social workers. She advocates the conflict model's emphasis on alienation, rather than on deviance or pathology, in the assessment of clients' situations and needs. Moreover, Gould warns that practitioners who minimize the prevalence of social and institutional conflicts that wreak destruction in women's daily lives and relationships risk remaining oblivious to the scope and depth of women's victimization (Gould 1987:350). Two dangers, in her view, are attached to such oblivion: the danger of the practitioner's failure of empathy that stems from comprehending client coping behaviors without reference to their social causes and precipitating factors and the danger of neglecting to support the sustained forms of struggle that individual women and groups of women must wage if they are to end violence and discrimination at their workplaces, in their homes, and in their community's institutions.

Change as Adaptation A second conception of change that empowers emanates from the ecosystems paradigm of social work thinking. Two social workers, Germain and Gitterman, have written extensively about their view of the transactional nature of the "continuous reciprocal exchanges" between individuals and their environments over time (Germain and Gitterman 1987:488–499, Germain and Gitterman 1980, Germain 1985, Gitterman 1989). They have stressed the action-oriented and strategic nature of adaptations achieved by persons and groups who are attempting to find a good life within their respective environments.

Such adaptations, in Germain and Gitterman's thinking, entail two concomitant streams of activity. Persons tailor their own behavior, relationships, and expectations in the light of changing situational givens while, at the same time, they join together to extract enhanced institutional sensitivity and response to their own particular needs and traditions. Activities are empowering for individuals and groups, according to Germain and Gitterman, when they involve clients in identifying and reconfiguring any element in their lives and contexts which blocks the fullest possible expression of their capabilities. For Germain and Gitterman, empowerment is a stream of successive, strategic modifications made by clients, with the help of social workers, of whatever parts of their external and internal universes that stand in the way of maximal growth and development. For some clients, empowerment will require modification of a contorted consciousness of themselves and their world. For others, it will mean changing personal and interpersonal patterns of behavior. For still others, empowerment will constitute the collective transformation of surrounding structures and cultures of daily life that constrain and impoverish them. For many vulnerable clients and populations, empowerment will involve active adaptations in all three of these domains of existence (Germain and Gitterman 1987:496, Gitterman 1991:1–32).

> Empowerment emphasizes efforts—jointly with clients where possible—to remove environmental obstacles and stressors and to increase the environment's responsiveness to clients' needs, rights, and goals, particularly for vulnerable groups. Under certain circumstances and with certain groups, it may include consciousness raising as a means of shifting from an unrealistic sense of personal inadequacy to a recognition of the sociostructural determinants in a stressful situation. In other instances, it may involve shifting a misperceived locus of control over

life events from impersonal societal forces to individual or collective responsibility. (Germain and Gitterman 1987:496)

Change as a Catalytic Process   The conflict view of empowering change focuses primarily on throwing over external impediments to equity and freedom. The adaptational perspective of empowerment eyes three targets: individual and environmental hurdles to development and happiness and the patterned interrelationship between those two kinds of hurdles.

The catalytic view of empowering change, by contrast, pays relatively little attention to stumbling blocks, whether of the external or internal varieties. Its spokespeople, like Weick and Falck, demote obstacles to personal and collective empowerment to a secondary status in analysis and action. They privilege, instead, the inner capacities of persons and groups, resources that are catalyzed and crystallized by interconnection with peers, client membership in clinical and mutual aid relationships, and professional attunement to and ongoing support for client strengths.

For the catalytic "school" of empowering change, vertical battles with leaders of hierarchical social structures or adaptational strategies in relation to environmental, interpersonal, and internalized barriers are considerations that are relevant to but secondary within the empowerment process. Vertical conflicts and adaptive strategies trail after, in the empowerment process, the primary tasks of identifying, supporting, and interconnecting the robustness and resourcefulness of local heroes who, in most cases, are unaware of their own heroism. "An initial phase of treatment of symptoms may be necessary, particularly if they are causing unusual distress. But the overall goal of intervention in a health model is to elicit the participation of individuals in a process that they are to direct" (Weick 1986:556).

Weick's emphasis on client healing and regeneration is paralleled and complemented by Falck's stress on the client as self-helper. The "self," for Falck, is the client who is a connected member of a purposeful clinical relationship with a social worker, with other clients with whom the client comes into face-to-face interaction, and with members of the client's "unseen group"—those meaningful others who are not present and observable in the client's helping group yet who currently influence (or who have influenced) the client and upon whom the client, in turn, has important influence (Falck 1988:64–66). The client acts as a self-helper, not in a condition of individualistic separateness, but, to the contrary, in a dyad with a professional helper and in a larger group with whom he or she interacts. Self-help takes the form of reporting, reenacting, and planning in conjunction with the social worker and other people significant to the client (Falck 1988:84–93).

Though Falck carefully avoids the use of the term *empowerment* to characterize his view of the change process that clients enter into, his conception, like Weick's, constitutes a contribution to empowerment thinking and practice within social work. Both understand empowering change to be a process of a client's recognizing and integrating her or his own latent capacities within the context of robust relationships forged with a social worker and others whom the client deems to be significant. The awakening of inner potentialities in conjunction with the consolidating of supportive interconnections form the basis of a client's self-empowerment.

FIGURE 8.1
SOCIAL WORKS VISION OF EMPOWERMENT: 1945-1994

SOCIAL WORKERS' SELF – CONCEPTIONS	METAPHORS FOR CLIENTS	CONCEPTIONS OF EMPOWERING CHANGE
Nurturers	Causal Agents	Conflict
Facilitators	Healers	Mutual Adaptation
Mobilizers	Survivors	Catalytic Dynamic
Social and Organizational Reformers		

Empowering Aspects of Social Work Practice: 1945–1994

Over the skein of years between 1945 and 1994, at least three elements of social work practice have been noteworthy as triggers to the self-empowerment of individuals and groups from historically marginalized populations. Social workers have emphasized the importance of: 1. phasing their interventions, beginning with direct responses to clients' requests, 2. encouraging clients' involvement in peer networks, and 3. acknowledging explicitly clients' knowledge, authority, and centrality in the change process.

First, as Cohen has identified in her extensive work with individuals who are both homeless and mentally ill, empowerment-oriented social workers have created stages of interventions, first engaging people by "gearing services to meet clients' perceived needs" (Cohen 1989:508). To overcome the deep fear and mistrust of professionals and their institutions felt by many homeless people, Cohen and the teams with whom she worked sought first to meet the human survival needs identified by clients, which often meant concrete services such as housing, money, food, and physical safety (Cohen 1989:506). Only then could other concerns recognized by professionals—medical, psychiatric, and substance abuse issues—be addressed by clients and social workers (Cohen 1989:506).

Empowerment-based practice, in short, is practice in phases, the first phase necessarily being a response to the needs identified by clients themselves as being primary. Both respect for clients and practicality give rise to this premise. Few members of historically vulnerable populations—whether homeless, poor, mentally ill, incarcerated, female, or black—will be inclined to trust professionals unless that which professionals offer first is a direct response to the clients' own definitions of need, which usually concern the most basic issues of survival.

A second element of professional practice since 1945 that has proved fundamental to effective work with previously disempowered individuals and groups is the encouragement of clients to join or form mutual aid groups. Mutual aid groups have transformed vulnerable individuals into members of a community, into sharers of information, into experts experienced with a given problem, into helpers of other people and of themselves, and into change agents shaping their environment (Martin and Neyowith 1988, Cohen 1989:507). Many social workers both before and after 1945 have relied on this time-honored approach to supplement, complement, and eventually replace altogether a client's need for professional services (Gitterman and Shulman 1986, Katz and Bender 1976, Levin, Katz, and Holst 1979). Reliance on mutual aid groups is especially pronounced since 1945—years punctuated by the rise of many political movements, such as the civil rights movement, the second wave of feminism, the welfare rights movement, the occupational safety and health movement, the gay rights movement, and the disability rights movement. In times of social movement fermentation and consolidation, self-help networks have become an organic part of formerly disempowered people's pursuit of equity, social justice, community, human services, and self-esteem.

Social work practitioners dedicated to client self-empowerment have incorporated a third crucial element, as well, into their repertoire of approaches. They have come to perceive clients from historically marginalized groups as indispensable architects of their own present and future environments, as people to whom professionals and other citizens need to turn for inspiration, ideas, direction, and participation in helping to construct a more humane and responsive residence, jobs program, workplace, outpatient clinic, neighborhood, or government. Empowerment-based social workers, consequently, have sought to involve clients as leaders, conceivers, planners, enactors, and evaluators of policies, agencies, programs, and services (Freire 1986, Rose and Black 1985).

For example, in Wichita, Kansas, young adults with spinal cord injuries and cerebral palsy have been encouraged by staff members and administrators of two residential settings there to take an active role in advising the management about priorities to honor in the residences. Social workers encouraged residents to form a residents' council and actively helped them learn a cluster of skills, including the use of parliamentary procedures, group participation and leadership, methods of dividing labor, negotiation, and bargaining. Over time, the residents' council has taken on interpretive, negotiating, advocacy, and advisory responsibilities within the two residences (Brooks 1991).

A long caveat needs to be attached to the claim that empowerment-based social work seeks to involve clients as shapers of their immediate and larger environments. The approach assumes an ongoing partnership between social workers and clients, not an abandonment on the part of professionals and government officials of involvement in the funding, planning, implementing, staffing, buttressing, and refining of programs and services to members of vulnerable groups. An authentic partnership depends upon a complementarity of partners' capabilities and sustained commitment. No federal or state government that is seeking to extricate itself as quickly as possible from financial and social involvement with a public housing project, for example, can consider itself a partner operating in good faith. To turn over ownership and leadership of a housing project to its tenants while simultaneously washing one's governmental hands of responsibility for stemming epidemic levels of violent crime, drug trafficking, illiteracy, AIDS, and joblessness that permeate and surround the project is to act cynically and to violate fundamental understandings of the meaning of partnership.

Conversely, residents of a public housing project cannot be bona fide partners with government in taking over and running their own project if they lack the wherewithal to do so. Residents, if they are to be genuine partners in empowerment require many things: 1. the ability to read and write contracts and regulations, 2. reliable living wages or income supports indexed to inflation from which they can pay rent steadily, 3. the capital funds for long-term maintainance and property improvements, 4. the power and authority to keep weapons, crime, and drugs out of the project, and 5. the know-how to budget and invest funds wisely, manage personnel, lead groups in a democratic fashion, nurture participation and leadership among project residents, resolve disputes, and intervene effectively when a resident's addiction, mental illness, abusive behavior, or irresponsibility threatens the safety or welfare of the community or a member thereof.

The inevitability of such abandonment renders duplicitous the "empowerment" rhetoric emanating from the White House in the Bush years. President Bush and his cabinet clearly conceived of empowerment as the abolition of a governmental role and of professional participation in the creation and maintenance of housing, jobs programs, and neighborhood restoration work. In direct opposition to this ideology, social work versions of empowerment presume that such projects are initiatives and responsibilities of the entire citizenry and its government as well as of the persons most directly affected. Social work thinking of an empowerment "stripe" also assumes that public and corporate funding is needed over a significant period of time to help disempowered and impoverished individuals and groups gain a secure foothold in a fast-changing community, polity, and economy. Furthermore, social workers know from long experience with many client groups that people who have spent decades in a despairing, alienated, and powerless condition require education in concrete skills, steady support, and time to become self-actualizing participants and citizens.

Full and thoughtful community and institutional membership on anyone's part grows out of an extended and mimetic process of observing the public service of others and of experimenting incrementally with leadership roles in one's own daily round. An empowered group of formerly disenfranchised people cannot be waved into existence by a cynical realpolitik that attempts to mask its systematic dismantling of the welfare state with oratory about the moral responsibility of individuals to take charge of their own lives.

In sum, empowering aspects of social work practice since 1945 include carefully sequenced interventions that respond first to the needs and issues clients have highlighted as primary, active encouragement of clients' participation in mutual aid networks, and the fullest possible involvement of formerly disenfranchised clients—in collaboration with a responsive and accountable professional and governmental corps—in contouring the programs that serve them and the environs in which they live their lives.

In chronicling recent social work history, it is important to note that the narrative since 1945, like all other tales of human effort, has an underside. It is to that nether region that we now turn—the paternalism within social work practice since World War II.

FIGURE 8.2
EMPOWERING ASPECTS OF SOCIAL PRACTICE: 1945-1994

Responsiveness to clients' presenting requests
Encouragement of clients' involvement in peer networks
Emphasis on the centrality of clients' agency in promoting
and sustaining change

Paternalistic Aspects of Social Work Practice

The nearly fifty years of social work undertaken between 1945 and 1993 yield abundant evidence of the continuing vitality of trained social workers' condescending, disrepectful, and disempowering attitudes and practices in relation to clients and colleagues from historically stigmatized groups. A triptych of salient paternalistic approaches employed by social workers since 1945 might well begin with a sketch of tokenism.

Tokenism is the process of placing a few members of a subordinate group within a larger entity that is dominated numerically by a majority group that constitutes 85 percent or more of the whole. Such entities are skewed toward the views, customs, and interests of the preponderant group that is represented. The few members of the minority category "can be appropriately called 'tokens,' because they are often treated as representatives of their category, as symbols rather than individuals" (Kanter 1977:966).

Tokenism need not be intentional. It can and does arise in groups, organizations, societal institutions, and social movements whose leaders and members earnestly are attempting to integrate their respective bodies by bringing in individuals from those subgroups of the larger population that have been wholly or mostly excluded in the past. If a critical mass of people are not brought in all at once to integrate an entity, the few who are incorporated become tokens, regardless of the intentions of the recruiters.

Social work, like other professions and like the broader society of which it is an integral part, has been complicit with tokenism. All too many social work agencies, particularly in the voluntary sector, have included only token representation of women, people of color, people with disabilities, and gays and lesbians in top leadership cadres. In the contemporary social work field, men "continue to hold two-thirds of the managerial jobs in a profession that is two-thirds women" (Zunz 1991:39).

From a study of the public health and welfare system of the state of Florida, Martin and Chernesky offer a statistical portrait of the extent to which women and people of color have been blocked from executive posts. Their data from 1987 reveal that white women and black men become senior officials in Florida's health and welfare system at a rate of approximately one-third of their paid representation in the entire organization. Meanwhile black women's rate of occupancy in senior officialdom is less than one-eighth of their total representation as employees in the public system. Contrast those figures with those of white men, who compose only 15 percent of all employees, but 50 percent of senior administration (Martin and Chernesky 1989:119–121). Earlier systematic studies of the demographic composition of managerial ranks in the social work field of the U.S. of the 1960s and 1970s told a similar story of the continuity of white male privilege in agency life (Austin 1988, Fanshel 1976, Fortune and Hanks 1988).

Tokenism within social work extends far beyond agencies' personnel practices. Few social work agencies involve clients in helping to design, evaluate, and redesign the contours of programs and services in anything but a token fashion. One or two client representatives on a fifteen or twenty-member board of directors or advisory council are clearly better than none. Nonetheless, this common practice of including only a tiny ratio of clients as managerial advisors continues a long-standing kind of tokenism in our field.

A second significant type of paternalism evident within the profession of social work since 1945 is the reductionist thought process and speaking process by which a client, patient, or neighborhood is treated as if he or she or it were nothing more than a disorder or pathology. To think and act in a reductionist manner is to oversimplify, to confuse a part with the whole, to place one attribute in the foreground and then to forget about all the rest. One thereby loses sight of the complexity, humanity, and strengths of a client or community in the process of focusing only on problems. If social workers were to examine themselves conscientiously, all but the most vigilant of social work staffs would be able to surface examples in any given week of passing comments about clients like "She's a borderline" or "He's the depressive I mentioned earlier." Such metonymic usages that are put to derogatory ends grow out of practitioners' unconscious search for psychic relief and distance from the oppressed humanity whom they are charged with helping and from the centrality of the medically derived DSM III and DSM III-R as diagnostic and reimbursement matrices in many social work agencies.

The third fundamental form of paternalistic social work practice that has been present in the field, especially since the early 1960s, is that which a feminist social worker from Great Britain, Annie Hudson, has designated as the danger of creating an "alternative victimology" (Hudson 1985:650). Her observations and analysis are based on her work with working-class and poor women and their families.

> Social workers need to take care that they do not fall into deterministic cul-de-sacs about the inevitability of women's positions and status. Such a "Yes, you have every reason to feel depressed. . . . You couldn't be anything else but feel fed up" syndrome reinforces images of women's passivity and inability to resist aspects of their oppressing circumstances. Empathy is obviously important but so is offering women clients strategies for action both at a personal and at a collective level. A focus on women's resources and strengths is crucial in forestalling the dangers of hooking clients into a fatalism about their circumstances. (Hudson 1985:650–651)

That familiar paternalistic trap, a preoccupation with the victimized parts of clients' experiences and a correlative oblivion to those elements of clients' lives that lie outside the static and narrow status of victim, ensnares some social workers on both sides of the Atlantic. If unaware of this preoccupation, well-meaning professionals may then collude with some oppressed clients' temptation to surrender to an overall conception of themselves as victims. Such collusion would constitute a blunder that would only serve to deepen clients' self-pity, hopelessness, and sense of powerlessness and that would be an unwitting betrayal of the century-old empowerment mission of social work. A professional misstep of this kind is particularly toxic for women clients, many of whom have grown up in or are accustomed to a "paternalistic setting" (Blechman 1980). A paternalistic social setting "is one in which a woman can rely on others to assume responsibility for her problems, is not expected to be able to cope with frequently occurring and stressful events, and is given little opportunity to take risks and perfect instrumental attitudes and behavior" (Ivanoff, Smyth, and Blythe 1992:7).

The empowerment tradition of social work practice has been constructed by men and women who inhabit unusually varied methodological and epistemological niches within the social work profession. Nonetheless, despite the heterogeneity of their assumptive worlds and practice paradigms, members of the empowerment tradition embrace a common mission, set of goals, and the unwavering premise that social workers are obligated in their working bonds with their clients to honor two charges. They must help clients expand their own sense of power and exercise of power within both the helping relationship and the larger world while, concomitantly, assisting clients to enhance their capacity to make their domestic and public domains safer and more fulfilling ones.

FIGURE 8.3
PATERNALISTIC ASPECTS OF SOCIAL WORK PRACTICE: 1945-1994

Tokenism
Reductionistic orientations to clients
Preoccupation with clients' victimization

As the next century nears, social workers in the United States, regrettably, face no shortage of disempowered clientele. Consequently, a sense of urgency as well as duty surrounds the project of shaping the future directions of empowerment practice with historically marginalized people. Practitioners in the empowerment tradition—despite the wealth of their century-old inheritance—still lack systematic strategies for extracting paternalism from practice and for empowering themselves as workers. The final chapter is a beginning inquiry into those two neglected subjects.

FIGURE 8.4

THE EMPOWERMENT TRADITION IN AMERICAN SOCIAL WORK

ERA	INFLUENCES OF THE ERA	VISIONS OF EMPOWERMENT		
		Professionals' Self-Conceptions	Metaphors for Clients	Conceptions Empowering Change
1893-1917	Populism Social Gospel Unionism Feminism Pragmatism Du Bois/Niagara Movement	Urban interpreters Educators of democrats Settlers	Active citizens Victims of industrial capitalism	Social investigation Linking of local and global action
1917-1945	Freudianism Garvey/Back-to-Africa Movement Existentialism Marxism and Socialism	Releasers of clients' potential Witnesses Organizers	Collaborators Members	Stimulation Demonstration Reconciliation of expert and public wisdom
1945-1994	Gandhi/Indian liberation Chinese consciousness-raising African movements Freire Civil Rights and Black Power "Maximum feasible participation" Liberation Theology New Left Self-Help Movement Feminism Gay and Lesbian liberation Disability rights	Nurturers Facilitators Mobilizers Social and organizational reformers	Causal agents Healers Survivors	Conflict Mutual adaptation Catalytic dynamic

EPILOGUE

We need experts and expert opinions, and experts can certainly help us to think about the important issues. But democracy is not the rule of experts. It is basic to the education of citizens that they learn how to evaluate expert opinion. . . . Weighing the moral implications of different options is what is fundamental. Here the citizen who has learned to pay attention in the family and the local community can generalize to larger issues. When the family is a school of democracy and the school is a democratic community, then the beginnings of such wisdom have already been learned.   —Robert Bellah et al.

Like the family and the educational system that Robert Bellah and his coauthors envision in the passage quoted above, social workers' professional relationships with their clients are a "school of democracy." Such a school is responsible for making sure that all parties to the relationship become fully able to perform two functions: 1. to weigh the implications of recommended courses of action and 2. to "pay attention," meaning to become concerned "with the larger meaning of things in the longer run, rather than with short-term payoffs" (Bellah et al. 1991:273).

Social workers of the empowerment tradition do not encourage clients to place their faith in the judgment of experts. Instead, they prompt clients to develop trust in their own capacity to discern, through dialogue and reflection, the respective merits and pitfalls of any recommendation, whether that of a professional, a government official, a supervisor at work, a friend, a support group, or a family member. Such discernment, for any of us, grows out of accrued experience in succeeding and failing in the lifelong project of making sense out of confusing, contradictory, and competing suggestions. Wisdom comes from repeatedly "unpacking" and then testing in daily life the meanings of ideas and ideals for oneself and one's family, social groups, and communal institutions. The work of empowerment-oriented social work, now and in the future, is to assist clients and their communities in fully attending, in Bellah's sense of that term, to those things that matter most to themselves.

Empowerment social work is also the art and science of being expert at helping clients to trust themselves and the "natural helping networks" or social supports that sustain their daily lives (Lee and Swenson 1978:366–367). Central to empowerment practice is the imperative of aiding clients to assess, tap, and contribute to the constructive friendships, family connections, links with neighbors, and community resources that they have built up long before as well as during the period of engaging a social work professional's help.

Self-Inspection

To honor this mission faithfully over time, social workers are obliged to keep watch continuously for paternalism in their own practice. In a professional culture and world of accelerating specialization, hierarchism, jargon, and technology, the "rule of experts" remains as fundamental a threat to client self-empowerment and to democracy as another, more obvious danger, that of the contempt in America for historically stigmatized subgroups.

Hopefully, this book has succeeded in establishing that paternalism within social work takes many shapes and ordinarily surfaces without the full awareness of the practitioner(s) responsible for it. Every social work professional, regardless of his or her political perspective or preferred practice modality, is at risk of unwitting participation in the tradition of paternalism. Therefore it behooves social workers who remain committed to empowerment practice to be on the constant lookout for paternalistic moments or elements of their own approach to practice and to clients. A short self-inventory follows that may prove helpful, if used periodically and conscientiously, in containing the erosive and omnipresent influence of paternalism.

Toward Empowerment: A Self-Inventory of Paternalism

1. With what degree of concentration do I listen to and consider the explicit and implicit communications of the clients or constituents to whom I am responsible?
2. Do I silently discount the opinions of any client, client group, or constituent? If so, why so? And what can I do to exchange my silence for dialogue with that person or group?
3. When I recommend a particular course of action to a client, do I take ample care and time to elicit from him or her alternative proposals *before* seeking agreement on the nature and sequence of steps to be taken?

4. Has any client given me feedback that I have been remote, intimidating, or inaccessible? If so, what more can I learn from that person about the basis for her or his impression of my unavailability?

5. Do I use acronyms, abbreviations, proper names, or specialized language that are foreign to clients in their presence without defining these terms?

6. When circumstances force me to rush a client or constituent or to keep him or her waiting, in what ways do I make amends?

7. When my professional duty requires me to violate a client's preferences, do I explain my actions and reasoning to that client in as open, direct, and respectful a manner as possible?

8. When I feel protective of a client, do I inspect the situation with special care to make sure that I am not underestimating the client or exaggerating my own importance or capability?

9. When I find myself thinking primarily about the problems that a client faces, do I make a conscious effort in my contemplation to pay closer attention to his or her strengths and imagination?

Interrupting Contempt

Empowerment-oriented social workers of the 1990s and the twenty-first century have a second obligation, as well, in addition to that of fending off the encroachments of paternalism on their everyday manner of practicing. In the United States, the expression of long-standing hatreds of stigmatized groups continues to damage members of those groups as well as to weaken the overall social fabric.

Contempt for the "other" has been culturally encoded, psychologically internalized, and institutionally perpetuated throughout the twentieth century. Scorn for members of minority groups remains robust in America of the 1980s and early 1990s. The bashing of the skulls of people of color and gays, the firing of striking workers, and the vilification of single women on welfare and of inner-city residents are but a few, flagrant examples of the polarization and exclusionism that imperil the social contract and civil peace of the United States.

Social workers are particularly well-positioned to witness and interrupt some of the face-to-face derision and discrimination directed at stigmatized peoples. They, more so than any other professionals except public health nurses, work directly with poor, old, sick, disabled, imprisoned, and homeless people. Consequently, social work practitioners have more opportunity than most Americans to document and disrupt the mean-spirited attitudes, behavior, and policies aimed at their clients and their clients' families and communities.

For a century, social workers in the United States have been refining the interventive tools with which to diminish the incidence of bias and discrimination and neutralize their impact. Social investigation, public testimony, public education, attentive administration, humane policy and program development, organizational innovation, and case and class advocacy are old social work approaches with multiple uses in the present and future. Of equal contemporary import are casework, case management, family social work, group work, and community organization with persons and neighborhoods who live and work on the social and economic margins. Social workers who are invested in client empowerment already have the necessary technical repertoire with which to battle the resurgence and effects of present-day hate. We need only mobilize the will and resources with which to do so.

Social Workers' Self-Empowerment

A third obligation also confronts contemporary practitioners who intend to contribute to client self-empowerment in the twenty-first century. Caught in the pincers of shrinking funding for social services and swelling client desperation, social workers need to summon their individual and collective strengths to stop the erosion of their working conditions and of their discretionary authority. Escalating caseloads and mounting paperwork, together with insufficient in-service training and supervisory supports, steadily disempower American social workers of the late twentieth century. Meanwhile, substandard salaries, benefits, office technology, and physical plants combine with scarce support services to diminish the quality of professional life and morale. As a consequence, the quality of professional programs and service suffers at the very time that spiraling social dislocation intensifies client demand.

The deterioration of the conditions under which social workers deliver services endangers directly their capacity to assist client empowerment. Overwork and underpay demoralize professionals, no matter how inspired and well trained they are. Common sense suggests that workers who face daily insensitivity, disregard, disrespect, and paternalism from their organizational superiors will displace some of their frustration, helplessness, and rage onto their clients, especially in times in which the larger public holds disdain for anyone connected to stigmatized groups, whether service recipient, service deliverer, neighbor, or one who mandates, administers, or funds such services. Disempowered workers are unable to sustain for long imaginative and empathic work on behalf of client empowerment. Their own degraded situation depletes their supplies of hope, energy, trust, and vision.

To halt and reverse social workers' disempowerment is a complex project, involving multiple avenues of activity that vary according to job level, organizational context, and field of social work practice. The complexity and variety of available strategies, tactics, and contexts mitigate against formulaic proposals for empowerment. Nonetheless, a review of some approaches to worker empowerment that have been successful in earlier periods of social work and other realms of work may prove useful to contemporary social workers in diverse settings and jobs.

Employee support groups are one measure whose selective utility has been demonstrated previously. Identifying the calculus of opportunities and constraints at work with a peer group of fellow workers is an important first step in assessing the degree to which one is losing, retaining, or gaining control over the conceptualization and enactment of one's responsibilities. A support group pools multiple views of the same work place and yields many more observations, reflections, and suggestions concerning worker empowerment and service delivery than one person alone can generate. Additionally, of course, peer groups offer solace, humor, mutual aid, and temporary relief from isolation and work-related stress.

Another approach to worker empowerment relevant to social work is job redesign. If a social worker's job becomes routinized, one-dimensional, or overtaxed with bureaucratic demands to the extent that he or she loses a sense of professional engagement, client importance, or organizational mission, then the reconfiguration of that position may well be in order. A greater variety of assignments, a larger role in program design and evaluation, intensified supervisory input, and increased opportunity to circulate as a responsible agent in the work place and community would, perhaps, help reverse his or her slide into apathy or alienation. If those measures fail to give the worker greater investment in his or her daily work life, a total change in responsibilities or organizational affiliation may be necessary.

A third method yielding enhanced empowerment for social workers is the systematic self-evaluation of the efficacy of social work programs and interventions. Social workers provide on a daily basis many forms of support, education, and succor, the constructive effects of which frequently remain undocumented, unexamined, and unmeasured. Therefore, the impact of social services is too often underestimated or misunderstood by elected and appointed leaders of the voluntary and public sectors who are responsible for reducing the incidence of poverty, sickness, and dependence and for bringing down, at the same time, the costs to America of maintaining its minimalist welfare state.

Social workers' empowerment is, in part, contingent upon recognition by the public and its officials of the contributions being made to the social whole by members of the profession. The most direct way of bringing about that recognition is through the careful documentation of the goals, methods, and effects of one's practice. In a nation preoccupied with cost containment, especially in relation to public expenditures and charitable contributions, social workers have a clear choice. They can yield to others the task of evaluating the efficacy their work or they can do it themselves. To surrender that evaluative function to others is to risk the development of criteria and measures that are premised upon oversimplified, distorted, and reductive analyses of the problems, interventions, impacts, and causal sequences of social work. That fate is already realized in many a program evaluated by people who lack direct experience in assisting clients and communities. The happier alternative, by far, is for social workers to shape evaluative premises, methods, and measures from within, so that those most knowledgeable about helping, mediating, and organizing within human services can determine suitable ways in which to weigh the outcomes and impact of their activities.

Professionals' unions can also be an aid to worker empowerment, particularly in large organizations in which executive-level managers have little face-to-face contact and consultation with line workers and limited opportunity for understanding the day-to-day imperatives encountered by direct service deliverers. If, despite earnest and sustained efforts to take part, professional employees find themselves repeatedly "out of the loop" of organizational decision making about the design, delivery, and evaluation of social service programs in which they work, they may need to organize a collective bargaining unit to assert their claim for a central and ongoing voice in such deliberations. Evidence of management's studied indifference to difficult working conditions, danger on the job, or inadequate pay and benefits may also signal the need for an employees' union. Such a group would be wise to concoct its expectations, customs, procedural rules, contract language, and bargaining approaches in a manner that resonates with the cultures of the specific organization and field of practice in which the union is being formed rather than to borrow indiscriminately from "factory-model" trade unionism.

Social Workers as Witnesses

Finally, the empowerment of social workers is ultimately contingent upon the larger society's willingness to acknowledge the membership, worth, and claims of those Americans who are most vulnerable and desperate. If, in the twenty-first century, the American pale is generally understood to exclude the most poor, sick, and wretched among us, then social workers should resign themselves to many more decades of scant resources, stigmatized programs and clientele, and disempowering terms of work. If, however, the majority of the American people can be persuaded that inclusive social policies and generosity of spirit serve the country's short- and long-term interests, strengthen its identity, and reinforce its heritage as a "strong democracy," then a totally different, more promising scenario is imaginable (Barber 1984).

No group of American workers are better positioned than contemporary social workers to bring forth fresh and persuasive documentation concerning the convergent interests shared by disempowered people and the larger public. By bearing witness in organizational and social reform campaigns and in research studies to the depth, breadth, and nature of social problems experienced by their clients, social workers can reinvoke a familiar posture and responsibility shouldered by many empowerment-directed social workers of past eras.

Present-day social workers have unrivaled opportunities to use their organizational influence as members of agency staffs to aid individuals, families, and small groups with whom they have direct contact. Similarly, they can use their professional organizations and employing agencies as bully pulpits from which to testify, advocate, and report about disempowered client groups' specific needs for resources and institutional responsiveness. Furthermore, social workers can use their talents and energies on both "company" time and their own time as "citizen-social workers" involved in social movements and community improvement activities (Weiner 1971).

It is sobering to realize that much more than the empowerment of clients and social workers is at risk in the debate over how widely to cast the net of social and economic membership in this society. The integrity and cohesion of the nation depend upon the magnanimous resolution of that issue.

References

Archival Sources

Archives, Boston School of Social Work, Columbia University Libraries.

Archives, Bryn Mawr College School of Social Work and Social Research, Bryn Mawr College Library.

Archives, New York School of Social Work, Columbia University Libraries.

Archives, Pennsylvania School of Social Work, University of Pennsylvania Library.

Mary Richmond Papers, Columbia University Libraries.

National Federation of Settlements, Lillian Wald Papers, Columbia University Libraries.

Russell Sage Foundation, Mary Richmond Papers, Columbia University Libraries.

Abbott, Andrew. 1988. *The System of Professions: An Essay on the Division of Expert Labor*. Chicago: University of Chicago Press.

Abbott, Edith. 1942. *Social Welfare and Professional Education*. Rev. ed. Chicago: University of Chicago Press.

—— 1943. *Twenty-One Years of University Education for Social Service, 1920–1941*. Chicago: University of Chicago Press.

Abbott, Grace. 1931. "The Children's Bureau . . . What It Is and How It Works." *Medical Women's Journal*, 38:55–59.

Abramovitz, Miriam. 1988. *Regulating the Lives of Women*. Boston: South End.

Abramson, Marcia. 1985. "The Autonomy-Paternalism Dilemma in Social Work Practice." *Social Casework: The Journal of Contemporary Social Work*, 66(7):387–93.

Adam, Barry D. 1987. *The Rise of a Gay and Lesbian Movement.* Boston: Twayne.

Addams, Jane. 1902. *Democracy and Social Ethics.* New York: Macmillan.

—— 1910. *Twenty Years at Hull-House.* New York: Macmillan.

—— 1930. *Second Twenty Years at Hull-House.* New York: Macmillan.

Albanese, Catherine L. 1988. *The Spirituality of the American Transcendentalists.* Macon, Ga.: Mercer University Press.

Alinsky, Saul. 1946. *Reveille for Radicals.* Chicago: University of Chicago Press.

—— 1971. *Rules for Radicals.* New York: Random House.

Allen, Frederick H. 1935. "The Influence of Psychiatry on Social Work." *Proceedings of the National Conference of Social Work.* Repr. 1939 in Fern Lowry, ed., *Readings in Social Case Work, 1920–1938,* pp. 694–709. New York: Columbia University Press.

Allen-Meares, Paula, Robert Washington, and Betty Welsh. 1986. *Social Work Services in Schools.* Englewood Cliffs, N.J.: Prentice-Hall.

American Association of Social Workers. 1930. "The Responsibility and Contribution of Social Workers in Unemployment Crises." *Compass,* December 1930.

Austin, David M. 1985. "Historical Perspectives on Contemporary Social Work." *The Urban and Social Change Review,* 18(2):16–18.

—— 1988. "Women's Career Choices and Human Service Organizations." *Social Work,* 33:551–52.

Austin, Michael J. and Neil Betten. 1977. "Intellectual Origins of Community Organizing, 1920–1939." *Social Service Review,* 51(1):155–70.

Axinn, June and Herman Levin. 1982. *Social Welfare: A History of the American Response to Need,* 2d ed. New York: Harper and Row.

Baines, Carol, Patricia Evans, and Sheila Neysmith, eds. 1991. *Women's Caring: Feminist Perspectives on Social Welfare.* Toronto: McClelland and Stewart.

Bakan, David. 1966. *The Duality of Human Existence: Isolation and Communion in Western Man.* Boston: Beacon.

Barbalet, J. M. 1988. *Citizenship: Rights, Struggle, and Class Inequality.* Bristol, Pa.: Open University Press.

—— 1989. *Citizenship: Rights, Struggle, and Class Inequality.* Minneapolis: University of Minnesota Press.

Barber, Benjamin. 1984. *Strong Democracy: Participatory Politics for a New Age.* Berkeley: University of California Press.

Barnes, Hazel. 1962. *Humanistic Existentialism.* Lincoln: University of Nebraska Press.

—— 1978. *Existentialist Ethics.* New York: Knopf.

Barrett, Michele. 1991. *The Politics of Truth: From Marx to Foucault.* Stanford: Stanford University Press.

Barry, Kathleen. 1988. *Susan B. Anthony: A Biography.* New York: New York University Press.

Bartlett, Harriett M. 1934. "Problems and Trends in Medical Social Case Work." *Family,* December 1934. Repr. 1939 in Fern Lowry, ed., *Readings in Social Case Work, 1920–1938,* pp. 462–73. New York: Columbia University Press.

Bayer, R. 1981. *Homosexuality and American Psychiatry: The Politics of Diagnosis.* New York: Basic.

Beauvoir, Simone de. 1953. *The Second Sex*. New York: Knopf.

Beck, Bertram. 1983. *Empowerment: A Future Goal of Social Work*. New York: Community Service Society Working Papers in Social Policy.

Bellah, Robert N., Richard Madsen, William M. Sullivan, Ann Swidler, and Steven M. Tipton. 1991. *The Good Society*. New York: Knopf.

Benson, Susan Porter. 1986. *Counter Cultures: Saleswomen, Managers, and Customers in American Department Stores, 1890–1940*. Urbana: University of Illinois Press.

Berman, Larry, ed. 1990. *Looking Back at the Reagan Presidency*. Baltimore: Johns Hopkins University Press.

Bettelheim, Bruno. 1979. *Surviving and Other Essays*. New York: Knopf.

—— 1990. *Freud's Vienna and Other Essays*. New York: Knopf.

Blechman, E. A. 1980. "Ecological Sources of Dysfunction in Women: Issues and Implications for Clinical Behavior Therapy." *Clinical Behavior Therapy Review*, 2:1–18.

Boswell, John. 1988. *The Kindness of Strangers: The Abandonment of Children in Western Europe from Late Antiquity to the Renaissance*. New York: Pantheon.

Boyte, Harry. 1984. *Community is Possible: Repairing America's Roots*. New York: Harper and Row.

Boyte, Harry and Frank Riessman, eds., 1986. *The New Populism: The Politics of Empowerment*. Philadelphia: Temple University Press.

Brager, George. 1968. "Advocacy and Political Behavior." *Social Work*, 13(2):5–15.

Brager, George and Francis Purcell, eds. 1967. *Community Action Against Poverty: Readings from the Mobilization Experience*. New Haven: College and University Press.

Brager, George and Harry Specht. 1973. *Community Organizing*. New York: Columbia University Press.

Braverman, Harry. 1976. *Labor and Monopoly Capital: The Degradation of Work in the Twentieth Century*. New York: Monthly Review.

Breckinridge, Sophonisba. 1921. *New Homes for Old*. New York: Harper.

Breines, Wini. 1982. *Community and Organization in the New Left: 1962–1968—the Great Refusal*. New York: Praeger.

Bricker-Jenkins, Mary and Nancy R. Hooyman. 1986. "A Feminist World View: Ideological Themes from the Feminist Movement." In Mary Bricker-Jenkins and Nancy R. Hooyman, eds., *Not for Women Only: Social Work Practice in a Feminist Future*. Silver Spring, Md.: National Association of Social Workers.

—— 1991. *Feminist Social Work Practice in Clinical Settings*. Newbury Park, Cal.: Sage.

Brieland, Donald. 1990. "The Hull-House Tradition and the Contemporary Social Worker: Was Jane Addams Really a Social Worker?" *Social Work*, 35(2):134–38.

Brooks, Nancy. 1991. "Self-Empowerment Among Adults with Severe Physical Disabilities: A Case Study." *Journal of Sociology and Social Welfare*, 13(1):105–20.

Bryan, Mary Lynn McCree and Allen F. Davis, eds. 1990. *100 Years at Hull-House*. Bloomington: Indiana University Press.

Bucher, Rue and Anselm Strauss. 1961. "Professions in Process." *The American Journal of Sociology*, 66(4):325–34.

Bullert, Gary. 1983. *The Politics of John Dewey*. Buffalo, N.Y.: Prometheus.

Cahm, Caroline. 1989. *Kropotkin and the Rise of Revolutionary Anarchism, 1872–1886*. New York: Cambridge University Press.

Campbell, T. D. 1978. "Discretionary Rights." In Noel Timms and David Watson, eds., *Philosophy in Social Work*, pp. 50–77. London: Routledge and Kegan Paul.

Camus, Albert. 1942a. *The Myth of Sisyphus (Le Mythe de Sisyphe)*. Paris: Gallimard.

—— 1942b. *The Stranger (L'Etranger)*. Paris: Gallimard.

Cannon, Ida M. 1952. *On the Social Frontier of Medicine: Pioneering in Medical Social Service*. Cambridge: Harvard University Press.

Cantor, Milton. 1978. *The Divided Left: American Radicalism, 1900–1975*. New York: Hill and Wang.

Carr, Charlotte E. 1930. "The Family Case Worker's Contribution Toward Higher Industrial Standards." *Family*, November 1930. Repr. 1939 in Fern Lowry, ed., *Readings in Social Case Work, 1920–1938*, pp. 731–35. New York: Columbia University Press.

Carruth, Gorton et al., eds. 1979. *The Encyclopedia of American Facts and Dates*. 7th ed. New York: Crowell.

Chambers, Clarke A. 1963. *Seedtime of Reform: American Social Service and Social Action, 1918–1933*. Minneapolis: University of Minnesota Press.

—— 1971. *Paul U. Kellogg and the Survey*. Minneapolis: University of Minnesota Press.

—— 1986. "Women in the Creation of the Profession of Social Work." *Social Service Review*, 60(1):1–33.

Chodorow, Nancy. 1991. *Feminism and Psychoanalysis*. New Haven: Yale University Press.

Cohen, Marcia B. 1989. "Social Work Practice with Homeless Mentally Ill People: Engaging the Client." *Social Work*, 34(6):505–9.

Cohen, Miriam and Michael Hanagan. 1991. "The Politics of Gender and the Making of the Welfare State, 1900–1940: A Comparative Perspective." *Journal of Social History*, 24(3):469–84.

Combs-Orme, Terri. 1988. "Infant Mortality and Social Work: Legacy of Success." *Social Service Review*, 62(1):83–102.

Cook, Blanche Wiesen. 1992. *Eleanor Roosevelt: 1884–1933*. Vol. 1. New York: Viking.

Cort, John C. 1988. *Christian Socialism: An Informal History*. Maryknoll, N.Y.: Orbis.

Cortes, Ernesto. 1984. "Empowerment." In Harry Boyte, ed., *Community is Possible: Repairing America's Roots*, pp. 125–59. New York: Harper and Row.

Costin, Lela B. 1983a. "Edith Abbott and the Chicago Influence on Social Work Education." *Social Service Review*, 57(1):94–111.

—— 1983b. *Two Sisters for Social Justice: A Biography of Grace and Edith Abbott*. Urbana: University of Illinois Press.

Coverman, Shelley. 1983. "Gender, Domestic Labor Time, and Wage Inequality." *American Sociological Review*, 48:623–36.

Coyle, Grace L. 1935. "Group Work and Social Change." *Proceedings of the National Conference of Social Work*, 62:393–405. Boston: National Conference of Social Work.

—— 1937a. "Case Work and Group Work." *Survey*, April 1937. Repr. 1939 in *Readings in Social Case Work, 1920–1938*, pp. 558–64. New York: Columbia University Press.

—— 1937b. "Social Workers and Social Action." *Survey*, May 1937. Repr. 1939 in Fern Lowry, ed., *Readings in Social Case Work, 1920–1938*, pp. 565–68. New York: Columbia University Press.

—— 1947. *Group Experience and Democratic Values*. New York: YWCA.

Cruz, Feodor F. 1987. *John Dewey's Theory of Community*. New York: Peter Lang.

Davis, Allen. 1967. *Spearheads for Reform: The Social Settlements and the Progressive Movement, 1890–1914*. New York: Oxford University Press.

De Schweinitz, Dorothea. 1935. "Social Legislation and the Family Case Worker." *Family*, January 1935. Repr. 1939 in Fern Lowry, ed., *Readings in Social Case Work, 1920–1938*, pp. 635–43. New York: Columbia University Press.

Dewey, John. 1935. *Liberalism and Social Action*. New York: Putnam's.

Dinerman, Miriam. 1986. "The Woman Trap: Women and Poverty." In Nan Van Den Bergh and Lynn Cooper, eds., *Feminist Visions for Social Work*, pp. 229–49. Silver Spring, Md.: National Association of Social Workers.

Dodd, Pamela and Lorraine Gutierrez. 1990. "Preparing Students for the Future: A Power Perspective on Community Practice." *Administration in Social Work*, 14(2):63–78.

Donovan, Josephine. 1990. *Feminist Theory: The Intellectual Traditions of American Feminism*. New York: Continuum.

Dore, Martha M. 1990. "Functional Theory: Its History and Influence on Contemporary Social Work Practice." *Social Service Review*, 64(3):358–74.

Driedger, Diane. 1989. *The Last Civil Rights Movement*. New York: St. Martin's.

Du Bois, W. E. B. 1903. *The Souls of Black Folks: Essays and Sketches*. Chicago: A. C. McClurg.

Dunham, Arthur. 1948. *The Job of the Community Organization Worker*. New York: Association for the Study of Community Organization and Community Chests and Councils of America.

—— 1958. *Community Welfare Organization: Principles and Practice*. New York: Crowell.

Dunham, Arthur and Ernest B. Harper. 1959. *Community Organization in Action*. New York: Association.

Edsall, Thomas and Mary Edsall. 1991. *Chain Reaction: The Impact of Race, Rights, and Taxes on American Politics*. New York: Norton.

Edwards, Richard C. 1980. *Contested Terrain: The Transformation of the Workplace in America*. New York: Basic.

Ehrenreich, John. 1985. *The Altruistic Imagination: A History of Social Work and Social Policy in the United States*. Ithaca: Cornell University Press.

Emerson, Ralph Waldo. 1971. *The Collected Works of Ralph Waldo Emerson*. Vol. 1. Ed. Joseph Slater et. al. Cambridge: Harvard University Press.

Erikson, Erik. 1950. *Childhood and Society*. New York: Norton.

—— 1956. "Identity and the Life-Cycle." *Journal of the American Psychoanalytic Association*, 4:56–121.

Erikson, Kai. 1976. *Everything in Its Path*. New York: Simon and Schuster.

Evans, Sara. 1979. *Personal Politics*. New York: Knopf.

Ewen, Stuart. 1976. *Captains of Consciousness: Advertising and the Social Roots of the Consumer Culture*. New York: McGraw-Hill.

Falck, Hans. 1988. *Social Work: The Membership Perspective*. New York: Springer.

Fanon, Frantz. 1967. *Black Skin, White Masks*. New York: Grove.

—— 1968. *The Wretched of the Earth*. New York: Grove.

Fanshel, David. 1976. "Status Differentials: Men and Women in Social Work." *Social Work*, 21:448–54.

Ferree, Myra and Beth Hess. 1985. *Controversy and Coalition: The New Feminist Movement*. Boston: Twayne.

Fisher, Jacob. 1936. *The Rank and File Movement in Social Work, 1931–1936*. New York: New York School of Social Work.

—— 1980. *The Response of Social Work to the Depression*. Cambridge, Mass.: Schenkman.

Flexner, Abraham. 1915. "Is Social Work a Profession?" *Proceedings of the National Conference of Charities and Correction*, 42:576–90. Chicago: National Conference of Charities and Correction.

Follett, Mary Parker. 1918. *The New State*. New York: Longmans, Green.

—— 1924. *Creative Experience*. New York: Longmans, Green.

—— 1927. "Leader and Expert." Paper presented in April 1927 to the Bureau of Personnel Administration. Repr. 1941 in Henry Metcalf and L. Urwick, eds., *Dynamic Administration*, pp. 247–69. New York: Harper.

—— 1928. "Some Discrepancies in Leadership Theory and Practice." Paper presented on March 8, 1928, to the Bureau of Personnel Administration. Repr. 1941 in Henry Metcalf and L. Urwick, eds., *Dynamic Administration*, pp. 270–94. New York: Harper.

Foner, Eric. 1989. *Reconstruction: America's Unfinished Revolution, 1863–1877*. New York: Harper-Row.

Foner, Philip S. 1947. *History of the Labor Movement in the United States*. Vol. 1. New York: International.

Fortune, A. and L. Hanks. 1988. "Gender Inequities in Early Social Work Careers." *Social Work*, 33:221–25.

Frankfort, Roberta. 1977. *Collegiate Women: Domesticity and Career in Turn-of-the-Century America*. New York: New York University Press.

Frankl, Viktor. 1984. *Man's Search for Meaning*. New York: Simon and Schuster.

Franklin, Donna. 1990. "The Cycles of Social Work Practice: Social Action vs. Individual Interest." *Journal of Progressive Human Services*, 1(2):59–80.

Freedberg, Sharon. 1989. "Self-Determination: Historical Perspectives and Effects on Current Practice." *Social Work*, 34(1):33–38.

Freeman, Jo. 1975. *Politics of Women's Liberation*. New York: Longman.

Freire, Paulo. 1970. *Pedagogy of the Oppressed*. New York: Continuum.

—— 1986. *Pedagogy of the Oppressed*. New York: Continuum.

—— 1990. "A Critical Understanding of Social Work." *Journal of Progressive Human Services*, 1(1):3–9.

Frothingham, Octavius. 1972. *Transcendentalism in New England: A History.* Philadelphia: University of Pennsylvania Press.

Gandhi, Mahatma. 1932. *Hind Swaraj.* 6th ed. Madras: G. A. Natesan.

—— 1958. *The Collected Works of Mahatma Gandhi.* New Delhi: Publications Division of the Ministry of Information and Broadcasting, Government of India.

Gans, Herbert J. 1982. *The Urban Villagers.* Rev. ed. New York: Free Press.

Garrison, Dee. 1975. *Apostles of Culture: The Public Librarian and American Society, 1876–1920.* New York: Macmillan.

Garrow, David. 1986. *Bearing the Cross: Martin Luther King, Jr., and the Southern Christian Leadership Council.* New York: William Morrow.

Garrow, David, ed. 1989. *We Shall Overcome: The Civil Rights Movement in the United States in the 1950s and 1960s.* Brooklyn, N.Y.: Carlson.

Gartner, Alan and Frank Riessman. 1977. *Self-Help in the Human Services.* San Francisco: Jossey-Bass.

Gartner, Alan and Frank Riessman, eds. 1984. *The Self-Help Revolution.* New York: Human Sciences.

Garvin, Charles D. and Fred M. Cox. 1987. "A History of Community Organizing Since the Civil War with Special Reference to Oppressed Communities." In Fred M. Cox, Jack Rothman, and John Tropman, eds., *Strategies of Community Organization,* 4th ed., pp. 26–63. Itasca, Ill.: Peacock.

Geertz, Clifford. 1983. *Local Knowledge.* New York: Basic.

Gelb, Joyce. 1987. *Women and Public Policies.* Princeton: Princeton University Press.

Germain, Carel B. 1970. "Casework and Science: A Historical Encounter." In Robert W. Roberts and Robert H. Nee, eds., *Theories of Social Casework,* pp. 3–32. Chicago: University of Chicago Press.

—— 1985. "The Place of Community Work Within an Ecological Approach to Social Work Practice." In Samuel Taylor and Robert Roberts, eds., *Theory and Practice of Community Social Work,* pp. 30–55. New York: Columbia University Press.

—— 1990. "Life Forces and the Anatomy of Practice." *Smith College Studies for Social Work,* 60(2):138–52.

Germain, Carel, ed. 1979. *Social Work Practice: People and Environments.* New York: Columbia University Press.

Germain, Carel B. and Alex Gitterman. 1980. *The Life Model of Social Work Practice.* New York: Columbia University Press.

—— 1987. "Ecological Perspective." In Anne Minahan, ed., *The Encyclopedia of Social Work,* 18th ed., pp. 488–99. Silver Spring, Md.: National Association of Social Workers.

Germain, Carel B. and Ann Hartman. 1980. "People and Ideas in the History of Social Work Practice." *Social Casework,* 61(6):323–31.

Getzel, George and Rosemary Masters. 1985. "Social Work Practice with Families of Homicide Victims." In Carel B. Germain, ed. *Advances in Clinical Social Work Practice,* pp. 7–16. Silver Spring, Md.: National Association of Social Workers.

Giddens, Anthony. 1982. *Profiles and Critiques in Social Theory.* Berkeley: University of California Press.

Gilbert, Neil and Harry Specht. 1987. "Social Planning and Community Organization." In Anne Minahan, ed., *The Encyclopedia of Social Work*, 2 vols., 18th ed., 2:602–19. Silver Spring, Md.: National Association of Social Workers.

Gilligan, Carol. 1990. *Mapping the Moral Domain*. Cambridge: Harvard University Press.

Gitterman, Alex. 1989. "Building Mutual Support in Groups." *Social Work with Groups*, 12(2):5–21.

—— 1992. Personal correspondence.

Gitterman, Alex, ed. 1991. *Handbook of Social Work Practice with Vulnerable Populations*. New York: Columbia University Press.

Gitterman, Alex and Carel B. Germain. 1981. "Education for Practice: Teaching about the Environment." *Journal of Education for Social Work*, 17(3):4–51.

Gitterman, Alex and Lawrence Shulman, eds.. 1986. *The Mutual Aid Group and the Life Cycle*. Itasca, Ill.: Peacock.

Goffman, Erving. 1963. *Stigma: Notes on the Management of Spoiled Identity*. Englewood Cliffs, N.J.: Prentice-Hall.

Goldberg, Gale and Ruth Middleman. 1974. *Social Service Delivery: A Structural Approach to Social Work Practice*. New York: Columbia University Press.

Goldmark, Josephine. 1953. *Impatient Crusader: Florence Kelley's Life Story*. Urbana: University of Illinois Press.

Goldstein, Howard. 1973. *Social Work Practice: A Unitary Approach*. Columbia: University of South Carolina Press.

—— 1990. "Strength or Pathology: Ethical and Rhetorical Contrasts in Approaches to Practice." *Families in Society*, 71(5):267–75.

Goodwyn, Lawrence. 1978. *The Populist Moment*. New York: Oxford University Press.

—— 1986. "Populism and Powerlessness." In Harry Boyte and Frank Riessman, eds., *The New Populism: The Politics of Empowerment*, pp. 19–29. Philadelphia: Temple University Press.

Googins, Bradley with Dianne Burden. 1987. "Balancing Job and Homelife Study: Managing Work and Stress in Corporations." School of Social Work, Boston University, unpublished manuscript.

Gordon, Linda. 1988a. "The Frustrations of Family Violence Social Work: An Historical Critique." *Journal of Sociology and Social Welfare*, 15(4):139–60.

—— 1988b. *Heroes of Their Own Lives: The Politics of Family Violence, Boston 1880–1960*. New York: Viking Penguin.

—— 1992. "Social Insurance and Public Assistance: The Influence of Gender in Welfare Thought in the United States, 1890–1935." *The American Historical Review*, 97(6):19–54.

Gould, Ketayun. 1987. "Life Model Versus Conflict Model: A Feminist Perspective." *Social Work*, 32(4):346–51.

Gramsci, Antonio. 1990. *Selections from Political Writings, 1921–1926*. Ed. and trans. Quintin Hoare Minnesota: University of Minnesota Press.

Gran, Guy. 1983. *Development by People: Citizen Construction of a Just World*. New York: Praeger.

Gray, Sylvia S., Ann Hartman, and Ellen S. Saalberg, eds. 1985. *Empowering the Black Family: A Roundtable Discussion*. Ann Arbor: National Child Welfare Training Center.

Grosser, Charles. 1965. "Community Development Programs Serving the Urban Poor." *Social Work*, 10(3):15–21.

—— 1973. *New Directions in Community Organization: From Enabling to Advocacy*. New York: Praeger.

Grosser, Charles and Jacqueline Mondros. 1985. "Pluralism and Participation: The Political Action Approach." In Samuel Taylor and Robert Roberts, eds., *Theory and Practice of Community Social Work*, pp. 154–78. New York: Columbia University Press.

Gutierrez, Gustavo. 1973. *A Theology of Liberation: History, Politics, and Salvation*. Maryknoll, N.Y.: Orbis.

Gutierrez, Lorraine M. 1990. "Working With Women of Color: An Empowerment Perspective." *Social Work*, 35(2):97–192.

Hall, Helen. 1931. *Case Studies in Unemployment*. Philadelphia: University of Pennsylvania Press.

Hamilton, Cynthia. 1989. "Work and Welfare: How Industrialists Shaped Government Social Services During the Progressive Era. *Journal of Sociology and Social Welfare*, 16(2):67–86.

Hamilton, Gordon. 1931. "Refocusing Family Case Work." *Proceedings of the National Conference of Social Work*. New York: Columbia University Press. Repr. 1939 in Fern Lowry, ed., *Readings in Social Case Work, 1920–1938*, pp. 81–98. New York: Columbia University Press.

—— 1937. "Basic Concepts in Social Case Work." *The Family*, 18(5):147–56.

—— 1941. "The Underlying Philosophy of Case Work Today." *Proceedings of the National Conference of Social Work*, 68:237–53. Boston: National Conference of Social Work.

Handler, Joel. 1992. "Dependency and Discretion." In Yeheskel Hasenfeld, ed., *Human Services as Complex Organizations*, pp. 276–297. Newbury Park, Cal.: Sage.

Handy, Robert T., ed., 1966. *The Social Gospel in America, 1870–1920*. New York: Oxford University Press.

Hanmer, Jalna and Daphne Statham. 1989. *Women and Social Work: Toward a Woman-Centered Practice*. Chicago: Lyceum.

Hareven, Tamara. 1982. *Family Time and Industrial Time: The Relationship Between the Family and Work in a New England Industrial Community*. New York: Cambridge University Press.

Harrington, Michael. 1962. *The Other America*. New York: Macmillan.

Hartman, Ann. 1986. "The Life and Work of Bertha Reynolds: Implications for Education and Practice Today." *Smith College Studies in Social Work*, 56(2):79–94.

—— 1989. "Still Between Client and Community." *Social Work*, 34(5):387–88.

Hartman, Ann and Joan Laird. 1983. *Family-Centered Social Work Practice*. New York: Free Press.

—— 1987. "Family Practice." In Anne Minahan, ed., *The Encyclopedia of Social Work*, 2 vols. 18th ed., 1:575–89. Silver Spring, Md.: National Association of Social Workers.

Hartmann, Heinz. 1958. *Ego Psychology and the Problem of Adaptation*. New York: International Universities Press.

—— 1964. *Essays on Ego Psychology: Selected Problems in Psychoanalytic Theory.* New York: International Universities Press.

Hasenfeld, Yeheskel. 1987. "Power in Social Work Practice." *Social Service Review,* 61(3):469–83.

Hawkesworth, M. E. 1990. *Beyond Oppression: Feminist Theory and Political Strategy.* New York: Continuum.

Hegar, Rebecca. 1989. "Empowerment-based Practice with Children." *Social Service Review,* 63(3):372–83.

Hegar, Rebecca L. and Jeanne M. Hunzeker. 1988. "Moving Toward Empowerment-Based Practice in Public Child Welfare." *Social Work,* 33(6):499–502.

Heidegger, Martin. 1927. *Being and Time (Sein und Zeit).* Halle: M. Niemeyer.

Higham, John. 1988. *Strangers in the Land: Patterns of American Nativism, 1860–1925.* New Brunswick, N.J.: Rutgers University Press.

Hirayama, H. and K. Hirayama. 1985. "Empowerment Through Group Participation: Process and Goal." In M. Parenes, ed., *Innovations in Social Group Work: Feedback from Practice to Theory,* pp. 119–31. New York: Haworth.

Hobsbawm, E. J. 1962. *The Age of Revolution.* New York: New American Library.

Hochschild, Arlie R. 1989. *The Second Shift: Working Parents and the Revolution at Home.* New York: Viking Penguin.

Hoffman, Lily. 1989. *The Politics of Knowledge: Activist Movements in Medicine and Planning.* Albany, N.Y.: State University of New York Press.

Hopkins, Charles Howard. 1940. *The Rise of the Social Gospel in American Protestantism, 1865–1915.* New Haven: Yale University Press.

Horton, Aimee Isgrig. 1989. *The Highlander Folk School: A History of its Major Programs, 1932–1961.* Brooklyn, N.Y.: Carlson.

Hudson, Annie. 1985. "Feminism and Social Work: Resistance or Dialogue?" *British Journal of Social Work,* 15:635–55.

Ivanoff, André. 1991. Personal correspondence.

Ivanoff, André, Nancy Smyth, and Betty Blythe. 1992. "Empowering Women Effectively: Designing Empirically Based Models for Change." Presentation at the Annual Program Meeting of the Council on Social Work Education, Kansas City, Missouri.

Jacoby, Mario. 1990. *Individuation and Narcissism: The Psychology of the Self in Jung and Kohut.* New York: Routledge, Chapman and Hall.

Jefferson, Thomas. 1944. *Basic Writings of Thomas Jefferson.* Ed. Philip Foner. New York: Wiley.

Jenkins, Shirley. 1987. "Immigrants and Undocumented Aliens." In Anne Minahan, ed., *The Encyclopedia of Social Work,* 2 vols., 18th ed., 1:872–80. Silver Spring, Md.: National Association of Social Workers.

Jesudasan, Ignatius. 1984. *A Gandhian Theology of Liberation.* Maryknoll, N.Y.: Orbis.

Jimenez, Mary Ann. 1990. "Historical Evolution and Future Challenges of the Human Service Professions." *Families in Society,* 71(1):3–12.

Jones, Gareth S. 1984. *Outcast London: A Study in the Relationship Between Classes in Victorian Society.* New York: Penguin.

Jones, Jacqueline. 1992. *The Dispossessed: America's Underclasses from the Civil War to the Present.* New York: Basic.

Kafka, Franz. 1925. *The Trial (Der Prozess)*. Munich: Kurt Wolff.
—— 1926. *The Castle (Das Schloss)*. Munich: Kurt Wolff.
Kanter, Rosabeth. 1977. "Some Effects of Proportions on Group Life: Skewed Sex Ratios and Responses to Token Women." *American Journal of Sociology*, 82(5):964–90.
Karger, Howard Jacob. 1987. "Minneapolis Settlement Houses in the 'Not so Roaring 20s': Americanization, Morality, and the Revolt Against Popular Culture." *Journal of Sociology and Social Welfare*, 14(2):89–110.
Katz, Michael B. 1986. *In the Shadow of the Poorhouse: A Social History of Welfare in America*. New York: Basic.
—— 1990. "The History of an Impudent Poor Woman in New York City from 1918 to 1923." In Peter Mandler, ed., *The Uses of Charity: The Poor on Relief in the Nineteenth-Century Metropolis*, pp. 227–46. Philadelphia: University of Pennsylvania Press.
Katz, Michael, ed. 1993. *The Underclass Debate*. Princeton: Princeton University Press.
Katz, A. and E. Bender, 1976. *The Strength in Us: Self-Help Groups in the Modern World*. New York: Franklin-Watts.
Katzenstein, Mary and Carol McClurg Mueller. 1987. *The Women's Movements of the United States and Western Europe*. Philadelphia: Temple University Press.
Kellogg, Paul., ed. 1909. *Women and the Trades, Pittsburgh, 1907–1908*. New York: Charities Publication Committee, Russell Sage.
Kessler-Harris, Alice. 1982. *Out to Work*. New York: Oxford University Press.
Kieffer, Charles H. 1984. "Citizen Empowerment: A Developmental Perspective." *Prevention in Human Services*, 3(3):9–36.
Klein, Melanie. 1975. *Envy and Gratitude and Other Works, 1946–1963*. New York: Delacorte Press/Seymour Lawrence.
Kopp, Judy. 1989. "Self-Observation: An Empowerment Strategy in Assessment." *Social Casework*, 70(5):276–84.
Koven, Seth and Sonya Michel. 1990. "Womanly Duties: Maternalist Policies and the Origins of Welfare States in France, Germany, Great Britain, and the United States, 1880–1920." *The American Historical Review*, 95(4):1076–1108.
Kozol, J. 1991. *Savage Inequalities*. New York: Crown.
Kropotkin, Peter. 1989. *Mutual Aid: A Factor of Evolution*. New York: Black Rose.
Lappin, Ben. 1985. "Community Development: Beginnings in Social Work Enabling." In Samuel Taylor and Robert Roberts, eds., *Theory and Practice of Community Social Work*, pp. 59–94. New York: Columbia University Press.
Larson, Magali S. 1977. *The Rise of Professionalism: A Sociological Analysis*. Berkeley: University of California Press.
Lee, Judith A. and Carol R. Swenson. 1978. "Theory in Action: A Community Social Service Agency." *Social Casework*, 59(6):359–70.
Lee, Porter R. 1929. "Social Work: Cause and Function." Presidential address, *Proceedings of the National Conference of Social Work*, 56:3–30. Boston: National Conference of Social Work. Repr. 1939 in Fern Lowry, ed., *Readings in Social Case Work, 1920–1938*, pp. 22–37. New York: Columbia University Press.

Leiby, James. 1978. *A History of Social Welfare and Social Work in the United States*. New York: Columbia University Press.

Leighninger, Leslie. 1987. *Social Work, Search for Identity*. New York: Greenwood.

Lemann, Nicholas. 1991. *The Promised Land: The Great Black Migration and How It Changed America*. New York: Knopf.

Lenin, Vladimir. 1935. *Collected Works*. Moscow: V. I. Lenin Institute.

Lenroot, Katharine F. 1935. "Social Work and the Social Order." Presidential address, *Proceedings of the National Conference of Social Work*, 1935. Repr. 1939 in Fern Lowry, ed., *Readings in Social Case Work*, pp. 54–63. New York: Columbia University Press.

Leonard, Elizabeth Lindeman. 1991. *Friendly Rebel: A Personal and Social History of Eduard C. Lindeman*. Adamant, Vt.: Adamant.

Lerner, Steve. 1990. *The Geography of Foster Care: Keeping the Children in the Neighborhood*. Occasional Paper no. 4. New York: Foundation for Child Development.

Levey, Judith S. and Agnes Greenhall, eds. 1983. *The Concise Columbia Encyclopedia*. New York: Columbia University Press.

Levin, Lowell L., Alfred H. Katz, and Erik Holst. 1979. *Self-Care: Lay Initiatives in Health*. 2d ed. New York: Prodist.

Lewin, Kurt. 1951. *Field Theory in Social Science*. Ed. Dorwin Cortwright. New York: Harper.

Lewis, Marcus Garvey. 1988. *Marcus Garvey: Anti-Colonial Champion*. Trenton, N.J.: Africa World.

Lichtenberg, Philip. 1990. *Undoing the Clinch of Oppression*. New York: Peter Lang.

Lifton, Robert J. 1970. *History and Human Survival*. New York: Random House.

Lindeman, Eduard. 1921. *The Community: An Introduction to the Study of Community Leadership and Organization*. New York: Association.

Linn, James. 1935. *Jane Addams*. New York: Appleton-Century.

Lipsky, Michael. 1980. *Street-Level Bureacracy: Dilemmas of the Individual in Public Service*. New York: Russell Sage.

Lovejoy, Arthur O. 1936. *The Great Chain of Being: The History of an Idea*. Cambridge: Harvard University Press.

Lubove, Roy. 1975. *The Professional Altruist: The Emergence of Social Work as a Career, 1880–1930*. New York: Atheneum.

Lurie, Harry, ed. 1965. *The Encyclopedia of Social Work*, 15th ed. New York: National Association of Social Workers.

Lyon, Larry. 1987. *The Community in Urban Society*. Philadelphia: Temple University Press.

McCann, I. Lisa and Laurie Perlman. 1990. *Psychological Trauma and the Adult Survivor*. New York: Brunner-Mazel.

McCord, Elizabeth. 1937. "The Part of the Worker in the Community's Acceptance of Social Work." *Family*, January 1937. Repr. 1939 in Fern Lowry, ed., *Readings in Social Case Work, 1920–1938*, pp. 582–591. New York: Columbia University Press.

McLellan, David, ed. 1983. *Marx: The First Hundred Years*. New York: St. Martin's.

McMillen, Wayne. 1945. *Community Organization for Social Welfare.* Chicago: University of Chicago Press.

Malraux, Andre. 1934. *Man's Fate (La Condition humaine).* New York: H. Smith and R. Haas.

Maluccio, Anthony. 1979a. *Learning from Clients: Interpersonal Helping as Viewed by Clients and Social Workers.* New York: Free Press.

—— 1979b. "Promoting Competence through Life Experiences." In Carel B. Germain, ed., *Social Work Practice: People and Environments,* pp. 280–302. New York: Columbia University Press.

—— 1981. *Promoting Competence in Clients. A New/Old Approach to Social Work Practice.* New York: Free Press.

Mandler, Peter., ed. 1990. *The Use of Charity: The Poor on Relief in the Nineteenth-Century Metropolis.* Philadelphia: University of Pennsylvania Press.

Marable, Manning. 1986. *W. E. B. Du Bois: Black Radical Democrat.* Boston: Twayne.

Marcel, Gabriel. 1927. *Metaphysical Journal (Journal Metaphysique).* Paris: Gallimard.

Marieskind, Helen. 1976. "Women's Self-Help Groups." In A. Katz and E. Bender, eds., *The Strength in Us: Self-Help Groups in the Modern World,* pp. 27–32. New York: Franklin-Watts.

Marshall, T. H. 1950. *Citizenship and Social Class and Other Essays.* Cambridge: Cambridge University Press.

—— 1975. *Social Policy in the Twentieth Century.* 4th ed. London: Hutchinson.

—— 1977. *Class, Citizenship, and Social Development.* Chicago: University of Chicago Press.

—— 1981. *The Right to Welfare and Other Essays.* London: Heinemann Educational.

Martin, M. A. and S. A. Neyowith. 1988. "Creating Community: Groupwork to Develop Social Support Networks with Homeless Mentally Ill." *Social Work with Groups,* 11(4):79–93.

Martin, Patricia Yancey. 1990. "Rethinking Feminist Organizations." *Gender and Society,* 4(3):182–206.

Martin, Patricia Yancey and Roslyn Chernesky. 1989. "Women's Prospects for Leadership in Social Welfare: A Political Economy Perspective." *Administration in Social Work,* 13(3–4):117–43.

Marx, Karl. 1988. *The Economic and Philosophic Manuscripts of 1844 and the Communist Manifesto.* Buffalo: Pometheus.

Mattaini, Mark A. and Stuart Kirk. 1991. "Assessing Assessment in Social Work." *Social Work,* 36(3):260–66.

Melosh, Barbara. 1982. *The Physician's Hand: Work, Culture, and Conflict in American Nursing.* Philadelphia: Temple University Press.

Memmi, Albert. 1967. *The Colonizer and The Colonized.* Boston: Beacon.

Meyer, Carol H. 1970. *Social Work Practice: A Response to the Urban Crisis.* New York: Free Press.

—— 1973. "Purposes and Boundaries—Casework Fifty Years Later." *Social Casework,* 54(5):268–75.

—— 1987. "Direct Practice in Social Work: Overview." In Anne Minahan, ed.,

The Encyclopedia of Social Work, 18th ed., pp. 409–22. Silver Spring, Md.: National Association of Social Workers.

—— 1993. *Assessment in Social Work Practice*. New York: Columbia University Press.

Meyer, Carol H., ed. 1983. *Clinical Social Work in the Eco-systems Perspective*. New York: Columbia University Press.

Middleman, R. and Goldberg, G. 1974. *Social Service Delivery: A Structural Approach to Social Work Practice*. New York: Columbia University Press.

Miller, James. 1987. *"Democracy is in the Streets": From Port Huron to the Siege of Chicago*. New York: Simon and Schuster.

Miller, Jean Baker. 1986. *Toward a New Psychology of Women* 2d ed. Boston: Beacon.

Mills, C. Wright. 1967. *The Sociological Imagination*. New York: Oxford University Press.

Minahan, Anne, ed., 1987. *The Encyclopedia of Social Work*. 2 vols. 18th ed. Silver Spring, Md.: National Association of Social Workers.

Minnich, Elizabeth Kamarck. 1986. "Toward a Feminist Populism." In Harry Boyte and Frank Riessman, eds., *The New Populism: The Politics of Empowerment*, pp. 191–97. Philadelphia: Temple University Press.

Mitchell, Juliet. 1971. *Woman's Estate*. Harmondsworth, Middlesex: Penguin.

Moore, Edward C. 1961. *American Pragmatism: Peirce, James, and Dewey*. New York: Columbia University Press.

Morell, Carolyn. 1987. "Cause Is Function: Toward a Feminist Model of Integration for Social Work." *Social Service Review*, 61(1):144–55.

Morris, Aldon. 1991. "Introduction: Education for Liberation." *Social Policy*, 21(3):2–6.

Morris, Richard B., ed. 1976. *Encyclopedia of American History*. Bicentennial ed. New York: Harper and Row.

Morris, Robert, ed. 1971. *The Encyclopedia of Social Work*. 16th ed. New York: National Association of Social Workers.

Moynihan, Daniel Patrick. 1969. *Maximum Feasible Misunderstanding: Community Action in the War on Poverty*. New York: Free Press.

Muncy, Robyn. 1991. *Creating a Female Dominion in American Reform, 1890–1935*. New York: Oxford University Press.

National Conference of Catholic Bishops. 1986. *Economic Justice for All: Pastoral Letter on Catholic Social Teaching and the U.S. Economy*. Washington, D.C.: U.S. Catholic Conference.

Noddings, Nel. 1984. *Caring: A Feminine Approach to Ethics and Moral Education*. Berkeley: University of California Press.

New York Chapter of the National Association of Social Workers. 1992. *Report of the Task Force on Recruitment and Retention for Agency-Based Practice*. Unpublished report submitted to the board of directors.

O'Neill, William. 1969. *Everyone Was Brave: A History of Feminism in America*. New York: Quadrangle.

Oberschall, Anthony. 1973. *Social Conflict and Social Movements*. Englewood Cliffs, N.J.: Prentice-Hall.

Oliver, Michael. 1990. *The Politics of Disablement*. London: Macmillan.

Orfield, G. 1991. "Cutback Policies, Declining Opportunities, and the Role of Social Service Providers. *The Social Service Review*, 65(4):516–30.

Palmer, John L., Timothy Smeeding, and Barbara Torrey, eds. 1988. *The Vulnerable*. Washington, D.C.: Urban Institute.

Pennell, Joan. 1990. "Knitting Empowering Configurations." In Joan Turner, ed., *Living the Changes*, pp. 188–96. Winnipeg: University of Manitoba Press.

Pernell, R. 1985. "Empowerment and Social Group Work. In M. Parenes, ed., *Innovations in Social Group Work: Feedback from Practice to Theory*, pp. 107–17. New York: Haworth.

Petchesky, Rosalind. 1979. "Dissolving the Hyphen: A Report on Marxist-Feminist Groups 1–5," in Zillah Eisenstein, ed., *Capitalist Patriarchy and the Case for Socialist-Feminism*, pp. 373–89. New York: Monthly Review.

Peterson, Merrill D. 1985. *The Jefferson Image in the American Mind*. 2d ed. New York: Oxford University Press.

Pettit, Walter W. 1925. "Community Organization in Relation to Other Forms of Social Work." *Proceedings of the National Conference of Social Work*, 52:117–37. Boston: National Conference of Social Work. Repr. 1939 in Fern Lowry, ed., *Readings in Social Case Work, 1920–1938*, pp. 576–81. New York: Columbia University Press.

Pincus, A. and Anne Minahan. 1973. *Social Work Practice: Method and Model*. Itasca, Ill.: Peacock.

Pinderhughes, Elaine. 1983. "Empowerment for Our Clients and for Ourselves." *Social Casework*, 64:331–38.

—— 1989. *Understanding Race, Ethnicity, and Power: The Key to Efficacy in Clinical Practice*. New York: Free Press.

Piven, Frances and Richard Cloward. 1982. *The New Class War*. New York: Pantheon.

Pomata, Gianna. 1986. "A Common Heritage: The Historical Memory of Populism in Europe and the United States." In H. Boyte and F. Riessman, eds., *The New Populism: The Politics of Empowerment*, pp. 30–50. Philadelphia: Temple University Press.

Practice, Programming, and Supervision Faculty. 1990. A subdivision of the faculty of the Columbia University School of Social Work.

Pumphrey, Muriel W. 1973. "Lasting and Outmoded Concepts in the Caseworker's Heritage." *Social Casework*, 54(5):259–67.

Radin, Norma. 1989. "School Social Work Practice: Past, Present, and Future Trends." *Social Work in Education*, 11(4):213–25.

Rappaport, Julian. 1981. "In Praise of Paradox: A Social Policy of Empowerment Over Prevention." *A Journal of Community Psychology*, 9(1):1–25.

—— 1987. "Terms of Empowerment/Exemplars of Prevention: Toward a Theory for Community Psychology." *American Journal of Community Psychology*, 15(2):121–45.

Reynolds, Bertha C. 1934. "Between Client and Community." *Smith College Studies in Social Work*, 5:5–128. Repr. 1982. Silver Spring, Md.: National Association of Social Workers.

—— 1935. "Social Case Work: What Is It? What Is Its Place in the World Today?" *Family*, December 1935. Repr. 1939 in Fern Lowry, ed., *Readings in Social Case Work, 1920–1938*, pp. 136–47. New York: Columbia University Press.

—— 1942. *Learning and Teaching in the Practice of Social Work.* New York: Rinehart.

—— 1946. *Re-thinking Social Case Work.* San Diego, Cal.: Social Service Digest.

—— 1951. *Social Work and Social Living.* New York: Citadel. Repr. 1975. Silver Spring, Md.: National Association of Social Workers.

—— 1963. *An Uncharted Journey.* New York: Citadel.

Richmond, Mary. 1917. *Social Diagnosis.* New York: Russell Sage.

—— 1922. *What is Social Case Work?* New York: Russell Sage.

—— 1930. "The Retail Method of Reform." In Joanna C. Colcord and R. Z. S. Mann, eds., *The Long View: Papers and Addresses by Mary Richmond,* pp. 214–21. New York: Russell Sage.

Riessman, Frank. 1986. "The New Populism and the Empowerment Ethos." In Harry Boyte and Frank Riessman, eds., *The New Populism: The Politics of Empowerment,* pp. 53–63. Philadelphia: Temple University Press.

Roberts, Albert R. and Linda Farris Kurtz. 1987. "Historical Perspectives on the Care and Treatment of the Mentally Ill." *Journal of Sociology and Social Welfare,* 14(4):75–94.

Robinson, Virginia. 1930. *A Changing Psychology in Social Case Work.* Philadelphia: University of Pennsylvania Press.

Rodriguez-Trias, Helen. 1992. "Women's Health, Women's Lives, Women's Rights." *American Journal of Public Health,* 82(5):663–64.

Rose, Anne C. 1981. *Transcendentalism as a Social Movement, 1830–1850.* New Haven: Yale University Press.

Rose, Stephen. 1990a. Personal communications at the Annual Program Meeting of the Council on Social Work Education, Reno, Nevada.

—— 1990b. "Advocacy/Empowerment: An Approach to Clinical Practice for Social Work." *Journal of Sociology and Social Welfare,* 17(2):41–51.

Rose, Stephen and Bruce Black. 1985. *Advocacy and Empowerment: Mental Health Care in the Community.* Boston: Routledge and Kegan Paul.

Ross, Dorothy. 1991. *The Origins of American Social Science.* New York: Cambridge University Press.

Ross, Edythe L. 1978. *Black Heritage and Social Welfare, 1860–1930.* Metuchen, N.J.: Scarecrow.

Ross, Murray. 1955. *Community Organization: Theory and Principles.* New York: Harper and Row.

Rothman, Jack. 1989. "Client Self-Determination: Untangling the Knot." *Social Service Review,* 63(4):598–612.

Rothschild, Joyce and James A. Whitt. 1986. *The Cooperative Workplace: Potentials and Dilemmas of Organizational Democracy and Participation.* New York: Cambridge University Press.

Saari, Carolyn. 1991. *The Creation of Meaning in Clinical Social Work.* New York: Guilford.

Sancier, Betty., ed. 1986–1992. *Affilia: Journal of Women and Social Work,* vols. 1–7.

Sartre, Jean Paul. 1938. *Nausea (La Nausée).* Paris: Gallimard.

—— 1943. *Being and Nothingness: An Essay on Phenomenological Ontology (L'Etre et le Neant).* Paris: Gallimard.

Schlesinger, Arthur M., Jr. 1986. *The Cycles of American History*. Boston: Houghton Mifflin.

Schwartz, Meyer. 1965. "Community Organization." In Henry Lurie, ed., *The Encyclopedia of Social Work*, 15th ed., pp. 177–90. New York: National Association of Social Workers.

Schwartz, Nancy. 1988. *The Blue Guitar: Political Representation and Community*. Chicago: University of Chicago Press.

Schwartz, William. 1974. "Private Troubles and Public Issues: One Social Work Job or Two?" In Paul E. Weinberger, ed., *Perspectives on Social Welfare*, 2d. ed., pp. 346–62. New York: Collier-Macmillan.

—— 1976. "Between Client and System: The Mediating Function." In Robert Roberts and Helen Northen, eds., *Theories of Social Work with Groups*, pp. 171–97. New York: Columbia University Press.

—— 1985. "The Group Work Tradition and Social Work Practice." *Social Work with Groups*, 8(4):7–27.

Scott, Anne Firor. 1964. "Introduction." In Anne Firor Scott, ed., *Democracy and Social Ethics*, pp. vii–lxxv. Cambridge: Harvard University Press.

Seligman, Martin E. 1992. *Helplessness: On Development, Depression, and Death*. New York: Freeman.

Seligman, Martin E. and D. Groves. 1970. "Non-transient learned helplessness." *Psychonomic Science*, 19:191–92.

Serrano-Garcia, Irma. 1984. "The Illusion of Empowerment: Community Development Within a Colonial Context." *Prevention in Human Services*, 3(3):173–200.

Shapiro, Herbert. 1988. *White Violence and Black Response: From Reconstruction to Montgomery*. Amherst: The University of Massachusetts Press.

Shelton, Beth Anne and Juanita Firestone. 1989. "Household Labor Time and the Gender Gap in Earnings." *Gender and Society*, 3(1):105–12.

Sherman, Wendy R. and Stanley Wenocur. 1983. "Empowering Public Welfare Workers through Mutual Support." *Social Work*, 28(5):375–79.

Shils, Edward A. 1975. *Center and Periphery: Essays in Macrosociology*. Chicago: University of Chicago Press.

Silva, G. V. S. de. 1979. "Bhoomi Sena: A Struggle for People's Power." *Development Dialogue*, 2:3–70.

Silverman, Phyllis. 1980. *Mutual Help: Organization and Development*. Beverly Hills, Cal.: Sage.

—— 1987. "Mutual Help Groups." In Anne Minahan, ed., *The Encyclopedia of Social Work*, 18th ed., pp. 171–76. Silver Spring, Md.: National Association of Social Workers.

Simkhovitch, Mary. 1917. *The City Worker's World in America*. New York: Macmillan.

—— 1926. Remarks at the Annual Meeting of the American Society for Organizing Family Social Work, 1926. Lehman Library, Columbia University.

—— 1938. *Neighborhood: My Story of Greenwich House*. New York: Norton.

Simon, Barbara Levy. 1990. "Rethinking Empowerment." *Journal of Progressive Human Services*, 1(1):27–39.

Siporin, Max. 1975. *Introduction to Social Work Practice*. New York: Macmillan.

Smith, Christian. 1991. *The Emergence of Liberation Theology: Radical Religion and Social Movement Theory*. Chicago: University of Chicago Press.

Smith, John E. 1978. *Purpose and Thought: The Meaning of Pragmatism*. New Haven: Yale University Press.

Social Work. 1962–1974. Vols. 7–19.

Solomon, Barbara Bryant. 1976. *Black Empowerment: Social Work in Oppressed Communities*. New York: Columbia University Press.

—— 1982. "Social Work Values and Skills to Empower Women." In Ann Weick and Susan T. Vandiver, eds., *Women, Power, and Change*, pp. 206–14. Washington, D.C.: National Association of Social Workers.

—— 1985. "Community Social Work Practice in Oppressed Minority Communities." In Samuel H. Taylor and Robert W. Roberts, eds., *Theory and Practice of Community Social Work*, pp. 217–57. New York: Columbia University Press.

Solomon, Barbara Miller. 1985. *In the Company of Educated Women: A History of Women and Higher Education in America*. New Haven: Yale University Press.

Solomon, Irvin D. 1989. *Feminism and Black Activism in Contemporary America: An Ideological Assessment*. New York: Greenwood.

Spicker, Paul. 1988. *Principles of Social Welfare: Am Introduction to Thinking About the Welfare State*. New York: Routledge.

Stadum, Beverly A. 1990. "A Critique of Family Caseworkers, 1900–1930: Women Working with Women." *Journal of Sociology and Social Welfare*, 17(3):73–100.

—— 1992. *Poor Women and Their Families: Hard Working Charity Cases*. Albany, N.Y.: State University of New York Press.

Staples, Lee. 1990. "Powerful Ideas about Empowerment." *Administration in Social Work*, 14(2):29–42.

Stehno, Sandra M. 1988. "Public Responsibility for Dependent Black Children: The Advocacy of Edith Abbott and Sophonisba Breckinridge." *Social Service Review*, 62(3):485–503.

Sterling, Dorothy, ed. 1984. *We Are Your Sisters: Black Women in the Nineteenth Century*. New York: Norton.

Stolorow, Robert and George E. Atwood. 1992. *Contexts of Being: The Intersubjective Foundations of Psychological Life*. Hillsdale, N.J.: Analytic.

Students for a Democratic Society. 1964. *The Port Huron Statement*. New York: Students for a Democratic Society.

Survey. 1949. Vol. 85.

Survey Graphic. 1947. Vol. 36.

Swift, Carolyn. 1984. "Empowerment: An Antidote for Folly." *Prevention in Human Services*, 3(3):xi–xv.

Takaki, Ronald. 1990. *Strangers from a Different Shore: A History of Asian Americans*. New York: Penguin.

Taylor, Barbara. 1983. *Eve and the New Jerusalem: Socialism and Feminism in the Nineteenth Century*. New York: Pantheon.

Thompson, E. P. 1966. *The Making of the English Working Class*. New York: Vintage.

Tobias, Mark. 1990. "Validator: A Key Role in Empowering the Chronically Mentally Ill." *Social Work*, 35(4):357–59.

Towle, Charlotte. 1936. "Factors in Treatment." *Proceedings of the National Conference of Social Work*, 63:89–121. Boston: National Conference of Social Work. Repr. 1939 in Fern Lowry, ed., *Readings in Social Case Work, 1920–1938*, pp. 319–30. New York: Columbia University Press.

—— 1969. "The Individual in Relation to Social Change." In Helen H. Perlman, ed., *Helping: Charlotee Towle in Social Work and Social Casework*, pp. 209–34. Chicago: University of Chicago Press.

Trattner, Walter. 1989. *From Poor Law to Welfare State*. 4th ed. New York: Free Press.

Trolander, Judith. 1987. *Professionalism and Social Change: From the Settlement House Movement to Neighborhood Centers, 1886 to the Present*. New York: Columbia University Press.

Tucker, Robert C., ed. 1978. *The Marx-Engels Reader*. 2d ed. New York: Norton.

Turner, Bryan S. 1986. *Citizenship and Capitalism: The Debate Over Reformism*. Boston: G. Allen and Unwin.

Turner, John B, ed. 1977. *The Encyclopedia of Social Work*. 17th ed. Washington, D.C.: National Association of Social Work.

Van Den Bergh, Nan and L. B. Cooper, eds., 1986. "Introduction," N. Van Den Bergh and L. B. Cooper, eds., *Feminist Visions for Social Work*, pp. 1–28. Silver Spring, Md.: National Association of Social Workers.

Van Maanen, John. 1988. *Tales of the Field: On Writing Ethnography*. Chicago: University of Chicago Press.

Wald, Lillian D. 1915. *The House on Henry Street*. New York: Henry Holt.

—— 1933. *Windows on Henry Street*. Boston: Little, Brown.

Walkowitz, Daniel J. 1990. "The Making of a Feminine Professional Identity: Social Workers in the 1920s." *American Historical Review*, 95(4):1051–75.

Warren, Roland. 1978. *The Community in America*. Chicago: Rand McNally.

Watson, Frank Dekker. 1922. *The Charity Organization Movement in the United States: A Study in American Philanthropy*. New York: Macmillan.

Weber, Max. 1958. *The Protestant Ethic and the Spirit Capitalism*. New York: Scribner's.

Weedon, Chris. 1987. *Feminist Practice and Poststructuralist Theory*. Oxford: Basil Blackwell.

Weick, Ann. 1982. "Issues of Power in Social Work Practice." In Ann Weick and Susan T. Vandiver, eds., *Women, Power, and Change*, pp. 173–85. Washington, D.C.: National Association of Social Workers.

—— 1986. "The Philosophical Context of a Health Model of Social Work." *Social Casework*, 67(9):551–59.

—— 1990. "Overturning Oppression: An Analysis of Emancipatory Change." Presentation at the University of Kansas symposium "Building on Women's Strengths: A Social Work Agenda for the Twenty-first Century," Lawrence, Kansas.

Weick, Ann and Loren Pope. 1988. "Knowing What's Best: A New Look at Self-Determination." *Social Casework*, 69(1):10–16.

Weick, Ann, Charles Rapp, W. Patrick Sullivan, and Walter Kisthardt. 1989. "A Strengths Perspective for Social Work Practice." *Social Work*, 34(4):350–54.

Weil, Marie and Jean Kruzich. 1990. "Introduction to the Special Issue." *Administration in Social Work*, 14(2):1–12.

Weiner, Hyman J. 1971. "Social Change and Social Group Work." Unpublished summary of a presentation made on December 14, 1971, to the Group Work Forum at the Columbia University School of Social Work, New York City.

Weisel, Elie. 1982a. *Night*. New York: Bantam.

Weisel, Elie. 1982b. *One Generation After*. New York: Schocken.

Wenocur, Stanley and Michael Reisch. 1989. *From Charity to Enterprise: The Development of American Social Work in a Market Economy*. Urbana, Ill.: University of Illinois Press.

Wenocur, Stanley, and Michael Reisch. 1989. *From Charity to Enterprise: The Development of American Social Work in a Market Economy*. Urbana, ILL: University of Illinois Press.

West, Cornel. 1986. "Populism: A Black Socialist Critique." In Harry Boyte and Frank Riessman, eds., *The New Populism: The Politics of Empowerment*, pp. 207–12. Philadelphia: Temple University Press.

—— 1993. "Race Matters." The Whitney M. Young Memorial Lecture, March 29, 1993, at Columbia University in New York City.

Westbrook, Robert B. 1991. *John Dewey and American Democracy*. Ithaca: Cornell University Press.

Wetzel, Janice Wood. 1986. "A Feminist World View Conceptual Framework." *Social Casework*, 67(3):166–73.

Whitman, Walt. 1964. *Prose Works*. 2 vols. Vol. 1. Ed. Floyd Stovall. New York: New York University Press.

Wiebe, Robert H. 1967. *The Search for Order, 1877–1920*. New York: Hill and Wang.

Wilson, Gertrude. 1976. "From Practice to Theory: A Personalized History." In Robert W. Roberts and Helen Northen, eds., *Theories of Social Work with Groups*, pp. 1–44. New York: Columbia University Press.

Wilson, William J. 1987. *The Truly Disadvantaged: The Inner City, the Underclass, and Public Policy*. Chicago: University of Chicago Press.

Wood, Gale Goldberg and Ruth R. Middleman. 1989. *The Structural Approach to Direct Practice in Social Work*. New York: Columbia University Press.

Wood, Gordon S. 1972. *The Creation of the American Republic, 1776–1787*. New York: Norton.

Young, Mary A. 1935. "Reexamination of Child Care Functions in Family Agencies." *Proceedings of the National Conference of Social Work, 1935*. New York: Columbia University Press. Repr. 1939 in Fern Lowry, ed., *Readings in Social Case Work, 1920–1938*, pp. 592–603. New York: Columbia University Press.

Zimmerman, Joseph F. 1986. *Participatory Democracy: Populism Revived*. New York: Praeger.

Zunz, Sharyn. 1991. "Gender-Related Issues in the Career Development of Social Work Managers." *Affilia*, 6(4):39–52.

Index